Assessment in the Classroom

Assessment in the Classroom:
Constructing and Interpreting Texts

George K. Cunningham

 The Falmer Press

(A member of the Taylor & Francis Group)
London · Washington, D.C.

UK   Falmer Press, I Gunpowder Square, London, EC4A 3DE
USA   Falmer Press, Taylor & Francis Inc., 1900 Frost Road, Suite 101,
        Bristol, PA 19007

First published in 1998

**A catalogue record for this book is available from the British
Library**

ISBN 0 7507 0733 x cased
ISBN 0 7507 0732 1 paper

**Library of Congress Cataloging-in-Publication Data are available
on request**

Jacket design by Caroline Archer

Typeset in 10/12 pt Times by
Graphicraft Typesetters Ltd., Hong Kong.

*Printed in Great Britain by Biddles Ltd., Guildford and King's Lynn on
paper which has a specified pH value on final paper manufacture of not
less than 7.5 and is therefore 'acid free'.*

*Every effort has been made to contact copyright holders for their
permission to reprint material in this book. The publishers would
be grateful to hear from any copyright holder who is not here
acknowledged and will undertake to rectify any errors or omissions
in future editions of this book.*

Contents

List of Appendices, Tables and Figures

Appendices

Tables

Figures

Preface

Assessment in the Classroom: Constructing and Interpreting Tests is intended to be used in two classroom settings: (1) teacher preparation courses that are not primarily devoted to classroom assessment, but for which assessment is an important topic and, (2) teacher preparation classes that have assessment as their major focus. It can be used as a quick reference for educators who need information about the best methods of constructing tests and other assessment instruments.

This book provides a rationale for why assessment is important and how it should be used. It is based on the belief that the purpose of educational assessment is to help teachers make decisions. The term 'assessment' is used to emphasize a teacher's need to make decisions in a wide range of settings.

The basic quantitative aspects of measurement (descriptive statistics, reliability, validity, and standard scores) are included in a single chapter. The actual computations associated with these are included in separate appendices. Separate chapters on objective tests (multiple-choice, true−false, and matching items), constructed response tests (short answer and essay), and alternative assessment (performance assessment, authentic assessment, and portfolios) are included. There also are chapters on standardized achievement, grading, and ethics.

The view that conventional tests are not the only assessment option that should be used is emphasized and the importance of other assessment techniques is strongly represented. Descriptions and discussions of a wide range of assessment techniques are included. At the same time, a strong commitment to the value of conventional assessment methods is maintained.

1   Introduction

In this chapter students will:

- learn why assessment is becoming increasingly important in our society;
- learn about the barriers that prevent good assessment practices;
- understand why teachers need to be better prepared to use assessment techniques;
- become familiar with the Standards for Teacher Competence in Educational Assessment of Students;
- understand the importance of assessment for decision making;
- know the requirements for good assessment procedures; and
- understand fundamental principles of measurement and assessment.

Education has gradually become one of the premier public policy issues in the United States. This has occurred in the presence of both hope and despair. The hope stems from the long held faith that education can solve the nation's social problems. Unemployment, drug use, unwanted teenage pregnancies, and sexually transmitted diseases are all problems that seem amenable to amelioration in our public schools. The despair stems from evidence that suggests that just when the need for better education is being most keenly felt, our schools are failing.

One of the earliest and most strident criticisms of American education appeared in a report commissioned by the National Commission on Excellence in Education, titled *A Nation at Risk* (1983). The report was prepared under the direction of Terrel Bell, Secretary of Education in the Reagan Administration. The report is replete with references to the failure of American education and includes the following famous quote, 'If an unfriendly foreign power attempted to impose on America the mediocre educational performance, that exists today, we might well have viewed it as an act of war.' Many other similar critical analyses of American schools followed. A further expression of this concern can be found in *The Learning Gap: Why Our Schools Are Failing and What We Can Learn from Japanese and Chinese Education* written by Harold W. Stevenson and James W. Stigler. In this study of Asian schools, the superior science and math performance of students in these countries is described. The most interesting part of the book is not the documentation of the differences in achievement between students from the two parts of the world, but the delineation of the reasons why this gap has emerged. The authors cite the existence of a single widely accepted curriculum and widespread commitment to the value of education as key reasons for the superior performance of Asian students.

There is also strong dissent from the view that our schools are in a downward spiral. These voices range from Gerald Bracey (in a series of columns and articles that have appeared in the *Phi Delta Kappan*); the Sandia Report, commissioned by the Bush administration to demonstrate the need for a large scale revamping of the nations schools which declared that pronouncements about the demise of public education were premature; and the recent book written by David C. Berliner and Bruce Biddle titled *The Manufactured Crisis: Myths, Fraud, and the Attack on America's Public Schools.*

Despite the differences in the ways our schools are perceived, the belief that our schools need to be changed is widespread. Ideas about how to improve the educational performance of our students have coalesced into the *educational reform movement.* A critical characteristic of most educational reform agendas is accountability. In practice this means a demand for more testing and/or different assessment techniques.

Many proposals for educational reform call for the increased use of alternative assessment, that is student evaluation techniques that go beyond the traditional pencil and paper techniques of true–false, multiple-choice, short answer and fill-in-the-blanks. Alternate assessment techniques usually include such techniques as performance tests and portfolios (both of these are discussed in Chapter 6). Another important aspect of educational reform is the need for increased participation by teachers in decision-making. As a result, teachers need to become sophisticated about the assessment issues surrounding decision-making.

Many teachers lack the skills necessary to effectively use assessment techniques or understand the assessment related issues associated with educational reform. The principles of measurement are technical, mathematical, and obscure. Those outside the field often find the code difficult to break. Even when assessment procedures are well understood, their implementation can be time consuming. Considering the amount of work they are required to do each day, teachers often conclude that it is not worthwhile for them to devote so much of their energy to developing their assessment skills.

The most obvious reason for the inadequate measurement skills of teachers is a lack of assessment courses in teacher certification programs. States, colleges, and universities responsible for the overall training of teachers, typically do not require coursework in assessment in their teacher education programs. Only fifteen states specifically include the successful completion of such courses for certification (Sullivan and Chalnick, 1991). Most states permit teacher training institutions to set higher standards, but only about half of these institutions have done so (Schafer and Lissitz, 1987). Furthermore, pre-service instruction in assessment has not been adequately augmented by appropriate in-service programming and follow-up studies of teaching practices, suggest that teachers have not retained or been willing to apply what they have learned. This lack of attention to assessment skills is not the result of difficulty in identifying what is most important, since the basic precepts of measurement and testing are well documented and accepted.

Standards for Teacher Competence in Educational Assessment of Students

In 1987, professional educational associations began developing a set of standards for evaluating teacher competence in student assessment. These organizations included the American Federation of Teachers, the National Council on Measurement in Education and the National Education Association. Work was completed on this document in 1990 and it was disseminated widely. It also was published in *Educational Measurement: Issues and Practices* (1990). These standards are not copyrighted and the committee that wrote this document encourages their widespread distribution.

The standards are based on two assumptions: (1) student assessment is an integral part of a teacher's role, and (2) good teaching and good testing go together. The impetus for the development of these standards came from the perception that teachers are not currently being well prepared in classroom assessment skills. Since accountability and assessment are included in educational reform programs, teachers need to prepare themselves for participation as knowledgeable decision-makers. Seven standards were proposed that are intended to prepare teachers to correctly use assessment techniques in their teaching, and better function in decision-making roles that require a knowledge of assessment.

1 *Teachers should be skilled in choosing assessment methods appropriate for instructional decisions.*

The implementation of this standard requires that teachers become aware of the importance of assessment in instruction, and be knowledgeable about the wide range of assessment techniques that can be used to make better instructional decisions. Teachers also need to be able to evaluate the commercially prepared tests that accompany instructional materials. They should know that these tests must be evaluated separately from the instructional material itself. Teachers need to be able to differentiate between good and bad assessment methods, in terms of their technical characteristics such as reliability and validity, and through the use of less formal, more subjective standards for evaluating overall quality.

Choosing the most appropriate assessment requires an understanding of the sort of decisions that will be made using the results of the assessment. In too many situations, tests are created and administered without any explicit delineation of why the assessment is being conducted.

2 *Teachers should be skilled in developing assessment methods appropriate for instructional decisions.*

Since teachers create most of the assessment tools they use, they need to be knowledgeable about test construction techniques. They should possess a wide range of skills encompassing a variety of approaches to the collection of assessment information on students. This knowledge should include both an understanding of formal and informal assessment methods.

3 *Teachers should be skilled in administering, scoring, and interpreting the results of both externally produced and teacher-produced assessment methods.*

Teachers need to possess the technical skills necessary to administer the assessment tools they are using. They also need to be able to correctly score and interpret them. Test scoring is seldom a problem when standardized tests are used because they can be machine scored accurately with the results reported to teachers in the form of standard scores. The evaluation of essay and performance tests may require enhanced skills not always possessed by teachers. Training and supervised practice in this type of assessment is particularly important when the results of the assessment will be used to make important decisions.

   4   *Teachers should be skilled in using assessment results when making decisions about individual students, planning teaching, developing curriculum, and school improvement.*

Teachers should be able to select the most appropriate assessment tools for making instructional decisions and be able to use the information appropriately. The accomplishment of this goal requires a broad range of assessment knowledge and skills, including an understanding of how to match specific assessment techniques with instructional goals.

   5   *Teachers should be skilled in developing valid pupil grading procedure which use pupil assessments.*

Teachers should be able to provide a rational basis for assigning grades. The explanation needs to be understood by both students and parents. Teachers should avoid grading methods that are justified by the need to adhere to existing policies or 'because these grading procedures have always been used.' In many cases, the grading methods that have been used in the past are less than ideal. Problems with grading often arise because teachers are unaware that there are alternative methods of assigning grades and/or that the approaches used in their school by other teachers are inappropriate.

   6   *Teachers should be skilled in communicating assessment results to students, parents, other lay audiences, and other educators.*

This standard requires that teachers be familiar with the interpretation and use of standardized scores. They need to be able to articulate to parents and the community *what* these scores mean as well as *how* and *why* the scores on subscales differ. It is particularly important for teachers to be knowledgeable about the advantages and disadvantages of different standard scores and be able to communicate that knowledge to parents.

   One of the most controversial aspects of the process of communicating results to parents and the public stems from the need to explain differences in performance among cultural-ethnic groups. Such communication needs to be handled with sensitivity. There is much that is not known about why student performance differs on such tests and teachers should be cautious about making generalizations about such matters. Teachers also need to be able to understand and explain how differences in student background can influence test performance.

   7   *Teachers should be skilled in recognizing unethical, illegal, and otherwise inappropriate assessment methods and uses of assessment information.*

There are many ethical problems surrounding the administration of standardized achievement tests. They pose two particular kinds of problems for teachers: (1) opinions differ regarding what is and what is not ethical; and (2) teachers often find themselves under pressure to act unethically. This pressure usually stems from a demand for higher test scores regardless of how they are obtained. Public officials, school boards, and principals — all the way down to the classroom teacher, feel this pressure.

Teachers need to approach student assessment with a commitment to fairness and employ the highest standards of ethical behavior. Ethical standards are particularly important for teachers because they are role models. When teachers violate the accepted standards of ethical behavior, we can hardly expect their students to be any better. Furthermore, when teachers use inappropriate or unethical assessment methods, students are likely to be the first to notice.

Awareness of ethical standards is not enough, teachers must make sure that their actions are guided by these standards. They also have a responsibility to ensure awareness and implementation of ethical practices in the larger community.

The Importance of Assessment in Decision Making

The need to make decisions is one of the most important characteristics of our world. In a sense, the capacity to make decisions is what makes us human. Teachers are required to make an enormous number of decisions during each school day, often in a short amount of time, and on the basis of what is known at the time. Assessment, both formal and informal, plays an important role in decision-making.

Formal assessments include conventional testing methods such as multiple-choice, true–false, short answer, and essay items and are characterized by precision and accuracy.

Informal assessments include such techniques as questioning, observing students while they work on tasks, asking students to read aloud or have them verbalize the working through of mathematics problems. Information obtained from these assessments lets teachers know whether their students understand the materials presented and assists them in making better decisions about what should be taught next. This can help the teacher decide whether there is a need for further review, or if the students are ready to have new material introduced. It also gives the teacher immediate feedback about the effectiveness of the teaching methods being employed. If students are not learning as they should, the teacher must decide whether or when to alter instructional methods.

Alternative assessment techniques represent an intermediate stage between the two. They lack the precision of formal assessments, but they are not as subjective as informal assessments.

Surveys of teacher behavior (Stiggins, Conklin, and Bridgeford, 1986) have shown that teachers prefer informal methods of assessment and use them more often than formal approaches. This is probably because informal methods require less preparation and skill. The pervasiveness of such assessments and the ease with which they are implemented can mask the complexities and difficulties with which they are associated. Informal assessments should be supported by careful record keeping to provide a defense against the charge that decisions are being made capriciously.

There are two types of decisions made by educators: socio-personal and instructional.

Socio-personal Decisions

We usually think of teachers as makers of instructional decisions, but teachers also make socio-personal decisions each teaching day. They may need to decide when and how to discipline a student who is misbehaving or determine the group into which a student should be placed. These decisions require the maintenance of a balance between the need to treat every student the same (in the interest of fairness), and the need to modify instructional activities according to individual differences. Consider the following decisions a teacher might make during a day.

1   Robert is talking to Ray at the next desk instead of doing his work. Ms. Jones puts Robert's name on the board. When Ray does the same thing, Ms. Jones puts her hand on his shoulder and quiets him with a 'shhhh'.
2   Ms. Jones is planning a group activity with three students in a group. The groups are supposed to imagine what will happen next in a story they have been reading in class. Ms. Jones has decided to let one group have four members because otherwise Mary will be excluded from the group made up of three of her friends. John has to work by himself.
3   During a class discussion, when Jamie calls out an answer she is told that she must raise her hand and wait to be called upon. When Betty calls out an answer Ms. Jones is quick to encourage her.

In each of these situations Ms. Jones has made a decision based on an assessment. It is conceivable that some form of standardized or formal assessment could have been used to inform these decisions, but it is unlikely. Instead, Ms. Jones has probably made a series of informal assessments. She has learned that Robert only responds to an assertive discipline approach, while her attention alone has a powerful influence on Ray. She knows how important social acceptance is for her students. Mary has been struggling for acceptance among a group of girls. To not allow her to participate as a member of their group would be devastating. From previous experience with this type of activity Ms. Jones has learned that John lacks the maturity to work productively with other students. She also has learned that if permitted, Jamie will answer every question and dominate any classroom discussion, shutting out other students. On the other hand, Ms. Jones has been trying all year to get Betty to become more actively involved in class discussions. The last thing she would want to do is discourage her the first time she attempted to make a contribution in class. You might not agree with the decisions that Ms. Jones has made, but a decision of some kind must be made in these circumstances and they must be made quickly. During a day, a teacher makes hundreds of such decisions.

Instructional Decisions

The three categories of instructional decisions are formative, summative, and placement.

Formative Instructional Decisions

Formative instructional decisions include the kind of day to day, lesson to lesson decisions that a teacher must make. While these decisions usually are not thought of as being part of the assessment process, they really are. These decisions are not made in a vacuum, but are based on data or information gathered by the teacher. Formative decisions can be further divided into *planning* and *process decisions*.

Planning decisions are made prior to instruction and involve alterations in the teaching of a lesson, based on observations and informal assessments. Examples of planning decisions follow:

1 Ms. Jones has her students watch a movie about the Boston Tea Party followed by a class discussion, rather than having them read the pertinent chapter in their textbook and answer the questions at the end of the chapter.
2 Ms. Jones decides to spend two class periods discussing the Declaration of Independence instead of devoting a single class period to this topic as was done last year.
3 Ms. Jones provides fewer examples and a shorter discussion of the Bill of Rights than she has in the past.

In each case Ms. Jones has altered the way instruction was presented based on assessments of student performance. In the first example, the assessment results indicated that the previously used method of instruction was not working and a different approach was needed. When the amount of time allotted to the discussion of the Declaration of Independence proved to be insufficient (in the second example), additional class time was allocated to the topic. In the third example, the teacher realized that the instructional goal of having students understand the Bill of Rights could be achieved more quickly than she anticipated in the past, so less time was allocated for this purpose.

Process decisions occur when alterations are made in how or what is being taught during instruction. Examples of these types of decisions follow.

1 Ms. Jones interrupts a lesson on parts of speech to present a review of verbs.
2 Ms. Jones finds that she doesn't need to spend as much time on prepositional phrases as she planned because her students understood the topic more quickly than anticipated.
3 Ms. Jones discontinues the whole group instruction on the events leading up to the Civil War and has her students convene in small groups and respond to questions she provides.

In the first example, Ms. Jones realized that she couldn't continue with her lesson on parts of speech because her students didn't understand verbs. In the second example, she realized that the time allocated for her lesson on prepositional phrases was too long and her students were getting restless so she moved on to another topic. In the third example, Ms. Jones realized that few of her students were responding in the whole class setting. For this reason, she switched to smaller groups with more structured questions.

Placement Decisions

To maximize student learning, students need to be placed in instructional settings that optimize their potential. This can occur at the classroom, school, or systemwide level. In the classroom, placement decisions could involve the determination of the reading group to which a student should be assigned. At the school or system level, decisions could be made about whether one child should go into a class for gifted students or another be assigned to a learning disability resource room.

Summative Decisions

Summative decisions, such as the determination of the grade a student is to be assigned or a change in placement are usually based on formal assessment procedures. Included in this category are decisions concerning the effectiveness of instructional programs and the identification of students who are falling behind their peers. A review of these results may require a more in-depth diagnosis of the specific learning tasks with which students are having difficulty, and the reasons for their learning problems. Ability tests are often used as part of the information base for making decisions about placements. These decisions include placement in special education, gifted or advanced classes. Ability tests are generally administered by school psychologists, school counselors, resource teachers, and/or other specialists rather than classroom teachers.

Requirements for Good Assessment Procedures

Good assessment is not a mysterious process — the building blocks for accomplishing it are well understood. There are four requirements for good assessment: (1) a knowledge of the correct procedures for student assessment, (2) a commitment of an adequate amount of time, (3) planning, and (4) a reflective analysis of the assessment process.

1   *A knowledge of the correct procedures for student assessment.*
Teachers do not arrive in the classroom with an instinctual knowledge of the rules for conducting valid and useful assessments. Appropriate instruction in these techniques, either pre- or in-service, is necessary. The assessment skills of teachers have declined along with confidence in the effectiveness of conventional testing

methodologies. The diminished appreciation of the importance of measurement in teacher preparation programs paradoxically, coincides with increased pressure for accountability at the national and state level.

2 *Time commitment.*

Employing good classroom assessment procedures takes time — this is unavoidable. When a teacher procrastinates and test construction is put off until it has to be rushed, the purpose of the assessment may not be achieved. Teachers must devote the time and effort necessary for effective planning, item writing, and follow-up evaluations of the items, in order for assessment to be effective.

3 *Planning.*

It is unlikely that useful information will be obtained from a test that is unplanned or minimally planned. As obvious as this might seem, the majority of teacher-made tests lack adequate planning. This is why students from elementary to graduate school often stare in bewilderment at a test, scratch their heads and try to figure out why the items are so different from what they expected.

The planning required for both instruction and test construction are inseparable, because assessment planning always begins with a delineation of instructional goals. The goal of good test planning is to ensure a match between the content of a test and what has been designated as important during instructional planning. This attribute of the test development process is called *content validity* and it is discussed further in Chapter 2.

4 *Analysis of results.*

At a minimum, a teacher should know how to compute means and medians so that they can understand how the typical or average student did on each test administered. These computations can be accomplished quickly and easily with a calculator. When Gullickson and Ellwein (1985) surveyed elementary and secondary teachers in a state that required a course in measurement for certification, only 13 per cent of teachers reported computing the mean and 12 per cent the median. This is a particularly dismal record since neither of these computations require much time or statistical sophistication. With the increased availability of personal computers in the school, and in teachers' homes, and more easily used and appropriate software, it should be possible to make more sophisticated procedures accessible. This is unlikely to occur if teachers are unwilling to utilize even the most basic summary statistics. Computer availability cannot replace good teacher training programs and appropriate in-service activities.

5 *Conclusions about improving assessments.*

Some important aspects of the test construction process — for instance good planning — don't require computational skills and should be in any good teacher's repertoire of skills. Bringing teachers to the point where they are able to recognize the importance of improving their own assessment techniques may be as important as conveying a knowledge of tests, measurement, and assessment. Teachers and teachers in training need to reach the point in their professional development where they understand that there are assessment methods that lead to increased student learning and embrace the idea that it is worth the effort to learn and apply these techniques.

Fundamental Knowledge about Measurement and Assessment

Before you can appreciate and understand what is to follow in this book, there are a few basic concepts that you need to understand. You need to be able to discriminate among the different terms related to assessment and you need to know a little about the underlying assumptions upon which this field is based.

Related Terminology

The title of this book suggests an emphasis on *assessment*, but the term *measurement* will also be used throughout. It is important for you to understand how these terms are related to *evaluation, statistics*, and *research*.

Assessment The preferred term for describing the sort of activity that is discussed in this book is *assessment*. In many publications on the topic it has replaced the use of the terms *measurement* and *evaluation*. *Measurement* is usually associated with formal assessment techniques while *assessment* can refer to both formal and informal assessments. It also seems more appropriate to use the term 'assessment' when referring to performance-based testing and portfolios.

Measurement The process of quantifying human characteristics by using numbers to indicate the degree to which an individual possesses a given trait is called *measurement*. Numbers are usually associated with traits through the use of tests, instruments, or scales. Measurement tends to be associated with conventional methods of assessing students.

Evaluation The meaning of the term *evaluation* has changed over the years. The term originally referred to individual evaluation and was used synonymously with measurement. Many textbooks include both terms, *measurement* and *evaluation*, in their title. The use of the term *evaluation* has changed over the years and it is now more likely to refer to *program evaluation*. A program evaluation is a formal process for assessing the success of a program, project, or grant.

Statistics The interpretation of individual student performance is usually simple and straightforward and there are many methods that can be used to give individual scores meaning. An examination of the scores of groups of students is more difficult because there is too much information for easy interpretation. Statistics can be useful for this type of interpretation because they can be used to summarize a group of scores into a single number and make them meaningful. The specific techniques of statistics will be described in the following chapter.

Research The use of scientific methodology to answer questions about the environment is called research. At one time, most research in education was quantitative and utilized statistics and measurement techniques. Other research methods which do not involve statistics and formal measurement techniques, which place less importance on objectivity are also accepted as legitimate. These approaches are called *qualitative* research.

Figure 1.1: An example of a continuum

— — — ————————————————————————————— — — — —

Little of the trait   Much of the trait

Domain Sampling and Constructs

Measurement has for its focus, the quantification of human attributes or character-istics. This is achieved by associating numbers with these characteristics, which quantify their presence or absence. The attributes being assessed are called *con-structs*. A *construct* is a generic term for a class of behaviors. For instance, the word 'creativity' refers to behaviors that, when present in sufficient quantity cause us to say that a person is creative. Examples of constructs are schizophrenia, para-noia, reading ability and rigidity. For our purposes, this quantification usually takes place through the administration of tests or other assessment instruments.

A construct is defined by all of the behaviors that are associated with it. The totality of these behaviors is called the *domain of observables*. For tests, the domain of observables would include all of the possible items that *could* be included and not just the actual items that appear on a particular test or measuring instrument. The goal of good test construction is to ensure that the items on a test are repres-entative of the entire domain. When this occurs, it is legitimate to claim that the score on a test represents an estimate of the quantification of a construct on the basis of item responses. At the same time, it is inappropriate for a teacher to focus instruction on the content of a specific test. Improving the performance of students on a limited number of items would not necessarily lead to improvement in per-formance across the entire domain. Consider a teacher who learns from standard-ized achievement test results that his or her students do not know which words are supposed to be capitalized. The teacher should not try to address this instructional weakness by teaching students to capitalize only those words that appear on the test itself. It is the domain of all words and the rules for capitalization that should be taught.

Continuums

When constructs are quantified with a single number it is best to think of these as being on a continuum. The right side of the continuum represents an abundance of the construct while the left side of the continuum represents little of the construct. The continuum is best conceptualized by a line which is broken at either end (see Figure 1.1). The broken line at the extremes indicates a lack of certainty about these parts of the continuum. We can always measure constructs best in the center of the distribution where most scores are. Our ability to conduct effective measurements decline as we move towards either end of the continuum.

The use of a single line to define a construct implies the existence of a unitary trait and the score from a test should represent only one trait. If the test is actually measuring several constructs, this should be indicated by multiple subscales and separate continuums.

Items correctly answered on a test serve the purpose of designating a person's position on the continuum. The numbers (often raw scores) used to designate position on the continuum are arbitrary and routinely are transformed into more easily understood metrics. For example, grade equivalents, percentiles, and standard scores can be used to indicate relative position on the continuum. These scores will be discussed in the following chapter.

Summary

The field of measurement and assessment is in the midst of a period of rapid change. Interest in assessment is increasing, as are criticisms and suggestions for change. With this change comes a need for teachers to improve their assessment skills and knowledge. The need for better teacher training has led to the development of the *Standards for Teacher Competence in Educational Assessment.*

A major purpose of student assessment is decision making. Assessment procedures are used to improve decision making, facilitate instruction, and improve placement decisions. To accomplish these purposes most effectively, teachers need to be informed about the importance of good test construction techniques and possess an understanding of why assessment is important.

Good assessment is dependent on a knowledge of the correct procedures for student assessment, time commitment, planning and careful analysis of results. There are several underlying principles of measurement that are important for understanding assessment including domain sampling, constructs, and continuums.

In order to understand the assessment techniques included in this book it is necessary that the reader be able to discriminate among terms such as assessment, measurement, statistics, research, and evaluation. It is likewise important to understand that the focus of assessment is on constructs which are defined by a domain of observables and best described graphically by a continuum.

Suggested Readings

AIRASIAN, P.W. (1991) *Classroom Assessment*, McGraw Hill: New York.
THORNDIKE, R.M., CUNNINGHAM, G.K., THORNDIKE, R.L. and HAGAN, E. (1991) *Measurement and Evaluation in Psychology and Education*, New York: Macmillan.

2 Interpreting Test Results

In this chapter students will:

- be able to differentiate between descriptive and inferential statistics;
- understand why a knowledge of statistics is important for teachers;
- understand how to compute and when to use the mode, median and mean;
- understand how to compute and when to use the standard deviation and variance
- know how variability is related to the normal curve;
- know how to interpret correlations;
- understand how to compute, use, and interpret grade norms, percentiles, and the different standard scores;
- be able to discriminate between reliability and validity;
- know the three approaches to reliability and when each should be used; and
- know how validity is determined and understand the evolving nature of its interpretation.

In addition to understanding how to construct different types of tests, teachers need to know how and when to use them. Accomplishing these two goals requires fundamental skills and knowledge in four areas: (1) descriptive statistics, (2) derived scores, (3) reliability, and (4) validity.

Descriptive Statistics

In measurement we attach numbers to the characteristics and traits (constructs) that we use to describe people. Instead of talking about a child being either good or poor reader, we provide reading scores that convey this information with a much higher degree of specificity and in a manner that lends itself to mathematical computations. We lose something when we do this because a single number cannot capture the richness and complexity of the words in our language.

Just because we can attach a numeral to a person to indicate the degree to which they possess some trait does not mean that we are justified in performing mathematical operations on these as though they were numbers. For instance, knowing the average value of numerals on the back of football jerseys tells us nothing useful about the teams or the players. Such a procedure would be of little use because the numerals were not intended for any purpose other than identification.

What this suggests is a need to discriminate among different types of numerals with their different mathematical properties. We call these different types of numerals, *scales* and each has its own mathematical properties.

Numbers can be of nominal, ordinal, interval, or ratio scale. These four scales represent a hierarchy. With *nominal scale date*, all we know is that the numbers are different, like the numerals on football jerseys. *Ordinal scales* convey information about relative standing in a group or rank order. An example of an ordinal scale is the rating of professional tennis players. They are ranked according to their success in tournaments. While higher rank implies greater ability and lower rank less, no assumptions are made about the intervals between players. It is possible that the first and second ranked players are nearly identical in ability, but there is a large gap between the second and third ranked players. With *interval scale data*, we do assume that the differences between individuals are the same. While test scores do not meet the standards for interval scale data, they are close enough to be treated as though they are. *Ratio scale* data is seldom encountered in educational assessment. Height and weight are examples of this scale. With ratio scale data, zero is meaningful, i.e., we know what zero height would be. It is reasonable to say that one child is twice as tall as another, but it is not acceptable to use reading test scores to assert that one child reads twice as well as another. The type of scores that will discussed in this chapter are for the most part considered to be of an interval scale so the reader does not need to know any more about the topic of scaling than has already been presented. A more detailed discussion of scales and assumptions can be found in Appendix A.

Inferential Statistics

While descriptive statistics provide a means for summarizing large amounts of data into meaningful metrics, inferential statistics are a primary methodology for quantitative research. Inferential statistics are used to understand the characteristics of a large groups of subjects called *populations*, by examining the characteristics of randomly selected subgroups from the population called *samples*. The results of the computations involving samples are called *statistics*, whereas those obtained from populations are called *parameters*. *Inferences* about parameters are made with statistics because it is usually impossible or inconvenient to collect data from an entire population. If you want to describe the reading level of all third-grade students in a school system, it would of course be possible to administer a reading test to all the students. This would be expensive and time consuming, but you would have precise information about the reading level of these students. Results that are almost as accurate can be obtained using a smaller subgroup, or sample, and it would be more cost effective to do so. While it is possible to administer a reading test to all third–graders in a school district, it would be impractical to do the same for all third–graders in the United States. If you want to know the average reading level of this group you would almost have to use sampling procedures. Inferential

Table 2.1: A distribution of test scores

Bill	23
Mary	17
Betty	26
Joe	22
Manuel	18
Brad	25
Jill	26
Jean	29
Charles	21

statistics provides tools for accomplishing this and also can tell you how likely it is that you have made an error in your estimate.

The Need for Statistics

After grading a test administered to thirty-four students. Ms. Greene is faced with thirty-four numbers, representing the performance of each student in class. Few people can process that many numbers in their head. Although it is possible to examine five or six scores, understand, and make sense of them, the human mind is generally not capable of adequately interpreting a larger set of numbers. Teachers need techniques for organizing scores and turning them into information. It should be understood that the process of summarizing data involves the loss of information.

Descriptive statistics can be classified into three main categories: central tendency, variability, and correlation.

Central Tendency

The central tendency of a set of scores is a single number that captures the essence of all the other scores. When you determine central tendency you have gained an understanding of the nature of the other scores, but some information about individual scores has been sacrificed. Other terms used to describe central tendencies are 'average' and 'typical score.' The three methods of determining central tendency are the mode, mean and median.

Mode

The *mode* is the value that comes closest to being a typical score and is the easiest of the three methods to compute. Simply put, it is the score that occurs most frequently. The mode works best when the distribution of scores is normally distributed, which makes the mean, median, and mode the same. Consider the scores listed in Table 2.1 where the number 26 occurs twice while the other numbers each occur once. The mode is therefore 26. This value does not represent the distribution very well. It is the second highest in the distribution. Of course part of the problem is the small size of the sample. The mode is more stable with larger distributions.

When two adjoining scores occur with equal frequency, the midpoint between the two is designated as the mode. If there are two scores that have the same highest frequency, but they are not adjoining, the distribution is designated as *bimodal* and the two scores are each considered a mode.

The mode is seldom used for the following three reasons: (1) when there is more than one mode, central tendency cannot be adequately described; (2) in some cases the mode is obviously not a typical score; and (3) the mode tends to be unstable. A change in the size of one or several scores can have a disproportionately large effect on the value of the mode.

Mean

The mean is computed by summing all the scores and dividing the value obtained by the number of scores. The sum of all the scores in Table 2.1 is 207. When that value is divided by 9 (the number of students) the resulting value is 23. This is the mean. It is much easier to calculate the mean than the other two methods of computing central tendency. The mean is the most commonly used statistical computation and it is usually the preferred method for defining central tendency.

Median

The median is the point (not necessarily the score) where there are as many scores above as there are below. If there aren't too many scores, duplicate scores do not occur at the midpoint, and there is an odd number of scores, computing the median is easy. You need only place the scores in rank order and pick the one in the middle. After placing the scores in Table 2.1 in order, the middle score or median is 23. When there are several scores with the same value in the middle of the distribution or an even number of scores, computing the exact median becomes more difficult. Elaborate mathematical procedures for computing the exact median under these circumstances are available or the integer closest to the midpoint can be designated as the median. This latter solution has become more common as a result of the growing belief that the more elaborate computations are neither necessary nor appropriate.

There are reasons for using the median. Extreme scores (scores much higher or lower than most) distort the interpretation of some descriptive statistics, and in particular they affect the mean, which is based on the magnitude of every score in a distribution. The median is not affected by extreme scores, which makes it the statistic of choice when there is a need to diminish the effect of outlying scores. Consider the numbers in Table 2.1. The largest value is 29. If that number were to be changed to 110 the mode would remain 26 and the median would still be 23. The mean, however, would change to 32. Which of these best represents the central tendency of the distribution? The answer depends on why you were computing the central tendency of the scores. If you want to disregard the outlying score, the median should be used. If you wanted your estimate of central tendency to be based on the magnitude of every score, the mean would be preferred.

Table 2.2: *Distributions with high and low amounts of dispersion*

Distribution A	Distribution B
76	34
78	89
75	76
76	50
78	22
77	99
77	55
76	67
75	76
77	33

The median is seldom used. There are three reasons why the median is used less often than the mean: (1) the value of the median does not reflect the magnitude of each score; (2) the scores must be placed in rank order before the median can be computed, which is difficult and time consuming; and (3) the mathematics required for the exact median's computation can be unwieldy.

Variability

The term *variability* refers to the degree to which a set of scores is dispersed. If all the scores in a distribution have the same or a similar value, it could be concluded that the distribution has little variability. Examine the scores in Table 2.2. The scores in Distribution A are all very similar ranging from a low of 75 to a high of 78. The scores in distribution B are more dispersed and range from a low of 22 to a high of 89. It should be obvious that Distribution B is more variable or has greater dispersion than does Distribution A.

There are three methods of computing variability: (1) the range, (2) the semi-interquartile range, and (3) the standard deviation/variance. The range and semi-interquartile range are seldom used and for this reason do not warrant further discussion in this chapter. It is enough for the reader to be able to recognize them as measures of variability that are inferior to the standard deviation/variance.

The standard deviation and variance are computationally related. The variance is the standard deviation squared — the standard deviation is therefore the square root of the variance. The standard deviation is a descriptive statistic that provides direct information about the dispersal of a distribution of scores. The variance is used in more advanced statistical analyzes. The discussion of variability in this chapter will focus on the standard deviation.

The Standard Deviation

The standard deviation is best interpreted as the average amount that scores differ from the mean. The actual computation is somewhat more complicated and directions for the computation of the standard deviation and variance can be found in Appendix B. When the standard deviation is small, scores can be expected to have similar values and there will be little dispersion in the scores. For instance, we would expect that the standard deviation for Distribution A in Table 2.2 would be small (it is 1.02) while the standard deviation for Distribution B could be expected to be larger (it is 24.28).

Test authors generally structure their tests in such a way that they have relatively large standard deviations. When a test has a small standard deviation it is difficult to discriminate among the students which makes decision-making more difficult.

Besides describing an important characteristic of a set of scores, the standard deviation is useful for two further reasons: (1) it can be used to equate scores; (2) it has an important relationship with the normal distribution.

Equating Scores

In evaluating students we often wish to combine several different scores to make a single score that can be used to assign grades. For example, teachers often find it necessary to combine the results of several tests or written assignments. The obvious way of accomplishing this is to add the raw scores. The combining of raw scores in this way constitutes one of the most common errors encountered in applied measurement.

Raw scores cannot be combined unless they have the same standard deviations because distributions with different standard deviations are on different scales. Adding raw scores from tests with different standard deviations is as incorrect as adding inches and centimetres. Inches and centimetres cannot be added because they are on different scales as are tests with different standard deviations.

The only way to ensure that two tests are correctly combined is to make certain that they have the same (or similar) standard deviations. This can be accomplished by transforming one of the scales into the other or changing both to a third scale. If you want to add inches to centimetres, you must first change the inches to centimetres or the centimetres to inches. In educational measurement, we usually change both incompatible scales into a third common scale. This is accomplished by transforming the distributions of scores into standard scores, which places them on the same scale. The use and computation of standard scores are explained in a following section of this chapter.

The Normal Distribution

Another important characteristic of the standard deviation is its relationship with the normal curve. The normal curve can be thought of as the tendency for a graph of either physical measurements or test performance to be bell shaped, with most scores in the center of the distribution and few at either extreme. Male height, as measured by US Armed forces doctors during the physical exams administered in

Figure 2.1:   *A normal curve*

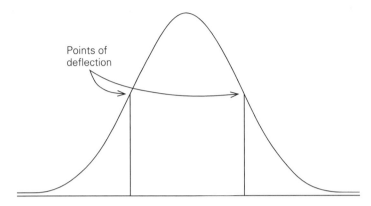

Points of
deflection

conjunction with induction, is normally distributed as are the measures of mental
ability they administer.

The normal distribution is also defined by a mathematical equation. The
capacity of formal mathematical equations to define the shape of naturally occurring measurements constitutes a fundamental building bloc of inferential statistics.
An example of a normal curve can be seen in Figure 2.1.

The standard deviation is related to the normal curve in two key ways. First
of all, the point of deflection, the place where the curve switches from being concave to convex, occurs one standard deviation on either side of the mean (this is
illustrated in Figure 2.1). Second, there is a fixed proportion of cases between any
two points on a normal distribution when these distances are expressed as standard
deviations. This characteristic is important because it makes the conversion of
standard scores into percentages possible and permits the computations associated
with inferential statistics. A more detailed description of this characteristic of the
standard deviation appears in Appendix C.

Naturally occurring curves, even when they look 'right' seldom fit the strict
mathematical requirements of the normal curve. However, the mathematical properties of the normal curve are very powerful, robust, and useful. Mathematicians
have discovered that when a distribution is close to being normal, it is possible to
assume that it is normal (or nearly normal) and take advantage of the mathematical
properties that accrue to such distributions.

Truly normal distributions are not usually found among classroom test score
data because the number of students is too small and the tests are usually too easy.
As a result, the scores of students tend to be piled up on the right side of the distribution. Furthermore, a normal distribution should not be expected when students
are not assigned to classes randomly. For example, a classroom made up of gifted
or low achieving students will not have a normal distribution.

A more completed description of a normal curve can be found in Appendix C.

Table 2.3: A distribution of reading and math scores

Student	Reading	Math
A	70	80
B	40	30
C	20	30
D	10	10
E	70	100
F	40	80
G	40	30
H	30	40

Correlation

In addition to information about central tendency and the amount of variability or dispersion in a set of scores, there is a need to understand the degree to which different scores (or other information about a student) are related. For example, we may have information about the educational level of the parents of students in a class and want to know if it is related to student scores on a test of reading comprehension, or we might wish to know if student performance on reading and math tests are related. If they are related, knowing a student's reading score would enable us to predict their math scores. It also could be said that the skills needed to be a good reader are similar to those needed to perform well in math. The simplest way of examining this relationship is by employing a scatter plot. Table 2.3 contains a set of reading and math scores for eight students.

A scatter plot of the eight pairs of scores from Table 2.3 is presented in Figure 2.2 below. As can be seen, the pattern created approximates a straight line rising from left to right. The linearity of the scatter plot suggests the existence of a positive relationship. A negative correlation would be illustrated by the pattern of a line rising from right to left.

A better way of quantifying the relationship between two variables is by using a correlation coefficient. The main advantage of correlation coefficients have over scatter plots is their use of a single value to define the degree of relationships. The correlation is a descriptive statistic, mathematically based on means and standard deviations. It can be no less than −1 and no more than +1 with values approaching +1 indicating that two variables are positively related and values approaching −1 indicating a relationship that is negative. Values near zero are indicative of the lack of any relationship between two variables.

This statistic has several different names including 'Pearson product-moment correlation,' 'product-moment correlation,' 'Pearson R,' 'Pearsonian correlation,' 'PM correlation,' or just 'correlation.' There are many variations on the correlation theme and it forms the basis for most of the important and sophisticated statistical methodologies used in measurement, statistics, and research.

To compute a correlation coefficient between two variables, two scores must be available for each individual. You cannot compute the correlation between two groups.

Figure 2.2: A sample scatter plot

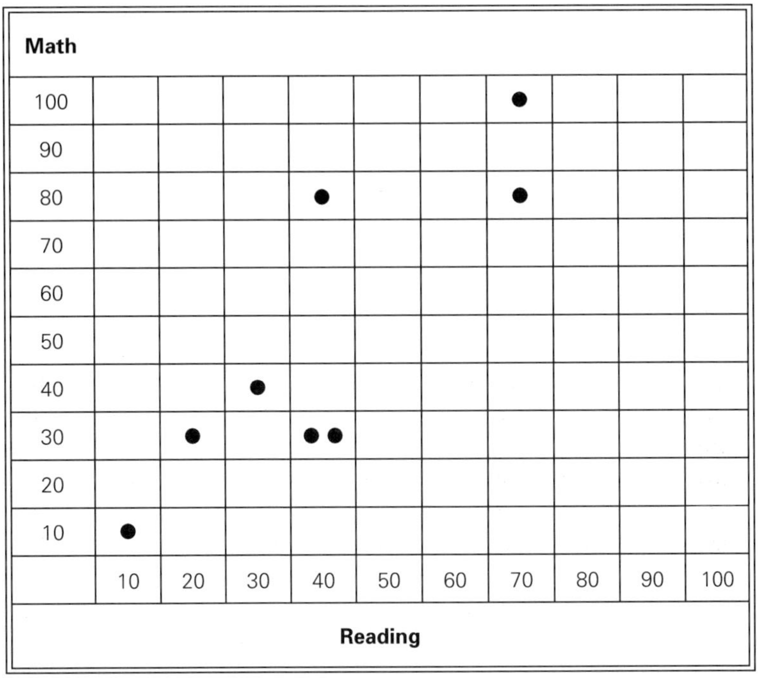

Positive and Negative Correlations

If there is a positive correlation between math and reading for a group of students, we could expect students with high scores in math to have high scores in reading. Likewise students with low scores in math would be likely to have low scores in reading. With negative correlations, high values in the first variable are associated with low values in the second, and vice versa. For example, across school districts, schools with the greatest proportion of students eligible for federally supported free lunches can be expected to have lower achievement scores. Schools with fewer students eligible for free lunches will usually have higher average achievement scores. It can therefore be said that there is a negative relationship between the number of students eligible for free lunches and school achievement.

As was true with the standard deviation, there is a definitional formula and several 'computational' formulas that can be used to compute the correlation between two scores. The computation of correlation coefficients can be found in Appendix D.

Interpreting Correlations

The first question most students ask about the interpretation of correlations is: how large must the correlation coefficient be before importance is attached to it? There

Table 2.4: *Examples of correlations*

Variable 1	Variable 2	Correlation
Score on test of programming skill.	Supervisor's rating of programming skill	.34
Childhood IQ (ten years)	Parental SES	.30
Combined Verbal and Math on SAT	Grades first year in college	.41
High school GPA	GPA in the first year in college	.52
WISC-R IQ	Stanford Binet IQ	.73

is no easy answer to the question, but we can start by saying that it depends on the variables. Table 2.4 provides a list of correlations that have been obtained between variables. The best way to develop a sense of how large a correlation should be is to examine the size of coefficients typically obtained between different types of variables.

Two, more concrete approaches to interpreting the size of correlation coefficients are *significance* and *index of determination*.

Significance of Correlations

The correlation between two unrelated variables will not be exactly zero. It will instead be a small positive or negative value. Such small coefficients are assumed to be chance occurrences. A coefficient large enough that it is not believed to have occurred by chance is considered *significant*. In measurement, research, and statistics the term 'significance' has a special meaning. 'Significance' in this case does not mean 'important,' it merely refers to a relationship that did not happen by chance. A correlation is considered significant if it can be expected to happen by chance less than 5 per cent of the time. The size of the correlation coefficient necessary for significance is mainly a function of sample size. For example, with a sample size of 100, a correlation could be as small as .19 and be significant. With a sample size of 10, any correlation less than .63 would not be considered significant. With a sufficiently large sample, any non-zero correlation coefficient would be significant. When you read a research article which bases its claim for the importance of a finding on 'significance,' you should be suspicious. Even very small correlation coefficients, which represent negligible relationships will be significant, if the sample size is sufficiently large.

Index of Determination

The *index of determination* provides an estimate of how well one score can predict another. It is obtained by squaring the correlation coefficient. Technically the *index of determination* is an estimate of the proportion of variance in a set of student scores that can be explained by knowing a second score for the same students. This is useful for the statistically oriented who choose to think of correlations in terms of the proportion of variance they can explain. For the more typical consumer of research information, the index of determination is not very informative because it is just a slightly different way of quantifying the same relationship.

Statistics are not always used to reveal the truth and use of the index of determination can be misleading. Most research seeks to establish the existence of relationships and therefore large correlation coefficients are desired. Sometimes the concept of 'significance' is used to make small correlations seem larger. Occasionally researchers have a different goal, they want to make a correlation seem smaller. Because correlations are always a decimal value, the square of a correlation coefficient will be smaller than the original correlation. A researcher who wants a correlation to appear to be smaller can use the index of determination to interpret its magnitude. The statement that Variable A explains only 25 per cent of the variance in Variable B seems to indicate less of a relationship than the statement that the correlation between Variable A and Variable B is .50.

Causality

In measurement, statistics, research, and science, causality is of great importance, but it is usually difficult to establish. The most common error made in the interpretation of correlations is the incorrect attribution of cause. Misunderstandings about causal relations occur frequently because our intuitive grasp of these relationships is so often flawed. When two events occur at the same time, there is a strong temptation to assume that one caused the other. Even if there is a causal relationship between the two, the direction of causation may not be clear. There is also the possibility that the correlation results from the effect of a third factor.

Confusing Cause and Effect

It has been established in numerous studies that there is a relationship between the score of students on a measure of self-esteem and their performance in class. It is often erroneously concluded that a child's self-esteem somehow determines his or her performance in class. This is used as a justification for classroom activity aimed at increasing academic performance by means of enhancing self-esteem. Raising the self-esteem of children may be a legitimate part of a child's education, and activities that enhance self-esteem may positively affect school performance, but the existence of a correlation between the two does not establish that this causal relationship exists. It is just as likely that a student who is successful in school will develop a good self-esteem as a result of his or her successes.

The same phenomenon occurs when researchers conclude that a high correlation between parental expectations and a child's academic performance justifies programs that endeavor to increase student achievement in school by raising parental expectations. In this case, an assumption is being made about the direction of causality that has little basis other than wishful thinking. It is far more likely that parents' expectations are affected by their child's past performance than the other way around.

In evaluating correlation coefficients, it is important to not jump to conclusions about what is caused and what is causal. All a correlation coefficient tells us is the strength of a relationship. It does not tell why that relationship exists.

Third Factors

The two examples above illustrate errors in identifying the direction of cause. Another common error occurs when a third factor affects both variables. In this situation the two variables may have no connection other than their relationship with the third factor. For example, across a large number of high schools, it is possible to obtain a sizable correlation coefficient between the number of books in school libraries and the percentage of graduates of these schools who attend college. This does not mean that there is a causal relationship between the two. It is unlikely that the number of students who go on to attend college can be increased by placing more books in school libraries. The most important factor is the socio-economic level of the community. Schools in well-to-do areas not only can afford more books for their school libraries, but the parents of their students are usually better educated and are committed to having their children attend college. Parents in such communities are also better able to afford to send their children to college.

In a number of states it has been found that students who take algebra in high school are more likely to attend college. This has led to the requirement that all students enroll in algebra in the mistaken belief that it is exposure to algebra that causes students to go to college. At the same time, as noted before, the average academic achievement of schools is negatively correlated with the proportion of students eligible for federally supported free lunches. No one would suggest that achievement could be improved by taking away student lunches, but that would be no more erroneous than the policy of requiring all students to enroll in algebra to increase college attendance.

Factors that Affect the Size of Correlations

There are many factors, besides the actual degree of relationship, that affect the size of the correlation coefficients. For instance, a substantial correlation coefficient can be obtained only when there is sufficient variability (large standard deviations) in the variables being correlated. When correlation coefficients are suppressed by low variability, the phenomenon is called *restricted range*. Another factor that can suppress the magnitude of a correlation coefficient is *non-linearity*. Only variables that are linearly related can be expected to have large correlations. The scatter plot in Figure 2.2, provides an example of a linear relationship. Figure 2.3 provides an example of the non-linear relationship between test performance and anxiety. As can be seen, performance is poor when anxiety is low. As anxiety increases, so does performance. When anxiety becomes too high, performance begins to decline.

Figure 2.3: Example of a non-linear relationship

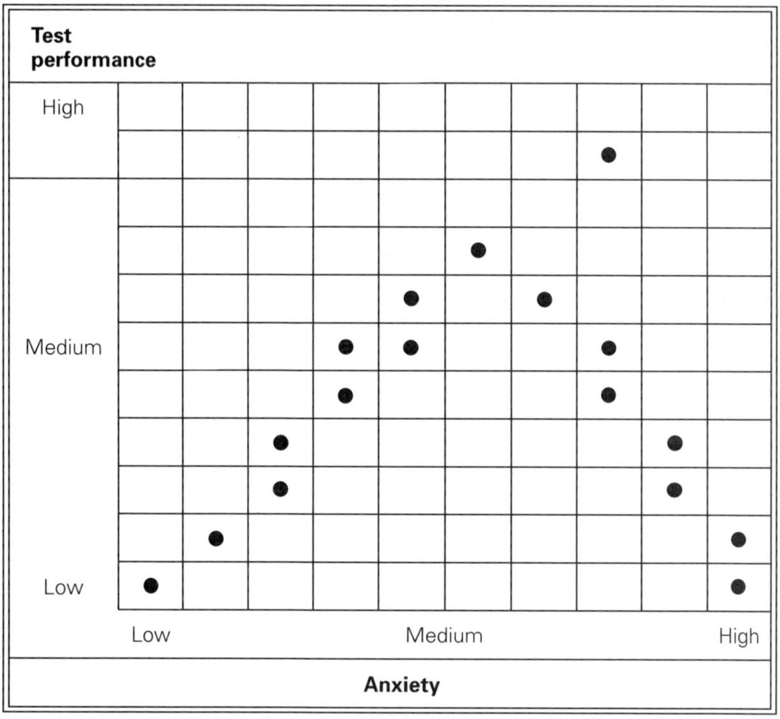

Test performance

High

Medium

Low

Low   Medium   High

Anxiety

The plot of such a relationship is better described as a curve than a straight line. Despite the obvious relationship between test performance and anxiety, the correlation coefficient between the two will be small.

Reliability is another important factor that affects the size of a correlation coefficient. Reliability is described in a following section in this chapter, but for now it is enough to know that it refers to the consistency or repeatability of a test score. When scores that are to be correlated are not reliably measured, small correlation coefficients can be expected. For example, the correlation coefficient between job aptitude test scores and on-the-job performance is small, typically in the .20 to .30s range. This is probably because assessments of job performance, which are usually based on performance ratings by supervisors, have low reliability.

Derived Scores

There is only a limited amount of information to be learned about student performance from an examination of raw scores, i.e., the number of items correctly answered on a test or the points earned in a classroom activity. Over-emphasizing the importance of raw scores is an error teachers often make when they evaluate students and assign grades. The number of items correctly answered on a test, by itself, does not tell us what students have achieved because it is so influenced by item difficulty. It is not easy to know, before test results are available, how many students should correctly answer an item. Items measuring the same instructional objective, even when they appear to be quite similar, may be correctly answered by students at different rates. The meaning of standardized tests is even more difficult to extract from raw scores because these tests are constructed specifically to have a level of difficulty that maximizes variability.

Telling a mother that her son correctly answered 36 out of 50 items on a reading comprehension test is likely to be more confusing than helpful in conveying to her an understanding how well her child is reading. There is no way for her to know whether this is a high, low, or in-between score, how it compares with the scores of other students in the class, or how much learning the score represents.

Raw scores can serve the purpose of rank ordering those who took a test, but in isolation they provide no basis for comparison. They may convey information about how a child is performing in school only when transformed onto scales that are understandable and interpretable. These transformations are called derived scores.

Grade Equivalents

Grade equivalents are used to interpret a student's performance according to how he or she compares with students at different grade levels. A child in the third grade who is doing very well might be described as reading at the 4.5 grade equivalent level, while a poor reader might be said to be reading at the 2.0 level. The popularity of grade equivalents stems from the ease with which they can be understood by teachers and interpreted to parents. Their simplicity, however, can be misleading because grade equivalents are imprecise and can provide a distorted description of student performance. The reporting of grade equivalents might lead teachers and parents to feel confident that they understand how a child is doing in school, but the picture they get may be distorted.

Limitations of Grade Norms

Grade equivalents provide a decimal grade value for each different raw score a student could obtain on a test. This makes it possible to interpret test scores in terms of how students at different grade levels typically perform on a given test. Grade equivalents promise more they deliver, however. There is no practical way to compare a child's performance with that of children in every other grade. To do this would require the administration of the same test to students in every grade. Such a practice would be unethical because students would be taking tests that were entirely inappropriate for them. It would also present a logistical nightmare. Instead, the test is administered in only a few contiguous grades and the equivalents for the other grades are estimated by means of extrapolation. Interpolation is used to determine the equivalents for scores between grades. If you know how fourth, fifth and sixth graders perform on a test intended for use with fifth graders, you can extrapolate above and below this grade to estimate how children in other grades might have performed if they had taken the test. These extrapolations tend to be inaccurate because they are based on the assumption that a child's achievement increases at a linear rate and we know this is not what really happens. In reading for example, the performance of children increases dramatically through the early elementary grades with less improvement between the seventh and twelfth grades. The lack of linearity is particularly pronounced at the secondary level, but exists across all grades. This is a major cause of the imprecision in grade equivalents. It is also the reason grade equivalents are used mainly with elementary school students.

It is not easy to make comparisons among different subject matter areas using grade equivalents because each is characterized by a different level of variability. For instance, there is much more variability in reading than math performance. Students can become better readers on their own by reading more, but there are limits to how much students can improve their performance in math without the benefit of formal instruction. It is possible that a fifth grade student who is at the seventh grade level in math and at the eighth grade level in reading is doing better in math than reading. Furthermore, grade norms cannot be used for subjects that are taught within a narrow span of years. For instance, it makes little sense to talk about a student's grade equivalent in biology, calculus, or home economics.

Finally, the meaning of grade norms is elusive. Consider the case of a fifth grade student who is at the seventh grade level in math. It is very important that the child's parents not be led to believe that their child can do seventh grade math. It would be better to describe the child's performance by stating that the child can do fifth grade math as well as a seventh grader can do fifth grade level work. This type of explanation is okay as far as it goes, but it doesn't work when a child is functioning below grade level. It is is illogical to say that a child can do seventh grade level math as well as a fifth grader can do seventh grade level math. Fifth graders have not been exposed to the curriculum necessary for success at this level and even the best fifth grade students should not be expected to have mastered that curriculum.

Grade norms provides only an approximation of how well a student is doing, and their magnitude really has little to do with the actual performance of students in other grades with whom the comparisons are presumably being made. As a result of the procedures used in their computation, the intervals between grade norms are not equal which renders their use in mathematical computations inappropriate.

Percentiles Ranks

Percentile ranks are a somewhat better method of communicating test score meaning than grade equivalents because they provide an indication of how an individual is functioning in comparison with others in the same grade. This characteristic means that percentiles avoid the biggest problem with grade equivalents, comparisons with students at different grade levels. Percentile ranks have the additional advantage of being appropriate for use with both high school and elementary students. Percentile ranks can tell us how a student compares with norms for the classroom, school, district, state, or nation. To correctly interpret percentile ranks, it is important to know the comparison group being used.

The first step in computing a percentile rank is to place the scores of students in rank order. Next each student's rank is divided by the total number of students in the comparison group. Like percentages, their value can range from 1 to 100. A percentile rank of an individual student tells us the proportion of students he or she has surpassed. A student at the 75th percentile has performed better than 75 per cent of the comparison group and in turn has been surpassed by 25 per cent. A percentile rank of 50 is the same as the median because both represent the midpoint in a set of scores. A more detailed description of the computation of percentile ranks can be found in Appendix E.

Percentile ranks are usually associated with standardized tests and are seldom used to describe in-class performance. When percentile ranks are used with standardized tests, tables of norms are prepared by the publisher. These norms are based on the administration of the test to a large and representative sample of students. A student's raw score is looked up in the table to find the equivalent percentile rank. This makes it possible to compare an individual with a national comparison group.

Limitations of Percentile Ranks

While percentile ranks are superior to grade equivalents in a number of ways, they have important limitations when compared with standard scores. There is a loss of information inherent in the process of computing percentile ranks because they are based on the rank-order position of students rather than actual scores. Reliance on ranking information causes percentile ranks to have a rectangular rather than a normal distribution shape, regardless of the shape of the original distribution. This means that there are always 10 per cent of cases between the 10th and 20th percentile ranks, just as there are between the 50th and 60th percentiles. With a normal distribution, most of the student scores are at the center of the distribution while there are far fewer at the extremes. As a result, differences among percentile rank values are not proportional to the differences among the raw scores upon which they are based. For this reason, percentile ranks should not be treated mathematically. If they are added, subtracted, or multiplied, the results will be distorted and inaccurate. For instance, one should avoid using the mean and standard deviation with percentile ranks. If such statistics are needed, they should be computed on the raw scores first and only then transformed into a percentile rank.

Standard Scores

Standard scores, unlike grade equivalents and percentiles, can be treated mathematically. On the other hand they are more difficult to explain to those who are not familiar with their use. Standard scores are transformations of scores that change the mean and the size of the intervals between scores. Depending on how they are computed, they may maintain the same shape as the distribution of raw scores on which they are based or they may be given the shape of a normal distribution.

Standard scores are defined by a fixed mean and standard deviation. This characteristic is important because scores that have been transformed onto the same scale can be legitimately compared and combined. There are many different standard scores, each with its own mean and standard deviation, and each intended for a different purpose. The proliferation of many forms of standard scores serves no real purpose and one standard score could serve the purpose of all the many available.

The reader may encounter terminology related to standard scores in other sources that is somewhat different from what is found in this section. Every effort to include the most accepted terminology has been made, but in some cases there is no agreement among experts and textbooks.

z-scores

The most fundamental standard score is the z-score. It is simply the difference obtained when a mean is subtracted from the raw score and that difference is divided by the standard deviation. It is defined by the following formula:

$$z\text{-score} = \frac{X - \overline{X}}{\sigma}$$

where:

X = a raw score
$\overline{X}$ = the mean
σ = the standard deviation

The z-score is used as a starting point for the computation of other standard scores. It always has a mean of 0 and a standard deviation of 1.

T-scores

The z-score has two disadvantages: (1) anytime the raw score is less than the mean, it is negative, and (2) it is usually reported as a decimal. To avoid these problems, the z-score is commonly transformed into a standard score with a mean of 50 and a standard deviation of 10.

Unfortunately, there is no consensus regarding what this standard score should be called. The authors of various measurement textbooks have identified this score as a T-score, a C-score, a Z-score or sometimes just as a standard score. The most common term is T-score and that is the term that will be used here. The formula for the T-score is as follows:

$$T\text{-score} = 10z + 50$$

To obtain a T-score, a z-score is computed which is multiplied by 10 and added to 50. Regardless of the scores you start with, after performing the above procedure the resulting standard scores will always have a mean of 50 and a standard deviation of 10. They also will be positive and can be used without a decimal point. The scores described above are not normalized. This means that the shape of the distribution of raw scores and the corresponding distribution of *T*-scores remain the same, as does the relationship among the scores. Normalized scores, on the other hand, not only have different means and standard deviations than the corresponding distribution of raw scores, but the shape of their distributions is normalized through changes in the relationship among the scores. A description of the computation of normalized *T*-scores can be found in Appendix F.

Standardized scores should only be normalized when the underlying construct being measured is normally distributed. For example, in the development of scales for intelligence tests, test authors can reasonably assume that the underlying intellectual traits are normally distributed. Therefore the standard scores developed to measure these scales are normalized.

College Entrance Examination Board (CEEB) Scores

The standard score used by the Educational Testing Service (ETS) for college and professional school aptitude tests are called CEEB scores. Examples of tests that use this type of score are the Scholastic Aptitude Test (SAT), the Graduate Record Exam (GRE), and parts of the Law School Aptitude Test (LSAT). The CEEB has a mean of 500 and a standard deviation of 100 based on its original administration. CEEB scores are normalized and are computed from the following formula:

$$CEEB = 100z + 500$$

The *z*-score used in the computation is not obtained using the *z*-score formula presented above, but is based on the same procedures described in Appendix F. As with any standard score, it is important to remember that all CEEB type scores are not normed on the same populations and therefore cannot be directly compared even though they appear to be on the same scale. A 500 on the GRE represents a higher level of functioning than the same score on the SAT because the norm groups are different. The norm group for the GRE consists of students in college who are contemplating going to graduate school while the comparison group for the SAT are high school students who are considering college.

ACT Scores

The American College Testing Program (ACT) is administered by the Iowa Test Bureau. Scores on this test can range from 1 to 36. The mean is now 20.7 and the standard deviation is 5. Like CEEB scores, ACT scores are normalized.

Intelligence Quotients (IQs)

In the United States, the first widely administered and generally accepted individual test of intelligence was published in 1916 by Lewis Terman and called the Stanford-Binet Intelligence Test. It was the first important test to use IQ scores. These scores were based on the ratio of mental age to chronological age, multiplied by 100, to eliminate the decimal. This was seen as an improvement over the mental age scores which Alfred Binet used to report intellectual functioning on the Binet-Simon test, the precursor for the Stanford-Binet. Ratio IQs are not an ideal way of reporting student intellectual functioning, because they share many of the same disadvantages of grade equivalents.

The second major individual intelligence test was the Wechsler-Bellvue developed by David Wechsler in 1937. One of the important advantages claimed for the Wechsler-Bellvue over the Stanford-Binet was the use of deviation IQs. These scores are computed in such a way that they have a mean of 100 and a standard deviation of 15 and they are normalized. The most recent version of the Stanford-Binet and some other group intelligence tests use a deviation IQ that is based on a standard deviation of 16.

Normal Curve Equivalents (NCE)

Since their inception, compensatory education programs such as Headstart, Follow-Through and Chapter 1 had to file reports of student progress with the appropriate federal agency. The selection of type of score used to report student performance was left up to the local sites. Many different types of derived scores were tried, but standard scores were usually avoided in favor of grade equivalents and percentile ranks. Often inappropriate statistical analyzes were performed on these scores. Those who did this were apparently unaware that it is improper to perform mathematical operations on grade equivalents and/or percentiles and that evaluations that include such computations, would be flawed.

To eliminate the use of inappropriate derived scores, all programs were required to use the same standard score. While it might have been best to replace the indiscriminate use of percentile ranks and grade equivalents with an existing standard score such as the *T*-score, a new type of standard score was developed instead. It is called the 'Normal Curve Equivalent' or NCE. Although the NCE is a normalized standard score with all the advantages of that type of scale, NCE scores look like percentile ranks. Perhaps the similarity in appearance was intentional in order to make the transition from percentile ranks to standard scores easier for practitioners. Their values range between 1 and 99, with these two values and 50 being the same as the corresponding percentile. The standard deviation of NCEs is 21.06.

Stanines

The term stanines is a conjunction of 'standard' and 'nine.' Stanines were first employed by the Army Air Corps in World War II. Only the integers between 1 and 9 are used and decimal values are never included. The choice of this particular range of integers was made because it fits conveniently onto a single column of a standard paper computer card. At one time computer cards were the most common media for communicating with computers.

Figure 2.4: Stanines

Stanine	1	2	3	4	5	6	7	8	9
Percentage of cases	4%	7%	12	17%	20%	17%	12%	7%	4%
Percentiles	1–4	4–11	11–23	23–40	40–60	60–77	77–89	89–96	96–99
z-scores		−1.75	−1.25	−.75	−.25	+.25	+.75	+1.25	+1.75

Although it might sound like an unusual and not very useful attribute, the most important characteristic of stanines is the lack of information that they provide. They are intentionally imprecise. Their use is justified in circumstances in which it is believed that parents are better off if they are not given detailed information about their children's performance. It is feared that parents are likely to attach undue importance to small differences in scores or slight changes from year to year. Parents might be upset to find out that their child had dropped from the 75th to the 65th percentile rank in reading in a year's time. If in both years they had been told that their child was at the 6th stanine they would be less likely to become upset.

As can be seen in Figure 2.4, the distance between each stanine is one half of a standard deviation. The easiest way to understand stanines is as a range of percentile rank scores. The 5th stanine is in the center and includes students between the 40th and 60th percentile ranks (the middle 20 per cent of students). The 6th stanine includes students between the 60th and 77th percentile ranks (17 per cent of students). The 4th stanine also includes 17 per cent of students, those between the 23rd and 40th percentile ranks. The 3rd and 7th stanines include 12 per cent, the 2nd and 8th 7 per cent; and the 1st and 9th 4 per cent.

Using Derived Scores

When a decision must be made regarding the form of derived score to employ, there are two considerations that should be kept in mind: (1) ease of explanation and (2) precision. The relationship between these two considerations can be seen in Figure 2.5. As this figure points out, the choice of a derived score requires a trade-off between ease of explanation and precision.

There is another way that derived scores differ. If a school district wishes to report year to year changes in student performance, the selection of the derived scores can be important. The same change in raw scores will appear to be much greater if scores are reported as percentiles. The difference will seem much less if NCE scores are used and will seem minuscule if *T*-scores are used.

Figure 2.5: *Comparing derived scores*

| Grade equivalents | Percentiles | Stanines | NCEs | Standard scores |

← Easily explained   Difficult to explain →

← imprecise   Precise →

Reliability and Validity

Measurements in psychology and education are of much lower quality than those employed in the so-called hard sciences. Assessments tend to be indirect and to refer to traits for which the precise meaning remains vague and open to contradictory interpretations. All measurements fall short of perfection and the assessment of the degree of this imperfection involves the determination of whether a test possesses two critical characteristics: (1) consistency (reliability), and (2) legitimacy of inferences about scores (validity).

A test score can be reliable without being valid, but before the inferences about test score can be considered valid they must first be reliable. If a test is measuring something consistently, it is considered reliable. Unless that *something* is what is intended, inference about the test scores would not be considered valid. Suppose an achievement test battery is assessing knowledge of science using multiple-choice items that assess student understanding of paragraphs about science. The test is mainly measuring reading comprehension which can be done quite reliably. At the same time, the inferences that can be made about how much students know about science are not necessarily valid. This test would, therefore, be reliable, but not valid.

Reliability is usually expressed by a single value that can range between zero and 1. With the aid of a computer, reliability can be computed quite easily and the technical manuals for standardized tests usually contain numerous pages filled with reliability data. The case for validity is more dependent on the force of narrative than on numerical indices and is seldom easily established. As a result, test manuals tend to devote far fewer pages to information about validity.

Reliability

Descriptions of test reliability usually begin with an examination of everyday measurements such as the repeated weighing of an object on a scale. If something weighs the same each time it is placed on a scale, it can reasonably be concluded that its measurement is reliable. If the same weight is not obtained each time, the measurement would be considered unreliable. The same could be said about a test that failed to yield the same score each time it was administered. There are two ways to quantify inconsistency on a test: the standard error of measurement and the reliability coefficient.

Standard Error of Measurement (SEM)

As psychometrists began to refine measurement techniques at the beginning of this century, there was a need to quantify the degree to which their measurements were imprecise. The concept of measurement error was first introduced by Charles Spearman (1924). He was seeking a way to quantify the degree to which an obtained score would differ from a true score. The obtained score is a student's actual score whereas the true score is the score a student would get if there were no error. Because errors are assumed to be random, when a student is repeatedly assessed, the obtained scores should be normally distributed around the true score. This distribution is assumed to be the same for each subject, and the standard deviation of this distribution is the standard error of measurement (SEM).

A useful characteristic of the SEM is that it can be used to compute confidence bands around a test score. For instance, if a student obtains a score of 36 on a test with a SEM of 3, we know that if we repeated the measurement many times, 68 per cent of the time the true score would be between 33 and 39 and 95 per cent of the time between 30 and 42.

The standard error is in the same scale as the data on which it is computed. For a classroom test it would be in raw-score form, and for an IQ test it would be in IQ points. This means that we cannot evaluate standard errors independently of their scale. For example, the SAT has a standard error of 30, whereas the American College Test(ACT) has a standard error of one. The difference in SEMs does not mean that the ACT test is more reliable. The SEMs for these two tests differ because each is based on a different scale. The size of the SEM is closely related to the size of the standard deviation and as a result, the SAT with its larger standard deviation has a larger SEM than the ACT.

The Reliability Coefficient

Unlike the SEM, the reliability coefficient is not based on the scale of any particular test and instead uses a universal scale that ranges from zero to one. The more reliable a test is, the closer it will approach 1. The reliability of any two tests can be directly compared using the reliability coefficient. There are three approaches to computing the reliability coefficient: parallel forms, test-retest, and the single administration methods.

Parallel Forms

The model for reliability most often recommended in measurement textbooks is called parallel forms reliability. It is so widely accepted that other methods of determining reliability are usually considered estimates of parallel forms reliability. To compute this form of reliability you must create and administer two tests which are equivalent. Ideally, the tests would be constructed of items randomly selected from the same pool of items. Reliability is defined as the magnitude of the correlation obtained between scores from the two test administrations. This method of computing reliability is easily understood and is consistent with conventional views of reliability. However, it is not often used because it is impractical. Generating enough items for one test can be difficult, but creating a second equivalent test requires more effort than most teachers are willing to expend. Time also must be set aside for the administration of two tests, either during the same testing session or with an intervening time separating the two.

Parallel forms reliability provides two types of information about reliability or consistency. First, it tells us whether students have changed between the administration of the two test (when there is a period of time separating the two administrations) which is one indication of consistency. Second, it tells us whether the items in the domain are measuring the same thing which is another type of consistency. This is because a high correlation between two parallel tests can be obtained only if the items in the domain from which they were selected, consistently measure the same construct. This characteristic is called *internal consistency*.

Test–retest Reliability

To compute test–retest reliability, the same test is administered twice and the correlation coefficient is computed using the scores from the two administrations. This method has the conceptual advantage of comparing separate test performances of students and can provide information about consistency in performance over time.

Test–retest reliability is generally considered a weak form of reliability because it tells us nothing about the relationship among items. It is possible to construct a test made up of items assessing unrelated constructs that still has high test–retest reliability. As long as students answer questions the same way across both administrations, they will obtain similar scores and the result will be a high correlation between the two administrations and therefore a high reliability coefficient. There is also a tendency for this form of reliability to reflect only the degree to which students can remember how they answered items the first time they took a test which inflates the magnitude of reliability coefficients computed in this way. Some students may even believe that their own consistency is being evaluated when they take the same test twice. This may cause them to try to answer questions the same way on the second test that they did on the first, even when they know their response on the first test was incorrect. The amount of time needed to administer a test twice is another disadvantage of this method of estimating reliability.

Single Administration Methods

There are several methods of computing reliability coefficients that require only a single test administration which avoid the problems of creating a second test. They also don't require students to take two separate tests, or the same test twice. The simplest single administration method is called *split halves*. In using this form of reliability, a test is divided in half and the scores from the two halves are correlated. A test can be divided in any manner that results in equivalent halves, but the division of items is usually accomplished by computing the correlation coefficient between odd and even items on the test. Because the split-half method compares two halves of the same test, the resulting correlation is based on only half as many items as the parallel forms approach. Split-half reliability can be thought of as an example of parallel forms reliability with both tests administered at the same setting.

Since the number of items included on a test directly affects reliability, the computation of split-halves reliability must include an adjustment for the effect of fewer items. The Spearman-Brown formula is customarily used for this purpose. The formula for its computation follows:

$$r_s = \frac{2r_h}{r_h + 1}$$

where

r_s = split half reliability

r_h = correlation between two halves of the test

If the correlation between two halves of a test is .50, the reliability using the Spearman-Brown formula will be .66.

$$r_s = \frac{2(.50)}{.50 + 1} = \frac{1.0}{1.50} = .66$$

Split-halves reliability is conceptually similar to parallel forms reliability which makes it easy to understand. Still, there are three reasons that this form of reliability is seldom used anymore: (1) the size of the reliability coefficient may differ depending on how the test was divided; (2) dividing the items on a test into those that are odd and those that are even is time consuming; and (3) there are other single administration methods of estimating reliability that are more precise and more easily computed.

The most often used single administration method of estimating reliability is Coefficient Alpha. It can be used for tests that are scored dichotomously (each item is scored right or wrong) or for tests made up of items for which students are awarded a range of points depending on the quality of their response. It also can be used with personality tests and attitude rating scales made up of items that are scored with a range of numbers representing differing levels of agreement with statements. A description of the computation of Coefficient Alpha can be found in Appendix G.

For tests that are scored dichotomously, there are single administration methods that provide an estimate of Coefficient Alpha. Their main advantage is their ease of computation. Unlike Coefficient Alpha, these formulas require the assumption that each item has the same difficulty. The simplest of these estimates of Coefficient alpha is KR-21. The main advantage of the use of this formula is that it requires only the mean, standard deviation, and the number of items for its computation. A description of its calculation can be found in Appendix G.

The Standard Error of Measurement (SEM) and Reliability

The reliability coefficient is directly related to the standard error of measurement, but each serve different purposes. The SEM is useful for describing the precision of an individual's performance on a test, while the reliability coefficient is better suited for making comparisons among tests. Although the SEM is defined in terms of repeated administrations of the same test, this is not how it is actually computed. In most cases, repeated administrations would be impractical. Instead, the SEM is computed indirectly using the reliability coefficient. The formula for computing the SEM using the reliability coefficient is as follows:

$$SEM = \sigma\sqrt{1 - r_{11}}$$
where
σ = the standard deviation of the test
r_{11} = the reliability of the test

To obtain the standard error of measurement, we subtract the reliability coefficient from 1, determine the square root of this value and multiply the result by the standard deviation of the test. If the reliability of a test is .91 and the standard deviation is 10, the SEM would be 3 (the square root of 1–.91 is equal to .3, which when multiplied by 10, yields a SEM of 3).

Measuring More than One Construct

Throughout this chapter, the reliability of test scores has been discussed in terms of how well they measure a construct. Of course, many tests are intended to measure more than one construct and this is reflected in the use of subscale scores. The reliability of each subscale should be computed separately. If the overall reliability of an assessment instrument is computed without taking into account the existence of separate subscales, the result will be an overall reliability coefficient that is smaller than the coefficient for separate subscales.

Methods of Determining Validity

Test scores are used to make inferences about the amount of a construct. The validity of a test is an indication of how good those inferences are. The first step in any discussion of validity is the establishment of the constructs about which we wish to make inferences. When someone asks whether a test is valid, the proper response is to answer the question by asking, 'Valid for what?' A test can be valid for one set of inferences, but not for others. For example, an interest inventory may be a valid indicator of interest in a particular job, but an invalid measure of aptitude for the same job. There is an almost unlimited number of inferences that can be made about a test score, some of which may be correct and some of which may be incorrect. Therefore, before the validity of a score can be evaluated, it is necessary to specify the interpretations or inferences that are to be made.

Validity is sometimes defined as the degree to which a test measures what it is supposed to measure. This is an incomplete definition of validity because inferences can be made about test scores that have no connection with what a test is supposed to measure. Some tests are quite useful even though they do not measure what their title implies or what their author intended. If legitimate inferences about test scores can be made for a particular purpose, then they can be considered valid even if they are different from the intended purpose of the test.

At one time, validity was defined by the three methods used to establish it. Most older measurement textbooks as well as the 1974 Joint Standards on Measurement and Testing focus on these three methods. The 1985 Joint Standards on Measurement and Testing changed the definition of validity, emphasizing that it is unitary, rejecting the use of separate methods for its computation. The 1985 Standards further stipulate that each method of assessing validity should be viewed as only one part of the evidence for validity. Several or all the methods should be employed whenever validity is being established. To further emphasize the unity of validity, '-related' is added to the titles of the three main types of evidence for validity. These include *content-related, criterion-related*, and *construct-related* validity. Face validity is sometimes included as a fourth, less important type of validity.

Content-related Validity

The content-related validity of a test is established by determining the degree to which the items on a test are representative of the instructional objectives the test is intended to assess. Content-related validity is most often used with standardized achievement tests, but it is also relevant for classroom tests. The simplest way of establishing this sort of validity is to list the objectives that a test is intended to assess and specify the items associated with each objective. A good starting point for the establishment of content validity is the construction of a *table of specifications*, which includes the association of items with instructional objectives. It also includes the number of items used to assess each objective, and the cognitive level of the questions (simple recall versus higher level problem solving). A description of how to construct a table of specifications is included in the following chapter.

Experts may also be used to evaluate the quality of items and the degree to which they match objectives. Unfortunately, content validation procedures are highly subjective and the case for validity is easily biased when it is presented by test authors. Content-related validity is probably best viewed as an argument in favor of a test's validity, which considering its source, will usually be positive.

You may have noticed that the definition of content-related validity is somewhat inconsistent with the definition of validity provided at the beginning of this section. This is because content validity is not really based on the inferences made from a test score. It is possible to provide convincing evidence for the content-related validity of a test even when inferences based on the test results may be entirely misleading. There are three ways this could happen. (1) A test could include items that assess each instructional objective, but the items could be so technically deficient that they cannot measure the intended construct. (2) A science test could include items that cover all the appropriate content, but the items could be written in such a way that a student's capacity to obtain the correct answer is more dependent on reading skill than knowledge of science. Such a test would be reliable since it is easy to construct reliable measures of reading achievement, but inferences made about level of science achievement would be misleading. (3) Finally, a test could have content-related validity but not be reliable. It is quite easy for a test with good content validity to have low reliability. This would occur if the domain being assessed was disparate to the point of being made up of different constructs. The items from the test, while being representative of the domain, could be so different that the test would lack internal consistency. As a result, such a test could have both good content-related validity and poor reliability.

Criterion-related Validity

The only type of validity that is based solely on an actual coefficient is *criterion-related validity* and it provides the most concrete form of validity. To compute criterion-related validity it is necessary to correlate the scores on a test with a criterion measure. The validation of academic aptitude tests provides a good example of the use of criterion-related validity. The criterion is the grade point average (GPA) earned in the first year of college. The size of the correlation between the academic aptitude test and GPA is used to establish the criterion-related validity of the academic aptitude test.

Although criterion validity appears to be the ideal way of determining validity, it has two important limitations: (1) it can only be used when an appropriate criterion measure is available, and (2) the reliance on the use of correlation coefficients introduces all of the problems associated with the interpretation of these statistics.

Identification of Appropriate Criterion Measures
It is often difficult to identify an appropriate criterion measure. The criteria that are available, too often are of low quality. A criterion validity coefficient can be no better than the reliability of the criterion measure used and poor criterion measures yield small validity coefficients. For example, the validation of job aptitude and civil service tests are usually not successful because they depend on supervisor evaluation of employees as the criterion measure for job success and these ratings tend to be unreliable.

The Use of Correlation Coefficients
The use of correlation coefficients can cause a myriad of problems. There are many factors that affect the size of correlation coefficients which in turn, influence the size of the validity coefficient. When the validity of a test is evaluated and the resulting coefficient is smaller than expected, the cause of this apparent invalidity may not be obvious. All the factors that influence the size of a correlation coefficient already discussed come into play in the establishment criterion-related validity.

If the range of scores on the test or the criterion is restricted, there will be not be much variability and as a result the ensuing correlation will be small. The correlation will also be suppressed if the test or the criterion is unreliable. Either, or both of these conditions will result in poor validity.

Construct-related Validity

Our language is rich in words used to describe classes of behaviors, such as intelligence, creativity, and reading comprehension. These terms refer to entities which exist only as descriptors of sets of behaviors. These descriptors are called constructs. A major purpose of measurement is the quantification of these constructs using scales that indicate how much of a trait an individual possesses. For instance, a teacher might be interested in the construct of self-esteem. Typically this construct is measured using a questionnaire that yields a numerical value indicating the degree to which individual students possess this trait. These questionnaires typically consist of a set of statements relevant to self-esteem to which students are asked to agree or disagree or respond with a numerical ratings to indicate how much they agree or disagree. By summing across student responses to statements, a score indicating the degree of agreement is produced. In this way an abstract construct (self-esteem) is turned into a concrete numerical index. Construct-related validity is intended to provide an indication of the degree to which the index really reflects the construct.

Designating the title of a test does not guarantee that the test will actually measure the construct it is intended to measure. The purpose of construct-related validity is the clarification of exactly what is being measured by a test. When first introduced, construct-related validity was considered to be only one of three types of validity. It was usually invoked when the other two were inappropriate, for example for the validation of personality tests. Content-related validity is not relevant for personality tests because there is no required content and they are often constructed in such a way that their true purpose is hidden. Criterion-related validity is inappropriate because personality tests usually are constructed when either no comparable instrument exists or there is a need to construct a better one.

Modern interpretations of validity suggest the need for a reordering of the relationship among the three different approaches to establishing validity. All validity should be defined as a form of construct-related validity. Content- and criterion-related validity need to be thought of as elements of, or evidence for construct-related validity. This perspective elevates construct-related validity to the forefront of test validation emphasizing that it has an important role to play in all test validation.

There is no single validity coefficient associated with construct-related validity. Instead, it is based on a logical validation, utilizing empirical data, in the form of an extended argument. Before we can accept the view that a test measures what it purports to measure, a logical case must be established for why inferences about a construct, based on test scores, are legitimate.

The accumulation of construct-related evidence takes place in three phases: (1) determining whether a single entity is being measured (unidimensionality); (2) describing the theory on which the construct is based; and (3) examining empirical evidence to determine whether the construct interacts with other variables in a predictable fashion.

Unidimensionality
For a test to be unidimensional, it must measure a single construct. There are statistical techniques that can be applied to a set of test scores to determine if the test is doing this. Prominent among these are factor analysis. Coefficient Alpha reliability also can be used to provide evidence for unidimensonality although it cannot be considered to be conclusive proof of that characteristic. A test that is unidimensional will have high coefficient alpha reliability while a test with poor coefficient alpha reliability is probably not unidimensional. Unfortunately it is possible for a test to be multidimensional and still have a satisfactory level of Coefficient Alpha reliability.

If a test does not measure a single construct, it cannot measure the particular construct it is intended to measure. Even if a test measures a single trait, and measures it well, it may not be measuring the right trait. Allen Edward's, now classic study (1953), demonstrated that on self-report personality tests, subjects tended to endorse items according to how socially desirable they perceived the items to be, rather than the degree to which the items applied to them. It is possible to obtain respectable Coefficient Alpha scores for such an instrument because it reliably measures a subject's ability to consistently identify items that are socially desirable. This does not necessarily mean it measures the intended construct.

Description of Theory
The second step in accumulating construct-related evidence of validity is less concrete than the determination of unidimensionality. It requires a description of the theory that underlies the construct being measured. For example, construct-related evidence of validity for the results of a test intended to assess self-esteem would include a detailed explanation of what is meant by 'self-esteem.' The theory should encompass a definition and delineation of the domain of observables that define the construct. In this particular case, it is necessary to describe how the trait is manifested and the instruments that can be used to assess its existence. In addition, the correlates of the construct must be described. This includes the way other measures are related to the construct, which variables show a positive relationship with the construct, and those for which the correlation would be negative. It also is necessary to list variables that have only a minor relationship with the construct under consideration.

Empirical Analysis
The third stage in accumulating construct-related evidence of validity requires the use of empirical evidence, usually in an *ex post facto* fashion. Much of this evidence is based on determining the correlation between the variable being validated

and other relevant measures. Evidence that the correlations are in the expected direction, as outlined in the theory of the construct, is used as evidence for construct-related validity.

Another empirical approach to establishing construct-related validity uses contrasting groups. To validate a measure of self-esteem, groups of students with high and low self-esteem could be identified using teacher rating scales or peer nominations. The results of the administration of a measure of self-esteem would be used to determine if the differences in self-esteem that teachers perceived were manifested in student responses to the scale.

Face Validity

A test has face validity when it *appears* to measure what it is supposed to measure. While this is obviously a less important means of establishing validity than the three previously discussed methods, there are some circumstances where it may be important. For instance, if an academic aptitude test does not have face validity, which means it does not contain the sort of items that students have come to expect, it will not be accepted as legitimate and students may not expend a sufficient amount of effort. Face validity is important for purposes of establishing rapport, but it is not required and in some cases it may not even be desirable. A test could be lacking in face validity and still be useful. An example of this would be the use of assessment instruments in research in which a knowledge of what is being assessed can not be shared with subjects. Of course most tests are constructed in such a way that they have face validity in order to maximize student effort.

Changing Definitions of Validity

The transition from the 1974 to 1985 version of the *Joint Standards on Measurement and Testing* was characterized by a decrease in emphasis on the separate methods of computing validity and the elevation of construct-related validity to a position of pre-eminence. There is now a trend towards a broader perspective on the topic and less reliance on construct-related validity as the only perspective from which to view validity.

The measurement field is awaiting the publication of a new set of joint standards. The aspect of measurement that seems to have caused the most problems for the authors of this document is arriving at a consensus about the definition of validity. The increased popularity of alternative forms of assessment has had a strong influence on how validity is viewed. Conventional definitions of validity tend to lead to the conclusion that alternative tests are not valid. Instead of using these findings as the basis for rejecting alternative assessment we have instead seen a process of questioning conventional approaches to validity. There have been modifications in the way validity is explained in order to accommodate these new forms of assessment. The validity of alternative assessment methods is discussed in Chapter 6.

The two most important developments in this new interpretation of validity have come from Messick (1989) and Linn, Baker, and Dunbar (1991). Messick, continues to strongly support the view that the most important form of validity is construct-related validity, but he also argues for the need to consider the consequences of testing when evaluating validity. The consequences to which he refers include the values inherent in the descriptions of the theory that underlies a construct as well as the social consequences of testing. Linn, Baker, and Dunbar (1991) list eight factors that they believe should be considered when the validity of a test is being evaluated.

- Consequences   The lofty goals of tests are not always fulfilled in their implementation. If the administration of a test leads to more effective teaching and increased learning on the part of students, this is important. If the use of a test distorts a curriculum and as a result students waste time on meaningless test preparation tasks, the validity of the test has been diminished.
- Fairness   Differences in student performance on tests intended to measure achievement should be the result of different levels of learning and achievement and not merely reflect differences in the income of the family, ethnic and cultural differences, test taking skills or level of intellectual functioning.
- Transfer and generalizability   There is a need to determine whether the performance on a tests can be generalized to performance and behaviors outside of the testing setting. Specifically, can a student who is judged to have good problem solving skills on a test be able to actually solve problems in the real world.
- Cognitive complexity   Many currently available tests are constructed to measure high level thinking skills while rejecting the importance of the recall of facts and isolated skills. Whether or not test authors are successful in achieving these goals can be difficult to determine, but this is an essential aspect of validity.
- Content quality   The items or tasks on an assessment need to be of sufficient quality that they are worthy of a student's time.
- Content coverage   This standard is similar to content validity as already discussed. It has particular significance for alternative assessment techniques that include only a few items. Content coverage is much more difficult to achieve with a shorter test than it is with one that is longer.
- Meaningfulness   This standard argues for placing test items or tasks into a meaningful context.
- Cost and efficiency   Traditional standardized tests are relatively inexpensive while alternative assessment techniques can be quite expensive. This consideration can not be ignored.

The change of emphasis in the way validity is viewed represents a movement away from the focus on the legitimacy of inferences as the cornerstone of validity. It also represents a change in emphasis away from viewing tests as primarily summative.

Summary

Teachers should possess the following technical skills to effectively conduct classroom assessments and play an active role in school and system-wide assessments: (1) descriptive statistics, (2) derived scores, (3) reliability, and (4) validity. A minimal knowledge of descriptive statistics includes familiarity with the three measures of central tendency including mean, median, and mode; two measures of variability, the standard deviation and variance; and correlation. Derived scores range from the most basic, and easily understood, but technically deficient grade equivalents and percentiles; to standard scores. Reliability is defined as the degree to which a test is consistent and is computed using parallel forms, test-retest, or single test administration methods. The validity of a test refers to the legitimacy of inferences made about test scores. Content-related, criterion-related, and construct-related validity are all used to assess the validity of tests, but it is construct-related validity that is considered to be the most important method of determining the validity of a test. With the increased use of alternative methods of assessments, definitions of validity have been expanded to accommodate these new techniques.

Suggested Readings

FELDT, L.S. and BRENNAN, R.L. 'Reliability,' in LINN, R.L. (ed.), *Educational Measurement*, 3rd ed., New York: Macmillan, pp. 105–46.

LINN, R.L., BAKER, E.L. and DUNBAR, S.B. (1991) 'Complex, performance-based assessment: Expectations and validation criteria,' *Educational Researcher*, **20**, 8, pp. 15–21.

MESSICK, S. (1989) 'Validity,' in LINN, R.L. (ed.), *Educational Measurement*, 3rd ed., New York: Macmillan, pp. 13–104.

Moss, P. (1992) 'Shifting conceptions of, validity in educational measurement: Implications for performance assessment,' *Review of Educational Research*, **62**, 3, pp. 229–58.

3   Planning Classroom Assessments

In this chapter students will learn:

- why planning is an important part of the assessment process;
- how different approaches to planning assessments differ;
- the differences between criterion- and norm-referenced assessment;
- how to write instructional objectives;
- how to construct and use a table of specifications; and
- how cognitive approaches for assessment planning differ from conventional methods.

Teachers are responsible for helping students achieve the instructional objectives designated for their classes. The purpose of assessment is to determine whether students have achieved these objectives. The objectives must come first. It is inappropriate to construct the test first and later select instructional objectives that match the test.

Instructional objectives may be mandated at the state, district, or individual school level. They may be formal, written objectives, designated by the state or written at the school district level. Alternatively, they may be authored by the teacher, based on experience, or the suggestions and/or expectations of fellow teachers. Instructional objectives exist even if they are only in the mind of the teacher and can be inferred from what is taught and/or what is assessed. Whether or not they are written formally, it is preferable for teachers to think about their objectives before they begin teaching or conducting assessments.

Formative and Summative Evaluation

Assessments are always used to make decisions. If no decisions are to be made, no assessment should be conducted. Decisions can either be formative or summative. Examples of summative decisions are the assessments used for assigning grades, the determination of whether a student is to be promoted or retained, or whether a student is to be accepted or rejected by an educational program. Formative evaluation can have an individual or group focus. For individuals, the emphasis is usually on the acquisition of diagnostic information to be used for remediation or academic acceleration. Formative evaluation can focus on the entire class or some portion of it. This sort of evaluation may include decisions about the rate that content is presented or whether there is a need to repeat what has already been taught.

Time Commitment

The construction of an effective, valid assessment instrument requires extensive planning and preparation. When teachers are unwilling to devote a sufficient amount of time to the test construction process, unplanned tests are often the result. Teachers are usually overburdened with responsibilities and they may feel that they don't have enough time to plan and create valid assessment tools, while continuing to accomplish everything expected of them. Unfortunately, there is no way to create a good test in a limited amount of time. There are shortcuts, but they should be approached with caution. Existing tests can be recycled, or the test items provided by the publishers of commercially prepared instructional materials can be used. Particular care needs to be taken with the latter source of items because their quality may not match that of the instructional materials.

Approaches to Test Planning

Literature on testing and test planning often emphasizes strategies that enhance the mastery of higher order objectives through the acquisition of subskills. It is assumed that 'the whole is equal to the sum of its parts' and that the mastery of these subskills ensures that the higher order objective will be mastered. Objective tests and *tables of specifications* (described later in this chapter) fit well with this planning strategy.

Instructional approaches that do not emphasize the acquisition of basic skills have emerged in recent years. For example, constructivist approaches to instruction tend to reject the importance of the establishment of an optimum sequence of basic skills. They view the acquisition of such skills as an outcome of effective instruction rather than as one of its prerequisites. Rather than sequencing basic skills through the use of a table of specifications, there is an emphasis on having students construct meaning holistically and thereby acquire higher level thinking skills.

Criterion-referenced Tests

Before the introduction of criterion-referenced testing there was no need for the term *norm-referenced testing*. The term was introduced to distinguish conventional assessment from the new assessment technique of *criterion-referenced testing*. The difference between these two approaches to assessment does not reside in the format of the items because the same item format can be used for both with minimum modifications. The two are distinguished by the way test results are interpreted and by the type of information they provide. Norm-referenced tests are evaluated by comparing an individual student's performance to that of others. The purest form of norm-referenced assessment is the rank ordering of students. Norm-referenced comparisons can be made at the classroom, local, state, or national level.

The results of criterion-referenced tests are evaluated by comparing student performance to pre-defined standards. This means that a decision is made prior to testing which specifies the level of student performance that is acceptable. A single score is reported for norm-referenced tests. For criterion-referenced tests, each objective is designated as mastered or not mastered.

The unique characteristic of criterion-referenced measurement is its capacity to provide information about *what* a student has learned. Consider a teacher examining the results of a test administered to third graders intended to assess their knowledge of multiple choice facts. All a norm-referenced assessment can tell a teacher is how students compare in terms of rank order. A criterion-referenced assessment utilizes absolute standards and can tell a teacher whether a student has correctly answered a sufficient number of items to be considered proficient in multiplication. Absolute standards are useful with concrete academic subjects like mathematics. It is easy to establish standards that can be understood and widely accepted for this type of course content. Teachers know how many multiplication facts a student should know in a grade at a specific point in the school year. It is much more difficult to make decisions about how many multiple-choice items a student should be able to correctly answer on a history test. Information about how students perform in comparison to others can be useful in this context.

Norm-referenced tests are intended to maximize the differences among student scores. This is considered desirable because it facilitates the task of rank ordering students. Obviously, if all students in a class were to obtain scores that were similar it would be difficult to discern the good from the poor students. This task is made easier if there is a lot of variability in student scores. On the other hand, with a criterion referenced test, the teacher will be pleased if all students reach the criterion even if there is little variability among the scores.

Criterion-referenced measurement has its roots in the programmed instruction movement which began in the 1950s. The publication of B.F. Skinner's article (1954), 'The Science of Learning and the Art of Teaching', signaled the beginning of programmed instruction. Programmed instruction is based on the belief that subject matter, no matter how complex, is most easily learned if it is first broken down into its smallest components and sequenced in an optimum fashion (Block, 1971). Instruction is presented using mechanical devices for exposing succeeding frames to students. Each frame contains instructional content.

For a short time, programmed instruction seemed destined to be the primary instructional technique of the future. It proved to be effective with some students and some subject matter, but never became a dominant instructional method, to the dismay of its proponents and the relief of its critics. There was one aspect of programmed instruction that had a sustained impact on curriculum, instruction, and learning theory for many years. This impact derived from the insistence of the developers of programmed instruction that its objectives be stated very concretely. Such objectives later were called *behavioral objectives*. Behavioral objectives are stated in such a way that a decision about whether they have been mastered is easily rendered because a criterion behavior is either present or absent.

Mastery Learning

Mastery learning is an old concept and its antecedents go back many years. The term itself was first used in the late 1950s. Mastery learning employs techniques similar to those first used with programmed instruction and was adopted by such learning theorists as Carroll (1963), Bloom (1968) and many others. This instructional technique requires the articulation of an overall instructional goal, followed by a series of correctly sequenced enabling objectives. The use of mastery learning is based on the assumption that maximum learning will occur when each student is given the optimum amount of time to master objectives. When a student is unable to master an objective, he or she is given further instruction and additional time. The student continues to be assessed until the objective has been mastered.

An attractive attribute of mastery learning is its de-emphasis on individual differences and the articulation of the view that all students can achieve at an acceptable level, regardless of ability, as long as the instructional materials are correctly sequenced, and an adequate time for mastery is provided. Mastery learning was introduced in the 1960s when concern about inequalities in our society was emerging — as was the belief that this problem could be solved through education. Here was a logical, common-sense educational technique that promised that all children could learn. It had the additional advantage of being supported by behavioral psychologists. There was a further bonus; using mastery learning, students are evaluated in terms of whether they have mastered objectives rather than by making comparison among them. As a result there is less emphasis on establishing hierarchies and the negative self-concepts associated with failure.

The underlying logic of mastery learning is attractive because it breaks the learning process down into more easily comprehended components. Educational researchers have a difficult time explaining how learning takes place or how it can be facilitated, but by breaking the process into its smallest components there is a promise of clarity. Those who believe that there is a simple explanation for even the most complex issues tend to be comfortable with mastery learning.

The Role of Criterion-referenced Measurement

Criterion-referenced testing was developed as a means of evaluating the individual instruction methods such as mastery learning. The use of the term *criterion-referenced* is generally traced to an article published by Robert Glaser and D.J. Klaus in 1962, 'Instructional technology and the measurement of learning outcomes: Some questions.' In this publication, the authors expressed their belief that norm-referenced tests could not be appropriately used to evaluate instruction based on behavioral objectives.

Nationally distributed standardized tests are specifically constructed to have content validity across a wide range of instructional methods and philosophies. The more specific these tests are made, the less marketable they become because of the variability that exists in curricula across the country. Glazer (1963) and later others

— in particular Popham and Husek (1969) — called for testing methods that were more appropriate and better able to meet the needs of mastery learning. Criterion-referenced assessment was created to serve this purpose. All of the factors already discussed, that made mastery learning appealing, also encouraged the proliferation of criterion-referenced measurement.

Minimum-competency Testing

Starting in the 1970s and continuing into the 1980s, there was a second development that promoted the use of some of the concepts underlying criterion-referenced assessment. This was the emergence of minimum competency testing (MCT) as an important educational policy. There was a series of events — from Sputnik, to failures in compensatory education programs; from declining SAT scores to the ascendancy of Japanese technology — that eroded faith in the nation's educational system. This disappointment soon became translated into political action as politicians came to recognize that this was an issue that could garner widespread support. Legislators and governors sought solutions. What they wanted was a strategy that, in effect, would make it illegal for a student not to learn in school. Those who failed to learn were to be punished by the denial of a diploma.

If this movement had occurred prior to the 1960s, it probably would not have gotten very far. The existing norm-referenced testing technology did not lend itself easily to MCT. It is illogical to insist that all students be above average, or some predetermined percentile. Norm-referenced assessments are relative and student accountability demands absolute standards.

Criterion-referenced testing provides a useful technology for the implementation of MCT. Using criterion-referenced assessment techniques, it is possible to determine which students have mastered and which have not mastered a given set of objectives based on pre-determined standards. Remediation, or at least the opportunity to retake the test, is provided for those who fail to reach the prescribed level. Those who don't succeed are denied a diploma and can aspire only to a certificate of attendance. The setting of performance standards, as is done in criterion-referenced measurement, was widely adopted for use in minimum competency and competency based assessment programs. These programs typically do not include feedback regarding the specific instructional objectives students have and have not mastered.

Measurement Driven Instruction (MDI)

When high stakes are associated with the use of behavioral objectives evaluated with criterion-referenced assessment, the resulting approach is called Measurement Driven Instruction (MDI). With this instructional model, teachers are supposed to focus their instruction on what is being assessed, which is in turn dictated by the instructional objectives upon which the test is based. With MDI, no distinction is made between the curriculum and the content of the tests used to assess it. Unlike norm-referenced assessment, the items used in MDI are not considered to be samples from a domain. Everything the student needs to learn is specified in the instructional objectives and is included on the assessment.

The criticism of assessment that has led to the heightened interest and application of alternative assessment stems from reactions against MDI. With MDI there is tremendous pressure on teachers to focus only on specified objectives because that is all that is on the exams. This is the main benefit of this system for those who believe instruction should emphasize the assembly of correctly sequenced basic skills. On the other hand, this impact on instruction is viewed with alarm by cognitively oriented educators. They believe that these practices lead to distortions in the curriculum and too much of a focus on trivia and basic skills, with not enough time spent on higher level curricula.

The Present Status of Criterion-referenced Measurement

Where does this leave criterion-referenced assessment today? If you equate it with mastery learning, minimum competency testing, and measurement driven instruction, its use has certainly declined. If the focus is instead on the standard setting aspects of criterion-referenced assessment and its non-norm-referenced characteristics, it is doing well, even thriving as alternative assessment. The term *criterion-referenced testing* itself, is seldom heard. This trend is documented by Hambleton (1994) in his quantification of the number of criterion-referenced measurement papers, reports and books appearing in the literature. In the years between 1989–91 the number had dropped precipitously from its peak in the years between 1977 and 1979. Undoubtedly the downward trend has continued.

The advocates of criterion-referenced measurement are not ready to concede the demise of criterion-referenced measurement. In a series of articles appearing in an issue of *Educational Measurement: Issues and Practices* (1994) commemorating the thirty years that have passed since Robert Glazer's brief essay introduced the term criterion-referenced measurement (1963), the continued health of the movement is defended. This defense is based on a re-definition of criterion-referenced measurement. Behaviorally stated objectives are no longer the focus of criterion-referenced measurement nor is the optimal sequencing of basic skills. What we are left with is an assessment technique which reports *what* a student has learned that is not norm-referenced. If the term is not used much any more, and if it is no longer used for its previous purposes, it is difficult to build the case for the continuing importance of criterion-referenced assessment.

Using Criterion-referenced Tests

The usual method of implementing a criterion-referenced testing program is to begin with instructional objectives and generate a set of items to assess whether students have mastered the objective. The selection of items requires great care in order to ensure that success on the items will validly reflect mastery of the targeted objective. A cut-off score must be established to determine the number of items that a student needs to correctly answer before the objective is considered mastered. The determination of this cut-off score or criterion, is one of the most important and difficult aspects of criterion-referenced assessment.

The rationale for the setting of a criterion is the acknowledgment of the imperfectability of classroom assessment. It is unrealistic to expect that students who have mastered an objective will correctly answer all the items used to assess it. Therefore, taking measurement error into account, the cut-off score is set below perfection. The determination of exactly where it should be set is determined intuitively, but 70 or 80 per cent correct is typical.

There are several statistical techniques for setting a cut-off score that incorporate the judgments of experts (Nedelsky, 1954; Ebel, 1972; and Angoff, 1971). Although these techniques have the appearance of objective psychometric procedures, they depend on subjective decisions by judges and each method may yield a different cut-off score. Setting cut-off scores using these methods is time consuming and it is difficult for teachers to implement them in a classroom.

For some course content, the categorization of students as having either mastered or not mastered an objective makes little sense. The mastery of an objective is better described as continuous than categorical. To select an arbitrary point on a continuum and declare that those above that point have reached mastery while those below have not, is nonsensical. When the performance of students approximates a normal curve, the majority of students are in the middle, at the point where we probably want to distinguish mastery from non-mastery. Cut-off scores set at this point are therefore likely to result in many errors.

Writing Instructional Objectives

For any type of assessment, expectations about what students will be able to do at the conclusion of instruction need to be clearly defined prior to instruction. For a criterion-referenced test, a student's performance on each objective must be assessed precisely enough for a teacher to be able to decide if the objective has been mastered. When student performance is evaluated globally, precise information about which objectives have been mastered is not necessary. Objectives in this latter setting are intended only to provide enough detail to ensure an adequate sampling of subject matter. They also help teachers focus on the level of student performance expected at the conclusion of instruction which can in turn improve instruction.

In most educational settings, institutional goals provide a frame of reference for the development of instructional material and curricula, and for selecting teaching methods. Unfortunately, they are usually too broad to provide accurate descriptions of what a student should know. They are likely to contain such statements as '. . . all students can learn at a high level,' or '. . . students must become effective problem solvers.' When only this type of goal is available, teachers need to write instructional objectives that define what is actually being taught. In some states and school districts, curriculum guides that include more precise statements of object-ives are available. There are other possible sources for objectives, such as the tax-onomies of educational objectives developed by Bloom (1956) and Krathwohl *et al.* (1964), but the ultimate responsibility for selecting appropriate objectives rests with the classroom teacher.

Effective objectives are not easy to write. They must be concrete and specific enough for a determination to be made about whether they have been mastered. At the same time, they should not be so specific that they assess only what is trivial. Effective objectives will have the following characteristics.

1 *Objectives should be stated in terms of student behavior, rather than learn-ing activities or teacher purposes.*

For example, 'Participates in a group discussion about the Crash of 1929.' is not a satisfactory statement of an objective because it merely describes an activity. It does not specify the quality of the participation or tell us why a teacher wants his or her students to participate in a group discussion. An analysis of the activities and contents of the course of study in which the objective appears might indicate that the teacher wants students to understand the causes of the economic failures of 1929. If this is the purpose of the task it might be better to state the objective as, 'Demonstrates knowledge of the Crash of 1929 through participation in a group discussion.'

The introduction of behaviorally stated objectives was intended to correct for the tendency of instructional objectives to be too vague, by identifying the behavior that will be used to determine whether an objective has been mastered. When the content is concrete, objectives are easily written. For example, it is easy to specify the overt behaviors necessary to achieve mastery on a math task. Most subject matter taught in school is not as concrete as math and the associated instructional objectives are likely to reflect shades of meaning and understanding. Such object-ives are not easily classified as either mastered on non-mastered. For instance, it is difficult to categorize a person as either having understood or not understood the motivations of Hamlet. The criteria that might be used to define successful accom-plishment of this objective are quite diverse.

2 *Objectives should begin with an active verb that indicates the behavior that a student should exhibit at the conclusion of instruction.*

The use of an action verb places the focus of the objective on what the student does. The objective should not merely list content. For example, the statement 'Washington, Jefferson, Madison, and Monroe were among the first presidents of the United States.' is a statement of content, not an objective. The objective should be restated in terms of the student's observable behavior, such as 'Identifies the early presidents of the United States.' Other examples of action verbs are as follows: applies, constructs, categorizes, describes, defines, distinguishes among, and lists. Of course there are many other similarly effective action verbs that could be used.

3 *Objectives should be stated in terms of behavior that is observable in the classroom or school.*

An objective such as: 'Always practices good citizenship' is not stated in observ-able terms. The inclusion of the word 'always' makes it impossible to determine whether a student has mastered the objective because it is not possible to observe students at all times. Another example of an item that includes an inappropriate term is 'Understands the issues surrounding the Missouri Compromise.' Words like 'knows' and 'understands' do not represent observable behaviors. A proper object-ive would specify what the student must do to justify the conclusion that he or she has mastered the knowledge or understands the process being assessed.

4 *Objectives should be stated precisely.*

Make sure that terms have a uniform meaning. For example, in the objective, 'Knows the causes of the Civil War,' the word 'knows' does not mean the same thing to everyone. To one teacher it may mean that the student can list three or four different causes of the Civil War. To another it may mean that the student can synthesize the disparate views of experts into a single coherent thesis.

5 *Objectives should be unitary.*

Each statement should relate to only one process. For instance, the objective, 'Can list the events leading up to the assassination of Abraham Lincoln and can create a videotape of the reenactment of some of these events' contains two processes, a cognitive process of recall of information and a performance activity involving constructing a videotape. The same objective should not be used to define both. If a student can master only one part of the objective, the teacher will be in a quan-dary about whether the task has been mastered. If both parts of an objective are important, each should be stated as a separate objective.

6 *Objectives should be stated at an appropriate level of generality.*

Objectives should not be stated so generally that they are meaningless. At the same time, they should not be so narrow and specific that they refer to only unimport-ant bits and pieces of information. If objectives focus on minutia, the number of objectives required is likely to be long and unwieldy.

7 *Objectives should represent intended outcomes of instruction.*

It should be obvious that an educational objective for eighth graders such as 'Increases in weight' would be ridiculous. Obviously, instruction is not directed toward making eighth graders weigh more. However, objectives are often written that refer to changes in attitudes, even though no instructional effort has been devoted to their development. Objectives which focus on attitude change should be included only if the instruction is devoted to this outcome.

8 *Objectives should be realistic.*

The writer of instructional objectives must consider the time available for teaching and the characteristics of the students. An example of an unrealistic objective for fourth graders would be, 'Understands the causes for violence in human societies.' This would provide a daunting task for college level students and the cognitive level needed for this item may be beyond the capacity of all but the most excep-tional fourth grade students.

Constructing a Table of Specifications

Formal planning for a test requires the construction of a table of specifications otherwise known as a *test blueprint*. The table of specifications is a means for

Table 3.1: A table of specifications for Piagetian cognitive development

Content		Objectives			Number of items	Percent of items
	Recognizes terms and vocabulary	Identifies principles, concepts and generalizations	Applies principles and generalizations to novel situations			
Sensorimotor stage	object permanence, reflexes, intensionality, egocentricity	At the beginning of this stage an infant will track an object only as long as it is in view. In the latter part of this stage the infant will search for even a hidden object.	An infant sees you place a desired toy under a blanket. Unseen by the child the toy also is covered by a handkerchief. When just the blanket is removed, what does the infant do?		15	25
Preo-perational stage	conservation, fantasy, centering, combinatorial thinking	At the beginning of the pre-operational stage, a child is likely to believe that when the shape of an object changes so also does it's volume.	If you show a child at this stage that two balls of clay are the same size and then you roll one into the shape of a sausage, which will the child think is larger?		15	25
Concrete operations stage	classification, spatial relations, correspondence, irreversibility, decentering	In the concrete operations stage, children learn how to classify objects according to more than one attribute.	Given a set of round and square object, some of them white and some of them black, how will a child at this stage classify the objects?		15	25
Formal operations stage	form vs content, hypothesis testing, operations on operations, metaphors	Students at the formal operations stage are able to consider form independently from content.	How would students at concrete and formal operations stages respond to the following syllogism: All children like vegetables. Boys are children. Therefore all boys like vegetables.		15	25
Number of items	15	30	15		60	
Percentage of items	25	50	25			100

describing the content and structure of assessment instruments. The table of specifications is sometimes referred to as a two-way table because it includes both content and cognitive objectives. The table of specification can serve purposes beyond providing a template to ensure proper coverage of content by items. It also can provide the basis for establishing the content-related validity of a test.

In the table of specifications shown in Table 3.1, content is listed vertically to the left of the table and the cognitive objectives are listed across the top. The matrix also contains the number of items to be included for each content topic and its accompanying instructional objective. In this example, sample content is included to provide the reader with an understanding of what should be included. It is not necessary for teachers to always include this much detail in the table of specifications itself.

In the example above, the student is expected to understand the four cognitive stages described by Piaget. For each they are expected to master three cognitive objectives. First they must be able to recognize terms and vocabulary. It is easy to construct multiple-choice or completion items that assess this objective. Second, they must be able to identify principles, concepts and generalizations. This objective also could be assessed using multiple-choice items. The third, which requires the application of principles and generalizations to novel situations could also be assessed using multiple-choice items, but it would require a more ingenious test author. The test used to assess student achievement in Piagetian cognitive development is to have sixty items, with the items divided according to the percentages provided in the table of specifications.

Although strongly advocated in measurement textbooks, tables of specifications are seldom used by teachers when they construct tests because their creation requires so much time. There are strong arguments for their use, however. (1) Tables of specification provide a means of ensuring *breadth* of content coverage by specifying the number of items required for each objective. In the process, the teacher can learn which objectives are overly represented by items and which are ignored. (2) The process also can help ensure *depth* of coverage by reminding the teacher to include different levels of cognition from recall, to application and problem solving. Teachers may not always aspire to have their students function at a high level of cognitive functioning on a particular test, but the construction of a table of specifications will make the cognitive levels being employed, more explicit.

Relative Emphasis on Content

The number of test items used to assess each instructional objective within a content area should correspond with the amount of instructional time devoted to the objective. These decisions are likely to be subjective, but the teacher should try to maintain the same emphasis on content that has been placed on instruction. Allocating a different number of items to each instructional objective is the most obvious way of weighting topics and objectives on the test.

Table 3.2: *Comparisons among three item types*

	Objective	Constructed response	Alternative
Type of information provided	How well students select correct answers in comparison with other students.	Precisely what students have learned and how well they can organize information	How well students can apply what they have learned
Directness of measurement	Very indirect	Intermediate in directness. Provides direct measure of objectives which focus on written expression	Is intended to provide a direct measure of what students are supposed to learn.
Precision	Can provide very precise comparisons among students. Scoring can be completely objective	There is a considerable amount of subjectivity in the scoring of such tests.	Not a precise measure. Much subjectivity in scoring. There tends to be a lack of consistency across tasks.
Reliability	Highly reliable	Subjectivity in scoring tends to lower reliability.	Reliability is adversely affected by scoring subjectivity.
Validity	Content validity is emphasized and is enhanced by the large number of items that can be included. The restrictions in the format may limit construct validity.	Good content validity can be achieved with the main limitation being the restricted number of items that can be included.	Conventional measures of validity are difficult to establish and its advocates sometimes need to resort to face validity. Content validity is usually difficult to establish because of the restrictions in domain coverage.
Advantages	1 Can be objectively scored. 2 Can measure a wide range of cognitive objectives. 3 Can include a large number of items which permits good coverage of content. 4 Cost effective and efficient.	1 Can assess creativity, organization, and expressive ability. 2 Provides students with an opportunity to practice expression skills. 3 Item preparation is relatively easy. 4 Students cannot gain an advantage by guessing.	1 Measures real-life skills. 2 Assesses student within a meaningful context. 3 Uniquely suited to assess a student's capacity to transform knowledge into action.
Disadvantages	1 Item writing can be quite time consuming. 2 Items are generally presented without any context. 3 Guessing is possible and can increase measurement error. 4 Cannot assess creativity.	1 The evaluation of responses tends to be subjective. 2 Students can sometimes successfully bluff and convince the reader that they have a better understanding of content than they really do.	1 Costly and inefficient. 2 Samples a narrow range of content. 3 Lacking in reliability and validity.

The initial weighting of objectives requires the assignment of percentages to each, with the total adding up to 100 per cent. Teachers must also decide which type of knowledge is to be emphasized. If more items are allocated to objectives that require the recall of information, than those that require the student to employ problem solving ability, a decision has been made to emphasize the recall of facts. The important aspect of this decision is that it is conscious. This is better than unplanned decisions about test construction. Too often, the teacher's only goal is to generate a sufficient number of items. If the teacher wants the test to have fifty items, he or she will start writing items and stop when there are fifty. With this approach, cognitive levels and content coverage become a function of item availability or ease of item writing rather than conscious planning.

Determining the Types of Items to be Used

In addition to listing content and instructional objectives, it is necessary to specify how progress towards the achievement of the objective will be assessed. There are three main types of assessment: objective, constructed response, and alternative. Objective items require students to make choices among possible responses. Examples of the objective format are multiple-choice and true–false items. Constructed response assessment can utilize either a restricted or extended response format. In some cases, alternative assessments require written responses similar to constructed response items, but they differ in other important ways. With constructed response items, decisions about whether a student has achieved an instructional goal are inferred from the response to the items associated with that goal. Performance on an alternative assessment test should so closely match the actual objective that it is indistinguishable. This means that no inferences are required.

In deciding whether to use alternative or more conventional assessment methods, it is important to consider how the results will be used. Instructional objectives which focus on the recall of information, or require cognitive processing are typically assessed using conventional pencil and paper tests. When precise, reliable, and valid assessments are needed, objective items are preferred. For example a decision about promoting a student to the next grade, should be made on the basis of a test with strong reliability. The main problem with objective items is that they are indirect and do not provide information about what a student knows and does not know. For making instructional decisions, such as whether or not a group of students has learned enough to justify moving to another topic, a performance test might be preferred. Performance tests have the advantage of being direct and concrete. They also provide information about what a student can actually do and they are more closely related to the problems a student will encounter in the real world. Where they tend to fall short is in their reliability and validity. Constructed response items can provide a compromise between objective and performance tests having some of the advantages and disadvantages of both. The three types of assessment are described in the following three chapters and an outline of the advantages and disadvantages of the three item types can be found in Table 3.2.

Determining the Total Number of Items for the Test

Students can be expected to answer only a few extended response (essay) questions at a single sitting. When more extensive answers are required, fewer questions can be included. In a 50-minute class period, a high school student might be able to answer three or four questions, each requiring extended answers of a page. For a short answer or objective test a much larger number of items can be included.

The total number of items included on a test needs to be of a sufficient size to provide an adequate measure of student achievement in each content area. The more content areas to be assessed, the longer the test should be. A weekly quiz can be short because it is assessing a limited range of content and fewer objectives. On a 6-week test or final examination, a larger number of items are needed because there is more content to be covered and more objectives are being assessed.

The time available for testing is a factor that limits the number of items on a test. On the typical teacher-made test, 90 per cent of the students should be able to attempt an answer for every item. There is little to be gained by including so many items that the test becomes a measure of how quickly a student can answer questions. Response rate is not the same as the ability to provide correct answers. The number of test items that can be asked in a given amount of time depends upon the following factors:

1 *The type of item used on the test.* A restricted response item which requires a student to write his or her answer is likely to take more time than a true-false or multiple- choice item for which a student is only required to select an answer from several choices. Extended response essay questions that require lengthier responses will take still more time.

2 *The age and educational level of the student.* Because the reading, writing, and computational skills of students in the primary grades are just beginning to develop, they need more time per test item than older students. Attention span also can be a problem with young children. They may lack the ability to concentrate on a test for a long period of time. Testing time for these students must be shorter which will further reduce the number of items that can be included on a test.

3 *The ability level of students.* High ability students, by definition, are more skilled in reading and have better writing skills. High ability students also have a better command of subject matter and more developed problem solving skills. For this reason, high-ability students can answer more questions per unit of testing time than low-ability students of the same age and grade. Thus, a test for a class made up of gifted students could be longer than a test for students of average ability. A test for a slow learning class would be shorter than either of the two.

4 *The length and complexity of the items.* If test items are based on reading passages, or graphs, time must be provided for reading and examining this material.

5 *The amount of computation or quantitative thinking required by the item.*
Students may work slower when dealing with quantitative materials than
when dealing with verbal content. If the items require mathematical computations, the time allotted per item must be longer than for a verbal item.

It is impossible to specify the exact number of items that should be included
on a test for a given amount of testing time. Through experience, teachers familiar
with the kinds of students they are likely to have in their classes will be able to
judge the number and types of items, that can be administered in a specified amount
of time. The typical student will require from 30 to 45 seconds to read and answer
a simple multiple-choice or true-false item and from 90 seconds to read and answer
a complex multiple-choice item requiring problem solving.

The number of items that a student can complete in a given amount of time
also is related to individual learning styles. It has been found, for instance, that girls
take more time than boys to respond to items and minority students may take more
time than non-minorities.

Determining the Appropriate Level of Difficulty for Items

Difficulty implies something different for an essay than for a short answer or
objective test. The difficulty of an essay item is appropriate when it is written in
such a way that each member of the class can produce a credible answer. An essay
test with appropriate difficulty is structured to elicit responses which vary in com-
pleteness, insight, and overall quality. In the case of an objective item, difficulty is
defined as the percentage of examinees answering correctly. For example, if an
item on a test is answered correctly by 40 per cent of the students who take the test,
the item also has a difficulty index of 40. An item which 75 per cent of the students
correctly answer would have a difficulty of 75. (This can be confusing because the
larger the difficulty index the easier the test.)

The difficulty of the whole test is the average of the individual item difficulties, or more simply, the average percentage of items students get correct on a
test. The level of difficulty has a strong effect on the capacity of a test to make
discriminations among students, a characteristic that is manifested in the reliability coefficient. The ideal difficulty level for maximizing a test's discrimination is
a point halfway between the proportion of items a student could get correct by
guessing and 100 per cent. On a test made up of four-option multiple-choice items,
the ideal difficulty level would be 62.5 (this is the point halfway between 25 per
cent, which is the number of items one could get correct by guessing, and 100 per
cent). The formula for determining the optimum difficulty for a test is as follows:

$$\text{Optimum difficulty level} = P + \frac{T - P}{2}$$

where,

P = the number of items a student could be expected to get correct by chance
T = the total number of items on the test

For a test made up of eighty-four-option multiple-choice items, the ideal difficulty level would be 50 because a student could be expected to correctly answer 20 items by chance.

$$\text{Optimum test difficulty level} = 20 + \frac{80 - 20}{2} = 50$$

The appropriate average difficulty and spread of difficulty differs for norm- and criterion-referenced tests. On norm-referenced tests, item difficulty is set at a level that will maximize variability. One advantage to the use of multiple-choice items is the ease with which their difficulty can be adjusted by varying the degree to which distracters are similar to the correct answer. The difficulty of a criterion-referenced test depends more on the subject matter. Exponents of the use of criterion-referenced tests usually assert that the difficulty of these tests should be 'natural' and not manipulated.

On a diagnostic test intended to identify students with learning problems, it is reasonable to expect a large number of perfect or near perfect scores, and few relatively low scores. This is because the purpose of a diagnostic test is to identify the few students who are having difficulty with the subject matter being assessed. On a test administered at the beginning of instruction for the purpose of determining what should be taught, a large number of near-zero scores could be expected, since it is assumed that some of the material will be unfamiliar to the students.

For pretests, criterion-referenced tests, or diagnostic tests, variability is not a primary goal of test construction. It doesn't matter whether everyone gets a perfect or zero score on these tests. Important information is still being obtained. When a test is being used to discriminate among a group of students to facilitate decision-making, a wide spread of scores is desirable. We want to be able to see a difference between the high achiever and the next highest achiever and the low achiever and the next lowest achiever. Ideally, every student should obtain a different score and there should be no one who gets a perfect score or misses every question.

In the process of achieving the desired average difficulty level on a four-choice multiple-choice item, the teacher is likely to produce some difficult items that are passed by only 30 or 40 per cent of the students taking the test and some easy ones that are passed by 85 to 90 per cent. This is okay as long as the majority of items have a difficulty level around 62.5. Achieving optimum difficulty levels is less important than ensuring that the items provide a good coverage of content and that each is passed more often by good than poor students. Item analysis which includes considerations of item difficulty is discussed in Chapter 4.

Cognitive/Constructivist Approaches

Historically, most instructional theory has been predicated on the belief that teachers should focus on the teaching of instructional goals and that the assessment of student achievement should be aligned with these goals. Mastery learning and measurement driven instruction represent two examples of strong adherence to these principles. The belief in this approach does not necessarily require adherence to the principles of behaviorism, but these instructional approaches are certainly compatible with that theory.

Conventional instruction is usually based on the principles of direct instruction which is teacher centered and utilizes whole class instruction. In a classroom where these techniques are used, the teachers begins with a clear idea about what students need to learn. These goals are achieved through the use of carefully written and sequenced instructional objectives. Student responses are expected to be convergent; that is, the teacher specifies in advance which answers are to be considered correct. The implementation of direct instruction dictates adherence to the model of instructional planning already outlined in this chapter.

In recent years, cognitive/constructivist approaches to instruction have risen to prominence. They are based on the belief that learning takes place most readily when students construct meaning from their environment. The mastery of a set of properly sequenced discrete skills is replaced by an emphasis on problem solving, synthesis, and application.

Cognitive/constructivist approaches can be thought of as being indirect and they tend to be more student-centered than teacher-centered. Within this system, useful learning opportunities can occur that are outside of the original intentions of the teacher. Student involvement and participation in the direction of instruction is encouraged. Students are expected to generate creative answers and are rewarded when they respond differently from other students.

Instructional planning in the presence of cognitive/constructivist approaches to instruction are not as obvious as those associated with the more highly structured direct instruction methods. Instructional objectives may still be identified, but they tend to be broader and to have a focus on the mastery of higher level functioning skills. These approaches are compatible with alternative assessment techniques that require the student to construct responses using their knowledge. The alignment of assessment with instruction is not a priority and may not even be considered desirable. Assessment is not given a high priority and therefore assessment planning is not an important aspect of cognitive/constructivist instructional systems.

Summary

An important but too often forgotten aspect of assessment is planning. The first step in this endeavor is the determination of the purpose of the assessment. To understand the purpose of an assessment it is important to examine the types of decisions that will be made using the assessment. For assessment to be effective, an adequate amount of time must be devoted to planning and the construction of assessment instruments.

Assessment is sometimes categorized as being either norm-referenced or criterion-referenced. The two differ in terms of how results are interpreted. Norm-referenced results are interpreted through comparisons among student performances.

Criterion-referenced results are interpreted in terms of specified standards. The same items can be used for each.

A set of guidelines for writing concrete and measurable instructional objectives are provided in this chapter. Formal test planning begins with the use of a table of specifications. This a method of ensuring both adequate content coverage and that the content is assessed at an appropriate cognitive level. The use of a table of specifications is most suitable for instructional approaches that emphasize the teaching of a set of discrete skills. Approaches to instruction that are based on cognitive theories of instruction would not usually employ a table of specifications and instead utilize more informal approaches to assessment.

Suggested Readings

AMERICAN FEDERATION OF TEACHERS, NATIONAL COUNCIL ON MEASUREMENT IN EDUCATION, AND NATIONAL EDUCATION ASSOCIATION (1990) 'Standards for teacher competence in educational assessment of students,' *Educational Measurement: Issues and Practices*, **9**, 4, pp. 30–2.

BERK, R.A. (Ed) (1984) *A Guide to Criterion-referenced Test Construction*, Baltimore: John Hopkins University Press.

GRONLUND, N.E. and LINN, R.L. (1990) *Measurement and Evaluation in Teaching*, 6th ed., New York: Macmillan.

MAGER, R.F. (1975) *Preparing Instructional Objectives*, 2nd ed., Belmont, CA: Fearon.

SLAVIN, R.E. (1991) *Educational Psychology*, Englewood Cliffs: Prentice Hall.

4   Objective Test Items

In this chapter students will learn:

- how objective and constructed response items differ;
- about the advantages and disadvantage of the objective item format;
- about the advantages and disadvantages of the true–false item format;
- how to write better true false items;
- about the advantages and disadvantages of the multiple-choice item format;
- how to write better multiple-choice items;
- about the advantages of the matching exercises;
- how to write better matching exercises;
- how to prepare the objective test for use;
- how to score the objective test; and
- how to perform an item analysis.

Throughout this book, different methods of assessing students are described. Among these are teacher-made pencil and paper tests, standardized achievement tests, performance tests, and portfolios. This chapter emphasizes the type of objective pencil and paper tests that are used to evaluate students. Other forms of classroom assessment, including teacher observations and performance tests are more likely to be used in formative evaluations to assist teachers in the modification of course material. These are also the appropriate methods to use in making decisions about whether or not to provide more instruction before moving to another topic.

The approach to assessment that a teacher uses should be determined by the type of decisions that need to be made. No single method of assessment is likely to be best for all decisions. The characteristics of an assessment technique that make it appropriate for one type of decision, may render it less useful for other types of decisions. For example, a decision about whether or not a teacher should extend his or her discussion of a topic and provide additional instruction, can be made using an informal assessment consisting of oral questions. However, when a decision must be made about the grade a student is to receive or if he or she should be promoted to the next grade, a more objective test with higher reliability may be a better choice. A distinction should be made between conventional tests, which include traditional pencil and paper techniques (discussed in this and the following chapter) and alternative assessment techniques, which include performance tests and portfolios. This type of assessment is discussed in Chapter 6.

Types of Paper and Pencil Tests

Conventional tests can be divided into two main categories. (1) *Objective items* that require students to choose answers from several choices. Examples of these are true–false, multiple-choice, and matching exercises. (2) *Constructed response items* for which the student must create and write out their response. These can be brief, as is the case with restricted response items such as short-answer, completion, and fill-in-the-blank. They also can be in the form of the extended responses associated with essay questions.

The remainder of this chapter is devoted to suggestion for writing good object-ive items. The following chapter, Chapter 5, contains instructions for writing con-structed response items.

Characteristics of the Objective Item

Until recently, most educational testing specialists have favored the use of object-ive methods of assessment over constructed response methods. The dominance of objective testing began to dissipate in the 1990s with increased criticism of the use of multiple-choice items for standardized testing. Much of the criticism focused on large scale testing, particularly the use of these items with measurement-driven instruction. States, school districts, and test publishers have begun to adopt altern-ate formats for evaluating instructional objectives such as constructed response items and/or different forms of performance assessment. Much of the early advo-cacy of alternative assessment was based on dissatisfaction with objective tests. Arguments in favor of alternative testing tend to rely more on descriptions of the weaknesses of objective tests than the presentation of evidence supporting these new forms of assessment.

Whenever objective and constructive response items are carefully compared, the advantages of the objective format usually are manifested. An example of this comparison appeared in an article written by Lukhele, Thissen, and Wainer, titled 'On the relative value of multiple-choice, constructed-response, and examinee-selected items on two achievement tests.' (1994) published in the *Journal of Edu-cational Measurement.*

The test they chose to study was the Advanced Placement (AP) testing Pro-gram of the College Board. This test is a good choice because the training of their examiners and the sophistication of the scoring methods used with the constructed response items on this test are 'state of the art.' The deficiencies in constructed response items the study reveals cannot be attributed to flaws in the training of examiners or the scoring methods they employ.

The article begins by making two important points: (1) constructed response items are very expensive, and (2) the information that can be obtained from them is not very different from what can be obtained from multiple-choice items. The authors state:

Constructed response items are expensive. They typically require a great deal of time from the examinee to answer, and they cost a lot to score. In the AP testing program it was found that a constructed response test of equivalent reliability to a multiple-choice test takes from 4 to 40 times as long to administer and is typically hundreds of thousands of times more expensive to score. (p. 234)

With respect to the uniqueness of the information provided by constructed-response items they state:

The primary motivation for the use of constructed response formats thus stems from the idea that they can measure traits that cannot be tapped by multiple-choice items — for example, assessing dynamic cognitive processes. (p. 235)

Their conclusions were as follows:

Overall, the multiple-choice items provide more than twice the information than the constructed response items do. Examining the entire test (and freely applying the Spearman-Brown prophesy formula), we found that a 75-minute multiple-choice tests is as reliable as a 185-minute test built of constructed response questions. Both kinds of items are measuring essentially the same construct, and the constructed response items cost about 300 times more to score. It would appear, based on this limited sample of questions, that there is no good measurement reason for including constructed response items. (p. 240)

On the basis of the data examined, we are forced to conclude that constructed response items provide less information in more time at greater cost than do multiple-choice items. This conclusion is surely discouraging to those who feel that constructed response items are more authentic and hence, in some sense, more useful than multiple-choice items. It should be. (p. 245)

Much of the criticism of the objective item format, published during the last five years, which has been voluminous, has focused on the ways these tests have been used. In particular they are based on criticisms of minimum competency and measurement driven instruction programs. Much of the dissatisfaction with these programs focuses on the incompatibility of these methods with the most current learning and instruction theories. Alternative assessment programs are preferred over objective tests for these forms of assessment. In many cases the alternative assessment methods proposed turn out to be the use of constructed response items. Most of the literature on this topic is heavy on criticism of objective testing, but does little to demonstrate the superiority of the constructed response format.

Advantages of Objective Tests

Despite heavy criticism directed towards objective testing, the essential quality of the format, having students choose among options, confers important advantages.

- It is always easier for a grader to decide if a student has chosen the correct option than to evaluate the quality of a student's response to a question.
- The scoring of tests made up of objective items can be accomplished with a high degree of accuracy, which is why they are called objective items.
- The use of this format permits the inclusion of a large number of items on a test, which makes a broad sampling of subject matter possible.
- Objective items make bluffing more difficult. In responding to constructed response items, clever students who are effective writers can often convey the impression that they know more than they really do.
- Objective tests can effectively assess higher level thinking skills as well as student knowledge of facts. Multiple-choice items are particularly useful for this latter purpose.

In summary, the capacity of this item type to assess a large number of students efficiently, reliably, and at a low cost, should not be underestimated or undervalued.

Disadvantages of Objective Tests

Tests made up of objective items also have some disadvantages. The time and effort required for their construction can be considerable. The difficulty associated with test construction usually means that the test items must be used more than once. The cost of creating a new set of items each time a targeted instructional objective is assessed is too high. In addition, the improvement in succeeding forms of a test that results from item analysis is lost if items are not re-used. In practice, this means that students cannot keep their tests. Students therefore are deprived of a useful aid to studying and a way of gaining insights into the kinds of errors they are prone to make. Going over a test in class helps, but it is not as useful as allowing the student to retain their tests.

When tests are re-used, teachers must be concerned about item security. In particular, there is a need to be concerned when the same test is used in succeeding classes. Students may find out about the contents of the earlier test. Permitting some students to have the advantage of knowing about the items that will appear on a test administered earlier is unfair.

Objective tests are often criticized for placing too much emphasis on trivial subject matter. Some objective tests indeed do this, either intentionally or unintentionally, but multiple-choice items can be constructed in such a way that they measure a wide range of cognitive skills, from simple recall of facts to application, problem solving, synthesis, and evaluation. Of course it is difficult to write items that assess these higher cognitive levels. Furthermore, the teacher must ensure that there is a match between the cognitive skills assessed and those that students are taught. If appropriate instruction is not provided, tests intended to assess the higher level aspects of instruction may end up primarily measuring underlying intellectual functioning. On the other hand, if the items too closely match the problem solving instruction presented in class, the test may be primarily a measure of the students' ability to recall what they were taught rather than higher level functioning.

Guessing

Guessing can be a problem for objective items and can distort the interpretation of test results. Guessing not only contributes to measurement error directly, but it can have an equally important indirect impact on error variance when the rate of guessing among students differs. Guessing is an inherent and variable personality trait. When some students guess, and others are reluctant to record an answer about which they are unsure, test scores will vary because the students who are willing to guess, will get more items correct by chance alone. The best strategy for countering this tendency is to encourage students to respond to every item whether or not they are certain they know the answer. If every student guesses, the variability associated with differing rates of guessing will be eliminated.

The effect of guessing can also be ameliorated in three other ways: (1) by giving students an adequate amount of time to respond to each item; (2) by including a sufficient number of items on the test; (3) and ensuring that the items are of appropriate difficulty. Giving students enough time to respond to each item can lessen the effect of guessing because students are more likely to guess when they are pressed for time. Including enough items is important because guessing can play a disproportionately large role in determining a student's grade on a short test. The effect of guessing also is related to item difficulty. When a test is too easy, there will be some items that nearly every student gets correct. This will cause a student's grade to be determined solely by the few items that have adequate difficulty. If the test is too difficult, guessing will be more prevalent because students are more likely to guess when they don't know the answer.

There are statistical techniques that can be used to penalize students for guessing. These *correction for guessing* formulas were at one time routinely used to adjust scores on standardized tests. Their use has declined because the assumptions upon which they are based are implausible. The use of these formulas requires the assumption that incorrect answers are indications of guessing. With these formulas, student scores are lowered more for incorrect answers than for not responding to an item. Only blind guessing is penalized and a student can improve his or her score through the use of 'educated' guesses. The main value of correction for guessing formulas is their capacity to intimidate some students into not guessing. Test-wise students know that even when a correction for guessing formula is employed, their scores can be improved by guessing. For these reasons, these formulas are seldom employed any more.

Testing Styles

The objective format itself tends to favor students who work fast and respond quickly. This can be a critical factor on long and difficult tests. Class instruction, on the other hand tends to favor carefully considered responses. Students who work carefully and respond only when certain, are likely to fare better on class work than on objective tests. This phenomenon has been used to explain why boys perform better than girls on objective standardized tests despite not doing as well in the classroom. Boys are typically more impulsive and have a greater willingness to

Table 4.1: *Types of objective items*

	Advantages	**Disadvantages**
True–false	• A large number of items can be included. • Items are easily written. • Good content coverage is possible.	• It is difficult to measure more than the recognition of facts. • Guessing is a major problem. • The level of item difficulty is not easily controlled. • Items tend to be too easy or if appropriately difficult, too obscure
Multiple-choice	• A very flexible item type. • Can be used to measure a wide range of cognitive skills. • Can be objectively scored.	• Item construction is time consuming and difficult. • Guessing is a problem, but not as much as with true–false items.
Matching	• It is possible to cover a lot of content in a small amount of time.	• Are not easily used to assess higher level skills.

respond quickly to items, even when they are not sure of the answer, while girls are socialized to work more carefully.

Types of Objective Items

There are three types of objective response items: true–false, multiple-choice, and matching. They are similar, differing mainly in the number of options provided. The true–false item has two options. Students indicate if they think an item is true or false (occasionally another variation such as 'yes' or 'no' is used). The multiple-choice item usually has four options although it may have three or five. Matching exercises have a larger number of options, although no more than ten pairs of premises and responses are recommended.

The number of options and the total number of items on a test determine how much guessing will influence test scores. Guessing will be more of a factor on a test made up of two-option true–false items than a four-option multiple-choice test.

It is somewhat easier to construct true–false items and matching exercises than multiple-choice items. On the other hand, multiple-choice items are often favored because of their flexibility and capacity to assess a wide range of cognitive skills. The advantages and disadvantages of the three objective item types are listed in Table 4.1.

True–False Items

True–false items have a long tradition of use by teachers, but are seldom included on commercially prepared tests. True–false items continue to be popular with teachers because they are easy to construct and score. It also is possible to include a large number of true–false items on a test because students can read true–false items quickly and complete more items than is possible with any other format.

Disadvantages of the True–False Item Format

1 *True–false items tend to be either too easy or too hard.*
True–false items that are straightforward and fair, tend to be too easy, while items that are sufficiently difficult to provide a reasonable amount of test variability, tend to achieve their difficulty by being 'tricky'. Tests that are too easy, as tests constructed using this format tend to be, lack variability and are therefore less reliable.

2 *Most content areas contain few statements, other than the trivial, that can be said to be unambiguously true or false.*
Even statements that appear to be straightforward and concrete, at least in the mind of the teacher authoring a test, may be ambiguous for those taking the test. It is difficult for a teacher to find statements that are clearly true or false. The interpretation of statements from different points of view and the realization that not every issue is easily classified as right and wrong are important lessons to taught in schools. The avoidance of ambiguity and the emphasis on absolute statements is a disadvantage of the true–false item format.

3 *Guessing tends to have a large effect on the scores of tests made up of true–false items.*
For each true–false item, a student has a fifty-fifty chance of selecting the correct answer. The importance of chance in determining a student's score on a true–false test contributes to the unreliability of this item type. The inclusion of more items, which is possible with this item format, can, to some degree, mitigate the effect of guessing.

Using True–False Items

The true–false item is most useful for assessing the acquisition of facts, preferably those that are easily categorized as true or false. For example, the Colonies either declared their independence from England in 1776 or they did not, and Ulysses S. Grant was either the leader of the Union forces at the end of the Civil War or he was not. Around this type of knowledge it is possible to write reasonable true–false items. Unfortunately, only a small fraction of the knowledge in any field is of this type, and much that fits the pattern is relatively unimportant. Recent research on instruction and test-taking behavior stresses the importance of having students construct meaning from related knowledge and experience. Because of the importance given to the context of information, the type of isolated facts assessed by true–false items may not be relevant to modern instruction. Furthermore, the lack of a frame of reference for such items makes judgments about the truth or falsity of statements too often dependent on the opinion of the test author.

An apparent advantage of true–false items, the ease with which a large number of items can be generated, may really be a disadvantage. Good true–false items are difficult to write and the process of constructing an entire test is time consuming. A true–false test made up of poor items may be easy to construct, but it usually will result in poor assessment. Although the same can be said about any item type, hasty, ill considered test construction seems to be a particular problem with true–false items, perhaps due to the ease of collecting the set of statements used in such tests.

Appropriate Uses for True–False Items

Before completely abandoning the true–false format it should be noted that with some subject matter it is possible to construct a test made up of these items that compares favorably with a multiple-choice test covering the same content. Advocates of the use of true–false tests (Ebel, 1979; Downing, 1992) concede that indiviual true–false items are inferior to comparable multiple-choice items, but assert that it is possible to include far more true–false items on a test. More items can be included because they are easy to construct and students can complete a larger number of such items in a given amount of time. Downing (1992) found that students can complete from 1.5 to 2.4 T-F true–false items for each multiple-choice item. The greater number of items that can be included on a true–false test may give them better content validity (see Chapter 2 for an explanation of content validity). Since reliability is dependent on test length, with some subject matter, the inclusion of a sufficiently large number of true–false items may result in a test with reliability comparable to what would be obtained if multiple-choice items were used.

Writing Better True–False Items

The true–false item format is not recommended. However, if a teacher still wishes to use this format, despite recommendations against it, the following section contains suggestions for how to write better items of this type.

    1 *Make sure that each item is clearly true or false.*
The goal of the writer of true–false items should be to make sure that experts would concur in labelling a statement as unequivocally true or false. Obviously, if the most knowledgeable students cannot select the correct answer to a true–false item, there is something wrong with it. With any item, there should be a linear relationship between a student's overall mastery of content and the probability he or she will get the item correct. True–false items often lack this important characteristic. It is easy to generate true–false items that both students who know nothing about the topic and students with the most knowledge, are likely to get wrong. With such items, only those students with a moderate amount of knowledge will select the correct response.

Example

Poor: *T* F   Christopher Columbus discovered America.

Although the item is keyed true, the student with the most knowledge about history is likely to conclude that there are a number of different claimants for the distinction of being first to set foot on this continent. The well-informed student might mark the statement false for this reason. On the other hand, the completely unprepared student might think that George Washington discovered America and mark the item false.

Example
Better: T̲   F   Christopher Columbus sailed to the new world in 1492.

Of course the above item also illustrates another weakness of this format. Even the 'better' item is assessing what might be considered a trivial historical fact, which brings us to the next rule about writing true–false items.

2   *Avoid trivial statements.*

The dilemma faced by the teacher endeavoring to write true–false items that are unequivocally true or false is that these items are often based on unimportant facts or references. Statements that refer to more important content are likely to be ambiguous because most of what is important in this world is not easily categorized as true or false. Items on any test, including those that include true–false items, should assess relevant and important content. When this is not possible using the true–false format, a different assessment format should be employed.

3   *Use your own words in writing statements.*

Requiring students to memorize exact passages from a text is seldom a legitimate instructional goal. True–false items are often used because it is an easy to generate items by copying statements from textbooks, but it is much better to write items in your words and have students apply what they have learned to a novel situation.

4   *Avoid the use of broad generalizations.*

Students quickly figure out that statements which include such words as 'all,' 'never,' 'no,' 'always,' or other absolute statements are likely to be false. Students are also likely to conclude that any statements including terms such as 'usually,' 'sometimes,' 'under certain conditions,' 'maybe,' or other broad generalizations, are likely to be true. The inclusion of such items favors the testwise student and renders the test an unfair measure of the instructional objectives being assessed.

Example
Poor: T   F̲   All five of the first presidents were from Virginia.
Better: T̲   F   James Madison was a native of Virginia.

5   *Do not use ambiguous and indefinite terms of degree or amount.*

People seldom interpret expressions such as 'frequently,' 'generally,' 'greatly,' 'to a considerable degree,' and 'in most cases,' the same. It should be the goal of the item writer to make sure that everyone who reads an item, interprets it in the same way. This will not occur when a student has to guess what the item writer had in mind. In the example that follows, the students may be troubled by the word 'generally' because he or she recalls that some states initially refused to endorse the Constitution because it lacked the guarantees later incorporated into the Bill of Rights. The student must decide how much reluctance qualifies as 'generally reluctant.' This leads to the practice of students trying to 'read the mind' of the teacher who wrote the items, which is not a legitimate instructional goal.

Example

Poor: T   F   The original 13 states were generally reluctant to endorse the Constitution without the inclusion of a bill of rights.

Better: T   F   The state of Virginia refused to sign the constitution without the inclusion of a bill of rights.

6   *Do not include more than one idea in a statement.*

The difficulty of a true–false item should not be increased by the inclusion of more than one idea. This practice only makes the item difficult to read and understand. Particularly confusing are statements that contain one true idea and one false idea. Items written in this way tend to be better measures of reading and problem solving ability than the achievement described in the instructional objectives. If complex statements are to be used, student attention should be directed toward the particular aspect of the statement that they are expected to evaluate as being true or false.

Example

Poor: T   F   The Lewis and Clark Expedition was sent by Thomas Jefferson to explore Southern California.

Better: T   F   The Lewis and Clark Expedition was sent by *Thomas Jefferson* to explore what was later to become the Northwest United States.

The student evaluating the 'poor' statement may not know the aspect of the statement that should be his or her focus. Is knowing who sent the expedition the critical aspect of the item? If so the statement is true because it correctly identifies Thomas Jefferson as the president who authorized the expedition. If the critical part of the statement concerns where they were sent, the statement is false because the expedition's destination was not Southern California. In the 'better' item, 'Thomas Jefferson' is underlined to indicate to the student that this is the aspect of the statement that should be evaluated. 'Southern California' is changed to 'Northwest United States' to remove the need for students to make this distinction.

7   *Avoid the use of negative statements, and particularly avoid double negatives.*

It has been determined that the time needed to answer a negatively stated item is greater than the time needed for an equivalent positively stated item. Therefore fewer items can be included on a true–false test that contains negatively stated items. Furthermore, the accuracy of student assessment will be lower when negatively stated items are used. The student is forced to perform elaborate mental gymnastics to untangle the meaning of negative statements. In addition, it is easy to overlook the 'no' or 'not' that makes a statement negative. Double negatives present even greater problems because they require the application of complex logical processes for the determination of the correct answer. These items tend to be better measures of high level cognitive functioning than mastery of course content.

Example

Poor: T̲   F   MacArthur never said he would not return to the Philippines.
Better: T   F̲   A famous picture from WW II shows MacArthur walking down the gangplank of a ship in his triumphant return to the Philippines.

8   *True statements should not be consistently longer than false statement.* Test writers are prone to make true statements longer than false statements because of the additional qualifications that are needed to make a statement unequivocally true. The testwise student will recognize this tendency and gain an advantage by marking long statements, about which he or she is uncertain, true. Of course some true statements can be long, if long false statements are also included.

9   *Include an approximately equal number of true and false statements.* Some teachers are hesitant to include a large number of false statements on a test fearing that students will remember the misinformation. To prevent this from happening, they include more true than false items. Again, the testwise student who recognizes this tendency, will label as 'true' any statement about which he or she is unsure.

10   *The source of a statement based on opinion should be included.* Students should not be asked to render a decision about the truth or falsity of a statement about which experts in the field are undecided. If the source of the statement is included, the item becomes a more reasonable measure of student understanding and knowledge.

Example

Poor: T̲   F   There is a long history of anti-intellectualism in this country.
Better: T̲   F   According to Hofstadtler, there is a long history of anti-intellectualism in this country.

Improving the True–False Item Format

It is possible to modify the true–false item to correct some of the limitations associated with this format. Modifications in the true–false item format are intended to accomplish one or more of the following: (1) increase the assessment of 'higher level' cognitive functioning, (2) reduce the ambiguity of the items; (3) reduce the effects of guessing on the scores; and/or (4) provide more specific information about how much a student knows.

1   *Assessing 'higher level' cognitive functioning.* Modern views of student learning tend to place more importance on a student's ability to solve problems and be engaged in 'higher level' thinking than to be able to recall or evaluate the truth or falsity of statements. Although true–false items are generally associated with the recognition of low level factual knowledge, there are ways of modifying this item format to permit the assessment of higher level cognitive functioning. For instance, students can be asked to distinguish between

statements that are based on facts and those based on opinion, or the student can be asked to distinguish between practices that are ethical (according to an identified code of behavior) and those that are unethical. Gronlund and Linn (1990) recommend the use of this format to determine if students understand cause and effect relationships. With such items, students are presented with two statements, both of which are true. The task of the student is to determine if the relationship is as stated.

Directions: Indicate if the two statements presented below are related in the manner stated by marking 'yes' if the causal relationship is as stated or 'no' if this is not the correct causal relationship.

Example 1

1. Students from wealthy school districts perform better on achievement tests

yes <u>no</u>   *because*

2. their schools have better and more expensive facilities.

Example 2

1. Levels of carbon dioxide in the atmosphere are increasing

<u>yes</u> no   *because*

2. increasing amounts of fossil fuels are being burned.

2 *Reduce the effect of guessing by underlining a word or clause in the statement.*
This is the simplest variation and it is intended to reduce ambiguity by focusing the attention of the examinee on the most important part of the statement.

Example

1. <u>T</u>   F   The ten years following the Civil War are called the <u>reconstruction</u>.

Underlining the word 'reconstruction' is important because students could be distracted by the number of years rather than focusing on the name of the historical period.

3 *Require students to correct false statements.*
When a student correctly labels a statement 'false' the teacher has not learned much about what the student knows. With only two options, luck can play a disproportionately large role in determining if a student chooses the correct answer. It is also possible that a student will choose the correct answer on the basis of misinformation. Consider the following item:

T or <u>F</u>   In the Battle of Gettysburg, which is considered the most important battle of the Civil War, the Confederate army defeated the Union Army.

A student may mark this item false because he or she does not believe the Battle of Gettysburg was the most important battle of the Civil War while accepting the statement that it was the Confederate army that prevailed in the battle. In this case, incorrect information leads to a correct answer. One way to prevent this from happening would be to require the student to correct all statements that are marked false. The item also could be improved by eliminating the part of the item that states that the Battle of Gettysburg was the most important battle of the Civil War. The key word or phrase also should be underlined to ensure that the student is focusing on the specific content that the teacher is trying to appraise. In the previous example, the words *Confederate* and *Union* would be underlined.

4   *Group short true–false items under a common question or statement heading.* An example of this true–false format is provided below.

Example

Directions: Place a T in front of each choice that is a correct answer to the question. Put an F in front of each choice that is NOT a correct answer to the question.

Which of the following countries sided with Germany in World War II?

(T)	1.	Spain	(F)	5.	China
(T)	2.	Italy	(F)	6.	France
(F)	3.	Britain	(T)	7.	Austria
(T)	4.	Japan	(F)	8.	Canada

The true–false format can be effectively used to assess a student's ability to place concepts into categories, classify characteristics, and assess the ability of a student to make simple applications. The format reduces the amount of reading that is required of the student and provides more context than is usually included with true–false items. To simplify the process further, the student can be asked place a check mark next to the statements that are true and leave the others blank.

5   *Use alternate-choice items.*
Alternate-choice items represent a compromise between true–false and multiple-choice items. Instead of evaluating whether a statement is true or false, the student is asked to choose between two related statements.

Example

The French helped the American Colonies in the war against Britain by (A) providing troop support (B) naval support.

Alternative-choice items have the advantage of being somewhat less ambiguous than conventional true–false items because they require comparisons rather than absolute evaluations of truth or falsity. At the same time, it is easier to write items using this format than conventional multiple-choice items and students can complete more alternative–choice than multiple-choice items. The inclusion of more items enhances both reliability and content validity. The main difference between alternate-choice and multiple-choice items is the number of options available to the student. The additional distracters associated with multiple-choice items can be difficult to generate and are sometimes so implausible that they would not be selected anyway. According to Downing (1992) this format should be considered as an alternative to other objective formats.

Writing Multiple-choice Items

The multiple-choice format is considered the best of the three *objective* item formats and is the most often used. It is flexible and permits the assessment of a wide range of cognitive objectives.

A frequent criticism of *objective* type items, in particular the multiple-choice format, is that they are useful only as a method of assessing the recall of facts, the mastery of basic skills, and the evaluation of content isolated from its context. The multiple-choice format is well adapted to these purposes, but it can do even more. Multiple-choice items can be written in such a way that they require the application of the cognitive skills of comprehension, application, synthesis, and evaluation.

Tests made up of these items can be scored with a high degree of accuracy and the error and unreliability that stem from scoring errors can be almost completely eliminated. A wide range of content can be covered by multiple-choice tests. As a result, a student is unlikely to be unjustifiably rewarded or unfairly penalized by the chance factors that surround the choice of the particular content included on a test. If care is taken in maintaining their security, items can be re-used, increasing test construction efficiency. This allows the teacher to spend time improving existing items rather than writing new ones.

There are four important learning outcomes that cannot be assessed using the multiple-choice format, including instructional objectives that: (1) require originality, (2) focus on a student's capacity to organize their knowledge, (3) assess the skill with which a student can present information, or (4) measure a student's ability to convert knowledge into action.

The Structure of Multiple-choice Items

A multiple-choice item is made up of two parts: (1) the stem, which can be in the form of a question, a statement to be completed, a blank to be filled or a command form (as in 'Please indicate which of the following . . .') and (2) four or five possible responses or options. The incorrect responses are labeled 'distracters' to differentiate them from the correct answer.

In general, the question or command format is easier than the completion format, particularly for students who lack well-developed reading skills. The main advantage of the completion format is that it allows items to be written in such a way that they include fewer words, making it possible for students to respond to more items during a testing session.

Multiple-choice items usually have four options, although some teachers and authors of standardized tests prefer the use of five options. The fifth option is intended to minimize the effect of guessing. The additional effort required to create an additional option seldom can be justified by the small decline in error resulting from guessing. A distinction should be made between the total number of options included in a multiple-choice item and the number of effective or functioning options that the item contains. The additional distracter included to bring the total number of options up to five may not be functional anyway. In the Poor Example below, written for a fifth grade test in history, there are five options, but it functions more like a two option item, because few students can be expected to think that Lyndon Johnson, Abraham Lincoln, or Jimmy Carter were Presidents during the first World War. The revised item presents four options and is likely to function as a four choice item because all the Presidents listed served in the same era.

Example

Poor: Who was the President of the United States during World War I?
    A. Lyndon Johnson
    <u>B</u>. Woodrow Wilson
    C. Theodore Roosevelt.
    D. Abraham Lincoln
    E. Jimmy Carter

Better: Who was the President of the United States during World War I?
    A. William Taft
    <u>B</u>. Woodrow Wilson
    C. Theodore Roosevelt.
    D. Warren Harding.

Suggestions for Writing Better Multiple-choice Items

All multiple-choice tests are not of uniformly high quality. The construction of good multiple-choice items requires a knowledge of the best way to write items and a willingness to expend the necessary time and effort. There are a set of rules that specify what should be done and what should be avoided to prevent students from getting items correct when they lack an understanding of the content being assessed. Likewise there are rules for avoiding item writing practices that result in capable students getting items wrong because they are not sufficiently testwise. There also are techniques for writing items in ways that increase their capacity to assess higher level cognitive functioning.

Maintaining Appropriate Levels of Difficulty

A test that is to be effective in making discriminations among students, must contain items that have an appropriate level of difficulty. You cannot obtain useful information from a test made up of items that are either too easy or too difficult because it will lack variability. When a test is too easy, only a few items may be of sufficient difficulty to permit an accurate differentiation among students. With only a few effective items, guessing and chance factors tend to play a too important role in determining a student's score. By varying the similarity between the correct response and the distracters, a teacher can control the difficulty of individual items and the whole test as well. In the previous example, the difficulty of the item is manipulated by changing the distracters. By including Presidents from the same era the item becomes more difficult.

In the Poor Example below, the item is too easy because of the heterogeneity of the distracters. In the Better Example, the item is made more difficult by selecting distracters that are more plausible.

Examples

Poor: Following the withdrawal of French troops from Vietnam, strategists in the US government recommended that American advisers and then troops be sent to support the South Vietnamese government. This was done in the interest of preventing the domino effect. What was the domino effect?
  A.   The tradition of domino playing among French soldiers.
  B.   The fear that Japan would again become dominant in the region.
  C.   The belief that if one country in the region adopted communism, all of them would.
  D.   Concern about nuclear proliferation in the region.

Better: Following the withdrawal of French troops from Vietnam, strategists in the US government recommended that American advisers and then troops be sent to support the South Vietnamese government. This was done in the interest of preventing the domino effect. What was the domino effect?
  A.   The fear that Russia would gain a warm water port in Asia.
  B.   The fear that Japan would again become dominant in the region.
  C.   The belief that if one country in the region adopted communism, all of them would.
  D.   Concern that if France left the region so would other European nations.

There are appropriate and inappropriate methods of increasing or decreasing the difficulty of an item. Difficulty is modified appropriately by adjusting the standards that students are required to meet in achieving instructional objectives.

Avoiding Characteristics That Make Items Too Easy

1   *Do not include implausible distracters.*
Distracters should be logically consistent with the stem and based on the common errors made by students at a particular grade or ability level. If the correct answer

can be selected by a student, without an understanding of the knowledge specified in the instructional objective, the item will be a poor discriminator.

In the Poor example below, students are likely to know that the Bill of Rights, the Articles of Confederation, and the Declaration of Independence were all documents created during the nation's founding and are therefore not consistent with the stem which refers to the freeing of the slaves during the Civil War. Students could get this item correct with a minimal knowledge of early American history.

Examples

Poor: Which of the following documents freed the slaves of the confederacy?
  A. Bill of Rights
  B. Articles of Confederation
  C. Emancipation Proclamation
  D. Declaration of Independence

One good approach to selecting plausible distracters for multiple-choice items is to identify the typical errors students make in solving a problem. This is a particularly useful technique for assessing a student's skill in using the correct procedures in mathematical computations.

2 *Avoid item characteristics that provide clues to the correct answer.*
Students can be expected to carefully examine items for clues that provides hints about the correct answer. A useful clue does not necessarily have to identify the correct answer. If it can be used to eliminate even one of the distracters, the test-wise student gains an advantage. The inclusion of such clues has two negative consequences. (1) If the clue is obvious, it will render the item too easy and it will fail to discriminate between students who have mastered the knowledge or skill measured by the item and those who have not. (2) If the clue is more subtle, it will cause the item to be easier only for the testwise student. A test containing too many of these items will yield a score that is an unpredictable combination of mastery of the instructional objective and skill in test-taking. Programs that teach students test-taking skills are sometimes advocated as a means of addressing the problem of poorly constructed objective tests. It is believed that instruction in test-taking skills will level the playing field for students who lack these skills. A better solution to this problem is for test authors to put more effort into advocating and constructing better tests, rather than enhancing the ability of students to identify and capitalize on test construction errors.

The following section includes examples of clues that will either make a test too easy for everyone taking it or give the testwise student an advantage. The revised items show how each of these faults can be corrected to make them more effective measures of student achievement and not merely assessments of how testwise a student is.

The term Clang association is used to describe the mistake of including the same word or phrase in both the stem and the correct answer.

Examples

Poor: Which Sioux chief led his warriors against Custer at the Battle of the Little Big Horn?
A.   Geronimo
B.   Chief Sitting Bull
C.   Crazy Horse
D.   Hiawatha

Better: Which Sioux chief led his warriors against Custer at the Battle of the Little Big Horn?
A.   Geronimo
B.   Sitting Bull
C.   Crazy Horse
D.   Hiawatha

The use of *specific determiners* such as 'always,' 'never,' 'all,' or 'none' in options, cue the student that the statement containing one of these terms is probably not correct. At the same time, options containing broad generalizations are more likely to be correct. Almost anything can occur 'sometimes' or 'occasionally' but relatively few things 'never' happen.

Examples

Poor: Which of the following statements best describes Abraham Lincoln?
A.   He was never a lawyer.
B.   He was president during the Civil War.
C.   He was always opposed to slavery.
D.   All of his relatives were wealthy.

Better: Which of the following statements best describes Abraham Lincoln?
A.   He was once the governor of Kentucky.
B.   He was president during the Civil War.
C.   He was at one time an advocate of slavery.
D.   His parents were wealthy.

Teachers sometimes make the correct answer longer by including qualifiers that make it unambiguously correct. This practice should be avoided because it will allow the testwise student to correctly respond even if they have not mastered the objective being assessed.

Examples

Poor: What was the contribution of the United States to the Allies in the early stages of World War II?
A.   The stationing of troops in France.
B.   Airborne assaults into Poland.
C.   A naval blockade of China.
D.   American workers produced an enormous number of the weapons, ammunition, ships and planes that were shipped to the Allies.

Better: What was the contribution of the United States in the early stages of World War II?

    A. The stationing of troops in France.

    B. Airborne assaults into Poland.

    C. A naval blockade of China.

    <u>D</u>. Shipments of food and ammunition to Europe.

Test authors need to be aware of any grammatical inconsistencies that might provide vigilant test takers with hints that will help them select the correct option or reject a distracter.

Examples

Poor: The Wright brothers are best known for their invention of the:

    A. penicillin.

    B. automobiles.

    <u>C</u>. airplane.

    D. pneumatic tires.

Better: The Wright brothers are best known for their invention of:

    A. penicillin.

    B. automobiles.

    <u>C</u>. airplanes.

    D. pneumatic tires.

3 *Do not use of 'all of these' or 'all the above' as an option on multiple-choice items.*

Test authors typically construct items using these options in two situations: (1) to provide a fourth option when only three can easily be generated or (2) to assess the ability of students to recognize lists of characteristics or traits. Items that include these options tend to be too easy because students only have to determine that two of the options are true, to realize that 'all the above (or these)' must be the right answer. Examine the Poor example below. Assume a student has been instructed to mark only one answer and knows that President Truman both became the president upon the death of Roosevelt and ordered the bombing of Hiroshima, but is skeptical about Truman being a clothing salesman. Since the student knows that two of the answers are correct, D, 'All the above' is the obvious choice. Students can therefore get such a question correct without knowing very much about President Truman.

Example

Poor: Which statement about Harry Truman is true?

    A. He became president with the death of Franklin D. Roosevelt.

    B. He ordered the use of the atomic bomb in the attack on Hiroshima.

    C. He was at one time a clothing salesman.

    <u>D</u>. All the above.

Characteristics of Items That Make Them Inappropriately Difficult

Test authors are usually striving for appropriate difficulty levels to enhance the capacity of items and entire tests to make good discriminations. In many cases this means increasing difficulty. Care must be taken to ensure that items are difficult because they require students to address instructional objectives at a higher cognitive level rather than as a result of extraneous characteristics of the item. Suggestions for avoiding irrelevant forms of difficulty are described below.

1 *The stem of the item should clearly formulate a problem.*
The student should understand what problem or question is being asked before examining the options. Look at the poor example below. When you have finished reading the stem, all you know is that the item is somehow related to the Constitution. You have to read the options to determine the purpose of the item. The answer choices that are provided are heterogeneous in content; that is, one relates to the purpose of the Constitution, one to when it was ratified, one to its interpretation, and one to authorship. The poor item is really nothing more than four true–false items with the words 'The Constitution' in common. The revised item provides a clearly formulated problem in the stem and a more homogeneous set of answer choices.

Examples

Poor: The Constitution:
    <u>A</u>.   established the United States government and its laws.
    B.   was immediately ratified by all states.
    C.   is interpreted by the individual states.
    D.   was written by Thomas Jefferson.

Better: The document that established the United States Government is called the:
    A.   the Declaration of Independence.
    B.   Articles of Confederation.
    <u>C</u>.   Constitution.
    D.   Bill of Rights.

2 *Keep the options short by including as much information as possible in the stem.*
Such a structure simplifies the process of responding to multiple-choice items. It also lowers the level of required reading skill and reasoning. Unless reading and reasoning skills are part of the instructional objectives being assessed, their influence should be minimized. To be avoided is the repetition of the same words and phrases in all the options, as occurs in the poor example below. It is better to rewrite the stem to include the repetitious material. Answer choices that are long in comparison with the stem usually occur when the problem is not clearly stated in the stem.

Examples

Poor: The Underground Railroad:

    <u>A</u>.   was a network of houses and other buildings used to help slaves escape to freedom.

    B.   was a network of houses and other buildings used to smuggle supplies to the Confederacy.

    C.   was a network of houses and other buildings used to help Union soldiers escape from Confederate prisons.

    D.   was a network of houses and other buildings used to help Confederate soldiers escape from Union prisons.

Better: The underground Railroad was a network of houses and other buildings used to help:

    <u>A</u>.   slaves escape to freedom.

    B.   smuggle supplies to the Confederacy.

    C.   Union soldiers escape from Confederate prisons.

    D.   Confederate soldiers escape from Union prisons.

3   *Do not include extraneous material in the stem.*

The stem should be as brief and sparse as is possible, but still include enough information to enable the knowledgeable student to select the correct answer. Lengthy stems filled with unrelated content will lead to items that are primarily measures of reading ability and short term memory rather than the intended objectives. Lengthy stems make students spend too much time on each item. As a result, the test may not have enough items. Some teachers include content unrelated to the item in the mistaken belief that tests should be used to teach as well as assess student achievement. This practice lowers the validity of a test by increasing the reading skills required for success on the test.

Examples

Poor: The worst economic period in American history occurred in 1929 when the stock market collapsed. A large number of banks and other businesses failed, putting many people out of work. This period lasted for ten years until the beginning of World War II. What is this period called?

    A.   The Great Collapse.

    <u>B</u>.   The Great Depression.

    C.   The Recession.

    D.   The Reverses of 1929.

Better: What is the economic collapse of 1929 called?

    A.   The Great Collapse.

    <u>B</u>.   The Great Depression.

    C.   The Recession.

    D.   The Reverses of 1929.

4 *Avoid the use of negative terms in the stem of an item.*

The inclusion of negative terms in the stem increases the reading difficulty of an item while requiring the student to perform difficult reasoning tasks. There is also the possibility that some students will not see the negative term and select an incorrect option as a result. As is true with true–false items, an indication that a student recognizes that something is not true, tells us nothing about what they do know.

There are some situations where the use of negative terms are justified. For instance a teacher may want his or her students to become familiar with a list of characteristics or conditions. It is certainly easier to create an item made up of three exemplars from the list of characteristics and one non-exemplar, than to find three plausible non-exemplars. There may also be situations where it is important for students to know the exception to a rule or be able to detect errors. When a negative term is included in a stem, it should be underlined, bold faced, and/or capitalized to ensure that it is recognized by students.

Example 1 below was written to measure if students knew the inventions for which Thomas Edison is given credit, but the item as written also focuses on the accomplishments of Alexander Graham Bell. Example 2 is a more direct way of assessing a student's ability to associate two famous inventors with their inventions.

Example 1

Poor: Which of the following was NOT an invention of Thomas Edison?
    A.   Electric light bulb.
    B.   The phonograph.
    C.   Telephone.
    D.   Talking motion pictures.

Example 2

Better: Which of the following was an invention of Alexander Graham Bell?
    A.   The electric light bulb.
    B.   The printing press.
    C.   The telephone.
    D.   The steam engine.

There are two reasons why the following example illustrates an appropriate use of a negative term in the stem of a multiple-choice item: (1) a common error made by students studying early American History is their tendency to confuse the Declaration of Independence with the Constitution; and (2) it would be difficult to come up with three other plausible distracters if the item was stated in a positive form.

Example 1

Good: Which of the following statements about the Declaration of Independence is *not* true? It:
    A.   stated that the American colonies were independent.
    B.   included the Bill of Rights.

    C.   denied that the King of England ruled the American Colonies.

    D.   proclaimed that all people have the right to life liberty and the pursuit of happiness.

5   *Avoid unfair ambiguity in the options.*

Only one correct option should be provided unless the student is expected to select the best answer from several that could be correct. In this latter case there should be one clearly best answer. Although the need to avoid including two equally correct options may seem obvious, to increase difficulty, test authors may construct items that either have two or more equally good answers or no good answer. In the following example, B is intended to be the correct answer, but some students could reasonably be expected to choose A because the United States was neutral during the first part of the war.

Examples

Poor: In World War I:

    A.   the US was neutral.

    <u>B.</u>   the US fought on the side of England and France.

    C.   Russia fought on the same side as Germany.

    D.   Japan attacked Pearl Harbor.

Better: In World War I:

    A.   the US sided with Germany.

    <u>B.</u>   the US fought on the side of England and France.

    C.   Russia fought on the same side as Germany.

    D.   Japan attacked Pearl Harbor.

6   *Avoid the use of the option 'none of these' or 'none of the above'.*

This type of option is sometimes added as the fourth distracter either to ensure that all options are examined carefully or because the author cannot think of another plausible distracter. It is most reasonably employed with items measuring spelling accuracy or the ability to perform mathematical computations where there is one, and only one, clearly correct option. However, all that is learned from such an item is how well students can eliminate incorrect options. It is possible to eliminate a wrong answer without any understanding of the knowledge assessed by the item. On a computation item in which the correct option is 'none of the above' a student might perform an incorrect computation and come up with the wrong answer. When this incorrect answer does not match any of the options, the student would choose 'none of the above.' The student gets the item correct without knowing how to perform the required mathematical computations. The short answer format should probably be used to assess ability and knowledge of this type.

    The terms 'none of the above' or 'none of these' should not be used with multiple-choice items written with a completion format, because this phrase does not complete the stem grammatically. It is also inappropriate to use this type of option with items for which the 'best' answer must be selected. A correctly constructed 'best answer' type of multiple-choice item will have several options that are not only plausible, but correct. Therefore the 'none of the above' option will never be the correct option with such an item. The following example illustrates the incorrect use of the 'none of the above' in a multiple-choice item.

Example

Poor: John F. Kennedy is best remembered because:
- A. He was the first Jewish president.
- B. He ended the Vietnam War.
- C. He lost his bid for re-election.
- <u>D</u>. None of the above.

Not only is the option 'none of the above' grammatically inconsistent with the stem, it also is logically inconsistent because option D does not refer to a characteristic of a president. Consider another similar item.

Example

Poor: Which of the following is the most important reason for John F. Kennedy to be remembered?
- A. He was the first Catholic president.
- B. He ended the Vietnam War.
- C. He lost his bid for re-election.
- <u>D</u>. None of the above.

The student addressing this item is faced with a dilemma. Among the first three options there is only one that is true, Option A. On the other hand, even though Kennedy was the first Catholic president, that is not the most important reason why he is remembered. Under these circumstances it would be reasonable for a student to choose option D, 'None of the above.' Even the best informed student is at a disadvantage with such an item.

The example given below represents another poor use of the 'none of the above' option. It is an item calling for a numerical answer about which historians are likely to disagree. Although there is general agreement that the WW II started in 1939, historians might differ in the interpretation of what 'begin' means in this context. It would not be unreasonable for a knowledgeable student to think that none of the years provided are correct.

Examples

Poor: When did World War II begin?
- A. 1935
- <u>B</u>. 1939
- C. 1942
- D. None of the above

Better: In what year did the United States declare war on Japan?
- A. 1939
- <u>B</u>. 1941

C. 1942
D. 1943

If a test author still wishes to include 'none of these' or its equivalent as an option, it should be used as frequently for the correct option as for any other answer choice, and the stem of the item should be phrased as a question. If the 'none of the above' option is to be designated as correct, the distracters must be completely untrue. This option should be used as the correct answer on some of the easier items at the beginning of the test to make sure the students realize it will sometimes be the correct answer.

Writing Items That Assess Higher Level Cognitive Skills

As has already been stated, a frequent criticism of multiple-choice items is that they only measure the recall of facts and isolated skills. This is not true. Multiple-choice items can be written to assess a wide range of higher level skills. Most of the examples provided so far have not been examples of the use of multiple-choice items to assess higher level cognitive skills. This is because the rules for writing good multiple-choice items are more easily illustrated with items written to assess lower level skills. The teacher constructing a multiple-choice test should try to include higher level items, particularly when the instructional objectives call for this type of student learning.

To measure a student's skills in application, novel material should be included. The example below illustrates how an item can be structured to appraise the ability of a student to apply information.

Examples

Rote memory: What was Martin Luther King's occupation before he became a civil rights leader?
A. A minister.
B. A medical doctor.
C. A judge.
D. A public school teacher.

Application: Which of the following scenes would best represent the 'Dream' of Martin Luther King?
A. A Black Supreme Court judge.
B. Black and white children playing together.
C. A school for Black males
D. The teaching of African history in schools.

An Example of Higher Level Assessment

In a high school psychology class, a teacher has been discussing Piaget's contributions to the understanding of the cognitive development of children. Specifically she has been emphasizing the acquisitions of *schemas* through *assimilation* and *accommodation*. These three terms are used in Piagetian explanations of the cognitive development of children. A multiple-choice test used to evaluate how much students have learned on this topic could include items assessing a student's understanding of these terms at a number of cognitive levels. The cognitive level at which students are assessed is specified in the table of specifications for the particular unit of instruction being assessed. Levels of understanding can be specified that range from the recall of facts, all the way to the evaluation level. An example of an item written at the knowledge level follows:

Example

1. According to Piagetian terminology, what are the basic building blocks in a child's cognitive structure?
    A. Concepts
    B. Constructs
    C. Schemata
    D. Factors

To get this item correct, the student would only need to be familiar with some of the basic vocabulary used in discussions of Piaget's theory of cognitive development. It would certainly be appropriate to include some items on a test that focus on knowledge level content, but all the items on a test should not be of this type. The next higher cognitive level is *comprehension*. An example of an item assessing this cognitive level follows.

Example

2. The term 'assimilation' refers to the process of:
    A. structural changes to accommodate more schemata.
    B. adaptation.
    C. the incorporation of more schemata.
    D. the achievement of a balance among mental structures.

To correctly answer the above item, the student must understand the meaning of a complex term and choose the correct option from several plausible distracters. When the correct response is exactly the same as the definition provided in the textbook or the one used in class, the item would be considered a lower level recall item. If the wording of the options was novel for the student and he or she could make a correct response only if the meaning of the options was well understood, the item would be at the *comprehension* level. The following example requires the student to apply a Piagetian principle.

Example

3. Bobby is a young boy just learning to talk. His family has a dog that he calls 'Woof-woof.' On a walk with his father they encounter a neighbor's dog. Bobby gets excited and calls this new dog 'Woof-woof.' The cognitive process that Bobby was exhibiting is called:

A. assimilation.
B. accommodation.
C. equilibration.
D. transformational reasoning.

It is not enough for a student to memorize a definition, he or she must be able to apply it in a novel situation to obtain the correct answer. A still higher level of cognitive functioning is *synthesis*. This requires the application of two or more principles in a novel setting. Consider the following example:

Example

4. A child shown two balls of clay of equal size and weight, watches while one is rolled into a tube. The child knows that the weight and volume of the two has stayed the same. This same child states that a child who accidentally breaks a valuable dish should be more severely punished than one who breaks an item of lesser value while exploring a cabinet he or she was told not to open. According to Piaget, at which stage of cognitive development is the child likely to be functioning:
   A. Sensorimotor.
   B. Pre-operational.
   C. Concrete operations.
   D. Formal operations.

To correctly answer this item, a student would need to be aware of two different characteristics of cognitive development. (1) A child's ability to recognize that mass is conserved, despite changes in form, is a characteristic of the Concrete Operations stage and (2) a mature understanding of the relationship between degree of culpability and the outcome of misbehavior is achieved only at the Formal operations stage. The student who recognized these principles and could understood the relationship, would be able to conclude that the correct answer was *C*, Concrete operations.

Cautions About Higher Level Testing

During the 1990s, the influence of behaviorally based instructional systems, with their focus on the mastery of basic skills as a prerequisite for the learning of higher level thinking, declined. At the same time, there was increased interest in constructivist approaches to instruction that de-emphasize the need for the acquisition of basic skills prior to exposure to higher level cognitive tasks. According to constructivist beliefs, education should be more than the memorization and subsequent regurgitation of isolated facts. These beliefs cause constructivists to be uncomfortable with objective testing techniques. The only type of objective assessment they can accept are those that measure higher level cognitive functioning.

The assessment of higher level thinking skills is not difficult to accomplish. There are many available standardized tests that can do this effectively. It is the assessment of higher level thinking skills in the context of specific subject matter areas that presents the greatest challenge. When multiple-choice items are used to assess a student's recall of facts, the teacher can be fairly certain about what is being assessed. If a student knows the vocabulary, recognizes relevant concepts, and can correctly identify dates and names, familiarity with content at least at some rudimentary level is assured. When higher level thinking skills are being assessed, the precise cognitive functioning being assessed may not be obvious.

This uncertainty illustrates an important disadvantage of the multiple-choice item format. A student's response tells us only whether or not the item was correctly answered, not what the student knows or doesn't know. It won't tell us anything about the underlying cognitive processes that were taking place. When high level items are used to assess a student's mastery of course material there are three things that can happen: (1) the student could correctly answer the question because he or she remembered a similar example from class; (2) the question could be answered without any knowledge of the content being assessed because the student possesses exceptional intellectual capacities; or (3) the student could correctly respond as a result of his/her mastery of the instructional objectives. Of course teachers are interested in only the final scenario as a way of describing the way the items are functioning. There is no way of knowing which of these scenarios best explains a particular student's performance on a given item. Test authors should be cautioned to avoid the premature conclusion that a student's response reflects the mastery of the intended cognitive skills.

Although the mastery of higher level cognitive skills is a worthy educational goal, it is difficult to address instructionally. The facilitation of higher level thinking skills, requires student practice on the application of what they have learned in a wide range of contexts. If students have not learned to make the desired applications, performance on high level multiple-choice items will be imperfectly related to student achievement. Bright students will perform better on tests of higher level functioning, even when their grasp of content is incomplete. At the same time, students who are well prepared may fail to respond correctly to such items because they lack the prerequisite cognitive skills. Including items on a test that require students to display the highest level cognitive functioning is legitimate only if this level of cognitive functioning is specified as desirable in the learning objectives and the students have been adequately prepared to function at this level.

Matching Items

A matching item can best be thought of as a more efficient presentation of a series of multiple-choice items. The two defining characteristics of a matching item are (1) their use of more options than the typical multiple-choice item, and (2) the use of the correct response for one item as a distracter for the other. A matching exercise consists of a series of statements called *premises* which are listed down the left-hand column of an exam and a series of *responses* listed down the right-hand column. The premises are placed in a random order, but the responses should be sequenced systematically. The premises are typically numbered and the responses are identified with letters. A space is provided adjacent to each premise where the student can enter the letter of the response that is believed to provide the best match with the premise.

Matching tests are most frequently used to assess a student's ability to make associations between terms and their meanings, dates and events, individuals and their achievements, symbols and chemical elements, authors and their books, etc. A matching exercise also can be constructed based on information derived from a chart, map, diagram, or drawing. The examinee can be asked to match names, functions, and so on, with numbered features on the figure. This technique can be used effectively to assess a student's mastery of study skills, science, or technology.

The most important disadvantage of matching exercise is that their use is restricted to the assessment of associations. They cannot easily be used to measure higher levels of understanding. Machine scoring is also difficult to implement with matching exercises because the number of options typically included on a matching exercise exceeds the five spaces allocated to each item on standard machine-scorable answer sheets. Answer sheets can be custom-made to record the responses of students on matching exercises, but this is time consuming and expensive.

Suggestions for Constructing Better Matching Exercises

1 *Include content that is homogeneous.*
If the list of pairs to be matched is a mixture of relationships, the task will be made artificially difficult. The exercise will be a measure of a student's ability to organize disparate information, rather than an assessment of the knowledge that the exercise is intended to assess. In the poor example that follows, it would have been better if all the choices were names of important historical figures, place, or events, but, not a mixture of the three. Homogeneous choices force the student to make genuine discriminations to arrive at a correct answer.

2 *Include no more than ten pairs of premises and responses.*
It is easier to maintain homogeneity in a matching exercise that is of this length or shorter. Longer lists force students to hold too many ideas in their short term memory. With more than ten premises, the task may be a better measure of this type of memory than a student's capacity to make associations.

3 *The response column should have the shortest statements.*
Students usually read the response column several times, and short statements increase the efficiency of the task. This practice also can decrease the effect of reading ability on test performance.

4 *Matching exercises should have more responses than premises.*
With an equal number of premises and responses, the testwise student will leave until last, the pairs about which he or she is least certain. Through a process of elimination, there will be fewer options to examine and the task will become progressively easier as more pairs are matched. By providing more responses than premises, the last associations are not made artificially easy. A larger number of answer choices will also reduce the influence of guessing on test scores.

5 *Arrange the responses logically.*

A student should not be required to exert an unreasonable amount of effort searching for a response that they already know. Arranging names in alphabetical order or dates in chronological order reduces the time required to find the answer.

6 *Include in the directions, a basis for matching the pairs if this is not obvious.*

All matching exercises should be made of homogeneous premises and there should be a common relationship between these premises and the responses. Students should not have to spend test time figuring out the nature of this relationship. One way of adding structure to the premises is to provide a heading for each column that accurately describes its content. If there is no appropriate heading that can reasonably define the content, the statements may be too heterogeneous.

The following example illustrates some of the common mistakes made in preparing matching items. First, the directions are vague and fail to specify the basis for matching. Second, the premises are too heterogeneous. The statements in Column I have very little in common except for referring to American history. Each response in Column II is a reasonable match for only one of the statements in Column I. In addition, the responses in Column II are not arranged in any systematic order. Even examinees who know the answer to a statement, have to search through the entire list in Column II to find it, which is time consuming. There are 8 statements in Column I and 8 answer choices in Column II. If a student knows the first 7, through a process of elimination, he or she can easily deduce the 8th association.

Poor Example

Directions: Place the correct letter to the left of each number. Use each letter only once.

Column I	Column II
(f) 1. Thomas Jefferson	a. Event leading to the Revolutionary War
(h) 2. Appomatox Court House	b. Boundary between North and South in Civil War
(a) 3. Boston Tea Party	c. Early revolutionary War volunteers.
(e) 4. Fourth of July	d. Ship that carried the Pilgrims to America
(e) 5. Mason Dixon line	e. National Holiday celebrating founding of nation
(c) 6. Minute Men	f. Author of the Declaration of Independence
(d) 7. Mayflower	g. Sewed the first official American flag
(g) 8. Betsy Ross	h. Place where Lee surrendered

Preparing the Objective Test for Use

In assembling items for a test, overall appearance should not be ignored. A good quality printer should be used to create clear, readable copies. The availability of laser printers and a wide choice of fonts can greatly enhance the appearance of a test. The following general rules for constructing a objective type test should be kept in mind.

   1   *Consider readability when arranging items on a test.*

A teacher must consider a number of sometimes conflicting rules when arranging test items on the page. First, a lengthy test, administered to many students can represent a sizable copying expenditure. Using smaller type, including as many items as possible on each page, and placing more than one option on each line can cut down the number of pages required. However, these steps will make the test-taking task somewhat more difficult and may not provide a fair assessment for students with visual impairments (tests for these students can be enlarged using a copier). One criterion to use in deciding how much to sacrifice page appearance to conserve paper is the age and sophistication of the test takers. Older, more experienced students should be able to handle a larger number of items crowded onto the same page, while this practice may have a more negative effect on younger students. Even at the cost of some extra pages, items should not be divided between pages since this arrangement will make the affected items unfairly difficult. If you are using stimulus material such as charts or maps and you cannot fit both this material and the items that refer to them on the same page, the stimulus material should be displayed on a separate sheet not stapled with the rest of the test.

   2   *Use separate answer sheet whenever possible.*

As students get older and more sophisticated in their test taking skills, separate answer sheets should be used. By the third grade, students can generally handle this task with equanimity. The main benefit to the use of separate answer sheets is ease of test scoring. This practice also can enhance test-taking skills and improve overall student performance on standardized tests.

   3   *Use test scanning equipment.*

Although scanning equipment is expensive, its use can dramatically increase the efficiency of objective format tests. Rudimentary scanners will print a count of the number of correct responses on the answer sheets, while more sophisticated scanners store student responses on the hard disk of an attached computer. Item analyses can be performed on this scanner output with a separate program.

   4   *Items with the same format should be grouped together.*

Because each objective format requires a different set of directions, it is not possible to write a concise and clear set of directions that will apply throughout each part of the test. Each time you change item type, the student is required to adjust their response set to the different item format. The examinee will be better able to maintain an appropriate response set if the items of the same type are grouped together.

   5   *Group items based on the same content together.*

This practice makes the test more coherent and maintains a consistent context for the student. It is also a good idea to have the items appear in the same sequence that was presented to students. This helps students see the items as part of a rational whole and not as isolated facts and relationships. As a further advantage, the teacher can use information about where in the test most errors occurred to pinpoint the areas in the curriculum where students are having the most difficulty.

6   *Arrange items so that the easiest items come first.*

This is of particular importance when testing time is limited and some items on the test will not be attempted by all students. The items that are not attempted because they are near the end of a test should be the most difficult. These are items that students would be less likely to answer correctly anyway. Starting off with easy items is particularly beneficial for young children and students who are anxious about being assessed.

Note: Suggestion 4, 5, and 6, in a sense, are contradictory. It would be impossible to structure a test in such a way that it was faithful to all three of these suggestions. The good test maker needs to keep all three in mind and structure their tests according to the age, level of cognitive functioning, and test-taking sophistication of his or her students.

7   *Provide separate directions for each item type.*

The directions should provide information about how answers should be recorded, the rationale for the way students should select answers, and the scoring procedures that will be used. For a test made up of mulitiple-choice items for which separate answer sheets are used, the following set of directions might be used.

Directions: Read each item and decide which choice best completes the statement or answers the question.

Mark your answers on the separate answer sheet. Do not mark them on the test itself. Indicate your answer by marking the space on the answer sheet below the letter corresponding to your choice.

Because your score will be based on the number of right answers, it will be to your advantage to answer every question, even if you are not completely sure which is the right answer.

Make sure your name is on your answer sheet.

8   *Check all the items on a test to be sure that one item does not provide clues to the answer to another item.*

Since the content of a test covers homogeneous content, there is always the possibility that one item will include clues or outright answers to other items. Consider the following example in which the multiple-choice item provides a clue to the correct answer to the true–false item.

Example

1.   T   F   John Smith was an English soldier who helped found the settlement of Jamestown.

2.   Who is credited with saving the life of John Smith, one of the founders of the settlement at Jamestown?
     A.   Pocahontas
     B.   Paul Revere
     C.   Powhatan
     D.   George Washington

9   *Avoid having the correct responses form a pattern.*

Some classroom teachers endeavor to make test scoring easier by establishing a pattern in the correct answers. For example, on a true–false test, two true items might be succeeded by two false items forming a repetitive pattern. On a multiple-choice test, a pattern such as D, C, B, A, D, C, B, A . . . might be employed. If this is done, some students may discover the pattern and use it to obtain correct answers to items. Sometimes patterns occur unintentionally. On a multiple-choice tests, there may be a tendency for the correct answer to appear more frequently in the second and third positions and less often in the first and last positions. This tendency, if detected, may result in testwise students choosing one of the two middle responses when they are unsure of the correct answer. It is best to distribute the correct answer among each of the four response positions.

10   *Review the test carefully before administering.*

It is a good idea to put aside a test and come back and review it later. This is a good way to catch errors that might otherwise be missed. Alternatively, the teacher could have someone else review the test for him or her.

Scoring the Objective Test

One of the most important advantages of objective type tests is ease and accuracy of scoring. The best way to score objective tests is with a test scanner. This technology can speed up scoring and minimize scoring errors. It also facilitates the item analysis procedures described in the following section of this chapter.

When using a test scanner, a scoring key is prepared on a machine-scorable answer sheet and it is read by the scanner first. After the scanner reads the scoring key, the student responses are read and stored on the hard disk of an attached computer. A separate program is used to score the student responses by comparing each response to the correct answer on the answer key. When this process is complete, each student's score, along with item analysis information is printed.

Test scoring and item analysis using a scanner requires some specialized skills and it may be too much to expect all teachers to be familiar with these procedures. An alternative is to centralize machine scoring and item analysis. With this system, teachers can bring their answer sheets to a central location where they can be scored, item analyzed, and returned to the teacher.

When machine scoring resources are not available, a scoring template can be used. First, the teacher prepares a scoring key on an answer sheet and, using a hole punch, makes holes where all of the correct answers are. This sheet can be placed over each student's answer sheet. When a bubbled response does not show through a hole, a mark is made through the hole with a colored marker. When the scoring key is removed, the teacher can count the number of colored marks to determine the number of wrong answers. This value can be subtracted from the total number of items on the test to determine how many items the students got correct. In comparison with a test scanner, the main disadvantage of this approach, in addition to being more time consuming, is that it does not provide item analysis information.

Once the test has been constructed, typed, reproduced administered and scored, the assessment procedure is not complete. The scores themselves must be interpreted. Raw scores can be quite misleading because tests differ in their difficulty. The proportion of items students have correctly answered actually tells us very little about student achievement. Standard scores can be useful in the interpretation of test results, but too few teachers take advantage of these useful computations. A description of their computation and the rationale for their use is provided in Chapter 2. Procedures for performing item analyses are described in the following section. It is important that this procedure not be omitted because it can help ensure that subsequent tests are improvements over their predecessors.

Item Analysis

Since objective tests, and in particular multiple-choice tests, are difficult to construct, items need to be used more than once. If the same items are used repeatedly with no change, the quality of the test will not improve and the possibility of a breach in test security will increase. When a teacher uses a test a second time he or she must make sure the items on the first test administration are working properly. The worst items should be eliminated and poor items that are worthy of being saved need to be modified. To accomplish these tasks, a method of determining which items to include on the next test is needed. The methodology for discriminating among good and poor items on a test is called *item analysis*.

Students are usually all too happy to point out the bad items on a test using a convenient operational definition — the bad items are the ones they got wrong. The ones they got correct, are the good items. Such criteria are not very useful for the teacher who is trying to create a better test. It is possible that an item that many students miss, is assessing something useful and should be retained, whereas an item that everyone gets right may not be a useful item because it contributes nothing to our understanding of how students compare. However, if the item covers a particularly important aspect of instruction, the teacher should certainly be pleased that everyone got it correct.

Students can also provide useful information about items that are flawed and their suggestions should not be discounted. However, categorizing items as good or poor by inspection alone is of limited value. Other than for purposes of identifying clearly flawed items, this practice provides little insight into the usefulness of items.

The Reasons for Conducting Item Analyses

Item-analysis procedures are generally associated with the construction of large-scale standardized tests, because test publishers have the financial resources to conduct elaborate item analyses. In that setting, careful and complete item analyses are indispensable. Item analyses are not used by teachers as often as they should be for two reasons. (1) Many teachers have never learned how to conduct an item-analysis, and do not possess the expertise necessary to interpret the results of an item analysis conducted by someone else. (2) Even when the necessary skills and knowledge are possessed by the teacher, the amount of effort necessary to accomplish this task may be too great. Teachers, should not be intimidated by the amount of work required. Some item analysis techniques can be implemented without an unreasonable amount of effort. Furthermore, the logistical problems can be addressed by personal computers and test scanners. New technology should make it possible in the future for a teacher to conduct item analyses with less effort than is currently needed.

Besides telling the teacher which items need to be improved or eliminated, item analysis provides the teacher with feedback about his or her item-writing skills. This process enables the teacher to become a better test-writer and the number of poor items should decrease. The item-analysis process also can provide feedback to the teacher about misinformation that students have acquired. If a large number of students provide the same wrong answer, a flaw in instruction should be suspected.

Item Difficulty

The most fundamental item analysis information is item difficulty. The difficulty of an item is simply the per cent of students who correctly responded to the item. This can be a little confusing because the higher the difficulty index, the easier the item. Difficulty is an important factor in an item analysis because the best items are those that are neither too difficult or too hard. In Chapter 3, Planning Classroom Assessment, procedures for computing the ideal difficulty for an entire test were presented. For a four option multiple-choice test, the ideal difficulty is 62.5. This means that, on average, students should correctly answer 62.5 per cent of the items. This does not mean that this should be the proportion of students who get each item correct, but the teacher should try to have the overall test be at this level.

Item-analysis Assumptions

Item-analysis procedures are intended to maximize internal consistency reliability, and do not directly address validity. These procedures focus on comparisons between items and the total score, which makes it necessary to assume that the total score itself is meaningful. If a test is not valid, the total score will be a poor criterion against which to compare items. The result will be a test that is reliable, but not valid.

The two primary methods of conducting an item analysis are (1) the discrimination method, and (2) the item-total score correlation method.

Table 4.2: *Item–discrimination analysis for a sample item*

| | **Responses** | | | |
	A	B	C*	D
Ten best students	2	1	6	0
Ten poorest students	5	3	2	2
Difference			4	

* Correct answer

$$D = \frac{RU - RL}{N} = \frac{6 - 2}{10} = .40$$

The Item-discrimination Method for Item Analysis

The item–discrimination method of conducting an item analysis has the advantage of being a technique that is appropriate for use by teachers who do not have access to machine scoring or computer analyses. This procedure provides the teacher with a numerical value (the discrimination index or D for an item) that can range from minus one to one. The greater the magnitude of D for an item, the more likely it is that the item is consistent with what the entire test is measuring. The student who correctly responds to one item should be more likely to obtain the correct answer for all items on the test. When a test is reliable, all or most of the items will be measuring the same thing. By altering or eliminating items with low D, the reliability of a test can be enhanced.

The first step in conducting an item analysis using the item-discrimination method, is to rank-order students according to the number of items correctly answered. Two groups are identified, the 27 per cent of the students at the top and a like number at the bottom. It is desirable to have as many students in each group as possible to increase stability; at the same time the two groups should be as different as possible to make the discriminations clearer. 27 per cent seems to maximize these two considerations. In actual practice, if you have between twenty-five and thirty-five students in your class, it is probably better to place ten students in each group. This simplifies the mathematical computations without any noticeable negative effect on the stability of the discrimination index.

The discrimination index (D) is computed by subtracting the number of students who got an item right in the lower group (RL) from the number who got it right in the upper group (RL) and dividing the difference by the number in one group. The formula is as follows:

$$\text{Discrimination index (D)} = \frac{RU - RL}{N(\text{each})}$$

Suppose that thirty-seven students took a test, 27 per cent of that number is ten (this is N in the equation), so you would select the ten students who did best on the test and the ten who did poorest. The responses of these students to one item are shown in Table 4.2. Six students got the item correct in the upper group (RU) and only two in the lower group (RL). The difference between the two is four; and when that is divided by ten a Discrimination of .40 is obtained. The same procedure would be used to compute discrimination indexes for each item.

The greater the magnitude of the Discrimination index, the more likely it is that those in the upper group got the item correct and the less likely it is that those in the lower group got it wrong. This is what the test author is looking for in an item.

A question that everyone gets right or everyone gets wrong will have a D equal to zero. If more students get a question correct in the lower group than in the upper group, the D will be negative. This is an unusual occurrence, but it can happen with an item assessing complex material, written in such a way that it is possible to select the correct response without any real understanding of what is being assessed. Poor students make a guess, select the obvious response, and come up with the correct answer. Good students may be suspicious of a question that looks too easy, take the harder path to solving the problem, and end up being less successful than those who guess.

The item-discrimination method of conducting an item analysis is straight-forward and easily understood by any teacher for a classroom test. The problem is that even with thirty students and a fifty item test, it will be necessary for the person conducting the item analysis to examine 1,000 items [20 students (10 in each group) × 50 items = 1,000]. This is more effort than most teachers are likely to be willing to expend.

Item-total Score Correlation Method of Conducting an Item Analysis

To conduct an item analysis using the item-total score correlation method, you need a computer and item analysis software, or at least a program that will compute correlations. Information about whether or not the item was successfully answered (usually a 1 if it is correct and a 0 if it is incorrect) must be entered into computer memory. Entering this much data into a computer by hand, is an arduous task, and for this reason, the item-total score correlation method is usually employed only when machine scoring is available. The computer compares the scoring key and the student response data and each item is scored as right or wrong. This data is then analyzed using item-analysis software, or an existing statistical analysis program. The outcome that is of most interest is the correlation between the item and the total score (the hand computation method for obtaining this correlation is referred to as the *point–biserial correlation*). It also is possible to have the computer generate item difficulties, item means, standard deviations, and the frequencies of responses to distracters. The correlations between the item and the total score are interpreted in the same way as the discrimination index.

Despite differences in their computation, both methods of determining the discrimination index for an item can be interpreted in the same way. The larger the discrimination index or the item-total correlation, the better the item. The size of the D or the item-total correlation needed to justify the retention of an item depends on several factors. First of all, it depends on the number of students taking the test.

When the number of students in a classroom is small, these indexes tend to be unstable. An item that might be effective in one class may not work with another. Subtle differences in the presentation of material, or the responses made by the instructor to a specific question in class, can alter the difficulty and effectiveness of an item. Another important consideration is the variability in the construct underlying the test. Variability strongly effects the magnitude of correlations. If most students are about the same in relation to the construct being measured, it will be difficult to obtain items that have high discrimination indexes. In a class with a wide disparity in performance, the indexes will tend to be higher.

A useful 'rule of thumb' is to retain items with the highest discrimination index (over .40), to eliminate those with the lowest index (below .15) and to modifying those in between. The first step in understanding why an item has a low index is to determine if the item is flawed in some way; i.e., if its construction violates the rules of good item writing set forth earlier in this chapter. Another important area of concern is item difficulty. The computation of item difficulty is described in Chapter 3, Planning the test. Items that are too easy or too difficult will usually be poor discriminators. Sometimes an item will be a poor discriminator because it is too difficult even though the computed difficulty might be in an acceptable range. This can occur when two of four distracters are completely implausible, leaving the correct answer and a plausible distracter. Even if the item is so difficult that only a few students can distinguish the right answer from the plausible distracter, half of the students can be expected to obtain the correct answer by guessing, since they need only guess between two responses. It is important to ensure that all the distracters are functioning effectively. Distracters that are not plausible make items too easy and those that are too close to the correct answer make an item too difficult.

Summary

There are a number of approaches that can be used to assess students. These can be teacher-made or standardized. They can have an objective, constructed response or performance format. The focus of this chapter is on objective tests. There are three types of objective items: true–false, multiple-choice and matching. In general, true–false items are not recommended, while multiple-choice items are generally preferred. In certain settings, where associations are of particular interest the matching item format can appropriately be used. The teacher authoring an objective item test, needs to realize that to create a good test it will be necessary for him or her to devote a sufficient amount of time to the task. It is also necessary for the test author to have some basic knowledge about how to write good objective items. There are a series of well-accepted rules for writing good items. They can be summarized into two general rules. First, avoid any practice that make items too easy or gives students with well-developed test taking skills a decided advantage. Second, don't make items artificially difficult by making the reading level too high or turning them into trick questions. It is not enough to apply good test construction practices. Item analysis techniques should be a routine part of test construction and administration. Two approaches to conducting an item analysis are presented: the *item discrimination* and the *item-total correlation* methods.

Additional Readings

CUNNINGHAM, G.K. (1986) *Educational and Psychological Measurement*, New York: Macmillan.

GRONLUND, N.E. and LINN, R.L. (1990) *Measurement and Evaluation in Teaching*, 6th ed., New York: Macmillan.

MEHRENS, W.A. and KAMINSKI, J. (1989) 'Methods for improving standardized test scores: Fruitful, fruitless, or fraudulent,' *Educational Measurement: Issues and Practices*, **8**, 1, pp. 14–22.

THORNDIKE, R.M., CUNNINGHAM, G.K., THORNDIKE, R.L. and HAGAN, E. (1991) *Measurement and Evaluation in Psychology and Education*, New York: Macmillan.

5   Constructed Response Items

In this chapter students will learn:

- the advantages of short answer items;
- the disadvantage of short answer items;
- how short answer items compare with objective items;
- how to write better short answer items;
- how to prepare short answer items for use;
- how to score short answer items;
- when essay questions should be used;
- the advantages to using essay questions;
- the disadvantage to using essay questions;
- improving writing skills with essay questions;
- how to construct better essay questions; and
- how to evaluate essay questions.

There are three main methods of assessing a student's performance in school: objective, constructed response and alternative assessment. Objective items were discussed in the previous chapter and alternative assessment will be discussed in the following chapter. The present chapter focuses on constructed response items.

There are a wide range of possible formats for constructed response items. At one extreme are *short answer items* that are brief, require a single word, sentence, or number as a response. These items share some of the characteristics of objective items. At the other extreme are *essay questions* which can be either in the form of a response that is brief or one that is more lengthy. A distinction also can be made between having a student write an essay and having students take an essay test. The writing of an essay requires more emphasis on style, the mechanics of writing, and other considerations of rhetoric than is usually required for an essay test. Generally speaking, the purpose of an essay test is to allow students to demonstrate their knowledge of a topic or their ability to perform the cognitive tasks stated in the item. The evaluation of spelling, grammar, and/or style are not usually the focus of tests that include essay questions.

Short Answer Items

The short answer item can be in the form of a question, a statement to be completed, or a statement containing blanks to be filled. None of the three is preferred over the other two, but younger and/or less adept students find the question format somewhat easier.

Advantages of the Short Answer Item

The short answer format appears to be an attractive alternative to the use of multiple-choice items because it gives students more flexibility in their responses and it is usually more straightforward and less likely to be 'tricky.' At the same time, there is less subjectivity than with more extended responses which facilitates test scoring.

Short answer items are most effectively used for assessing knowledge of vocabulary, names or dates, knowledge of principles and the ability to solve mathematical problems. Computation problems also are probably best structured as short answer rather than as multiple-choice items. It is only when machine scoring is mandatory, for example with large scale testing, that computation items need to be put into an objective response format.

The primary advantage of the short answer format is that it provides information to the teacher about exactly what a student knows and does not know. Multiple-choice items tell us how a student compares with others in terms of how well they can select the correct response to an item on a topic. What they do not tell us is what a student knows, and perhaps what is more important they do not tell us anything about what the student does not know. An examination of incorrect responses from a short answer question is much more revealing than an examination of which wrong answer was selected for a multiple-choice item.

Disadvantages of the Short Answer Item

The scoring of short answer questions tends to be subjective, and using this format, it is difficult to assess student achievement at other than the knowledge level. At the same time, the construction of a good set of short answer items for a test requires a considerable amount of time and effort. Without such preparation, a test made up of these items may only be assessing the acquisition of trivial information or be unscorable because of the multiplicity of plausible responses that could be made to an item the teacher assumed was unambiguous.

Teachers are tempted to use the short item format because it seems to have the advantages of both objective and extended response items. Unfortunately this format also has the disadvantages of both.

Comparing Short Answer and Multiple-choice Items

In many cases, the same instructional objective can be assessed using either a short answer or a multiple-choice format. When there is a choice, the most important advantage of the multiple-choice format over the short answer format is the elimination of ambiguity in scoring.

Example

Who was President when the Vietnam war began? (Answer: John F. Kennedy)

This is a fairly easy item for any student with a rudimentary knowledge of modern American history. The correct answer is of course John F. Kennedy. What if a student gives a different answer, such as Harry Truman or Dwight D. Eisenhower? Vietnamese nationalists began fighting the French not long after the end of the Second World War. It is not unreasonable to conclude that the war began during the Truman administration. The participation of the United States in the war began after the French were defeated at Dien Bien Phu. Some historians might consider the war to have begun (or at least the participation of the US) at this point, making the response of 'Eisenhower' correct. It is more likely that the teacher wanted to know who was president when the involvement of the United States was of a sufficient scale that one could reasonably conclude that the war had begun. Given these conditions, the obvious answer would be 'Kennedy.' If the teacher only wanted to know whether the students knew that Kennedy was president when US participation in the war began in earnest, and the history of the region during the fifties was not the focus of the class, a multiple-choice item such as the following might be preferred.

Example

Who was President when the Vietnam war began?

A.   John F. Kennedy
B.   Richard Nixon
C.   Gerald Ford
D.   Jimmy Carter

The multiple-choice format is a good choice when instructional objectives call for the assessment of concrete knowledge. A multiple-choice item assessing a student's knowledge of when the Vietnam war started could certainly be evaluated more easily and objectively than the same question asked using a short answer item. However, what is gained in objectivity by using the multiple-choice format is paid for in other ways. When a student selects the wrong response with a multiple-choice item, there is no way to know whether he or she believed it was the correct answer or merely guessed. Furthermore, ambiguity may be a critical aspect of what you want your students to understand and this might be better reflected in a short answer than a multiple-choice item.

Though short answer items have a simple, straightforward structure, it is not unusual to encounter poorly written items of this type. The most common faults found in these items are ambiguity, lack of precision, and triviality. In the following section, guidelines for improving the construction of short answer times are presented.

Writing Good Short Answer Items

The writing of good short answer items begins with the selection of the appropriate content to be assessed. This format should not be employed when a objective or an essay format could more effectively assess an educational objective. In constructing short answer questions, the teacher should place particular emphasis on ensuring that all students understand the meaning of each item. An item that seems unambiguous to the teacher who wrote the item, may have a different meaning for a student who encounters the item on a test.

1   *Avoid short answer items that measure only trivia.*
The knowledge for which a student is responsible on a short answer item should be important. It also should reflect what is specified in the instructional objective to which it refers. For each item, the teacher should ask whether either knowing or not knowing the answer will indicate competence in the target instructional object-ive. Both of the following short answer items assess trivial information. The only revision that might be suggested would be to change the focus of the instructional objectives to something more important.

Examples

The Gettysburg Address begins with the phrase 'Fourscore and seven years ago . . .' How many years is that? (Answer: 87)

John Wilkes Booth assassinated Abraham Lincoln in the year _____. (Answer 1865)

2   *Write each question or statement in such a way that it poses a specific problem.*
Short answer items should be written in such a way that students who know the content best are most likely to respond with the correct answer. This will not occur when there is uncertainty about what is being asked.

Examples

Poor: Where is the Capital of the United States? (Answer: Washington D.C.)

Better: What states border the Capital of the United States? (Answer: Maryland and Virginia)

The correct answer in the first example is intended to be 'Washington D.C.' However, as the question is written there are many other possible answers that would be factually correct, for example: 'on the east coast,' 'on the Potomac river,' and 'between Virginia and Maryland.' The problem needs to be more specifically defined as is done in the revised question.

3   *Recheck what you are going to consider a correct response.*
Examine the examples provided below. The test author intended to have Christopher Columbus be the correct answer, but there is considerable debate about the veracity of this generally accepted historical 'fact.' There is evidence that the Norsemen were here before Columbus and of course, indigenous civilizations were present

when Columbus arrived. The ancestors of the residents of these civilizations had 'discovered' America thousands of years before any Europeans arrived.

Examples

Poor: Who discovered America? (Answer: Christopher Columbus)

Better: What European first sailed to America in the 1400s? (Answer: Christopher Columbus)

4 *For questions that require a numerical answer, specify the units in which it is to be expressed.*

Specifying the units for numerical answers simplifies scoring and removes one source of ambiguity in a student's response. In the 'poor' item below, the expected answer is 1849. But students could answer 'in the 1800', 'the mid 1800s,' 'the nineteenth century' and so forth. The teacher evaluating student responses to such items must decide which of these is correct and which is not. The better example removes the ambiguity and makes it easier to evaluate the correctness of a student's responses.

Examples

Poor: When did the California Gold Rush take place? (Answer: 1849)

Better: In what year did the California Gold Rush take place? (Answer: 1849)

5 *Omit only key words in completion items.*

The fact or term that the student is expected to provide for a short answer item should address a specific instructional objective. Choose carefully the word or phrase to be omitted. Do not leave the verb out of a fill-in-the-blank-statement unless the purpose of the item is to measure knowledge of verb forms. In the sample item below, it is the word 'role' that is omitted. This is a poor choice because there are other words besides 'role' that might fit equally well, such as 'position,' 'place,' or attitude. Any of these words complete the meaning of the statement, making it difficult to argue for one answer over the other. In the first *better* item, the word 'impeached,' is omitted. This is a better choice, but it is not the only one that could be used in the sentence. The second *better* item assesses a more relevant aspect of the topic and 'Watergate' is the only answer that completes the sentence.

Examples

Poor: In response to President Nixon's _____ in the Watergate scandal there was pressure to have him impeached. (Answer: role)

Better: In response to President Nixon's role in the Watergate scandal there was pressure to have him _____. (Answer: impeached)

Better: In response to President Nixon's role in the _____ scandal there was pressure to have him impeached. (Answer: Watergate)

6 *In a fill in the blanks short answer item, do not leave so many words blank that the statement loses its meaning.*

Too many blank spaces in a statement can reduce the task to a guessing game. Only when the purpose of an item is to appraise creativity would the deletion of more than two related words be appropriate.

Examples

Poor: The most important _____ of the _____ War was fought at _____.
(Answers: battle, Civil, Gettysburg)

Better: The most important battle of the Civil War was fought at _____.
(Answer: Gettysburg)

7 *In a fill-in-the-blank item, put blanks near the end of the statement rather than at the beginning.*

Short answer items need to be written such a way that a student knows what is being asked before encountering the blank. If this is not done, short term memory will be the most important factor determining whether or not a student correctly responds to a question. This is why short answer items using a question format are somewhat easier than other short answer formats.

Examples

Poor: The _____ amendment guarantees freedom of speech. (Answer: First)

Better: Freedom of speech is guaranteed in the _____ amendment. (Answer: First)

Better: Which amendment guarantees freedom of speech? (Answer: The first)

8 *Use novel content in constructing completion items.*

Too often the statements used for completion fill-in-the-blanks items are sentences copied from a textbook with one or two words omitted. This is an unacceptable practice because a sentence out of context loses much of its meaning. Furthermore, constructing items in this way places too much emphasis on the rote memorization of textbook material, which is rarely a desirable instructional goal.

Preparing the Test for Use

Appearance and structure influence the effectiveness of all tests, but they are even more important for tests made up of restricted-response items. Teachers should select a test format that is easily understood by students which also facilitates the scoring of tests for teachers. Some suggestions that will help to achieve these goals are provided below.

1 *Provide separate answer sheets for students to record their answers.*

The teacher will find it easier to evaluate student answers if they are recorded in a uniform manner on a separate sheet. Students should be instructed to place their answers in the same order as the questions so that the grader does not have to search each student's paper for answers. Blue books or blank sheets of paper can be used with instructions that each answer be numbered to correspond with a question. Alternatively, an answer sheet can be provided which contains the number of each question and a line on which the student can record his or her answer. Since the size of handwriting varies with different students, an ample space for recording answers should be provided.

2   *Separate directions for each item type should be provided.*
The directions should be complete and clearly written. The following points should be included:

- how and where the students are to record their answers;
- the score value of each question;
- whether spelling will be considered in judging the adequacy of answers;
- (for quantitative problems) whether the student must display their computations or merely record the answer; and
- for short-answer questions, whether answers must be written in complete sentences.

3   *Group together items dealing with the same content or skill and place them in a sequence that follows class presentations.*
The use of this organizational structure reduces the perception that the test is made up of unrelated bits and pieces and provides better context for the test items. The student will also be able to concentrate on finding answers to questions instead of trying to figure out the aspect of the course content that is being assessed. Grouping items together that measure similar content also makes it possible for a teacher to see at a glance the content area where frequent errors are occurring. This practice makes it easier for the teacher to focus instruction on the aspects of the content students understand and those which could have been taught better.

Scoring the Test

Although the format of the short answer item is objective, the evaluation of student responses is not always easy and straightforward. Care should be taken in the construction of short answer items to ensure that they can reliably and accurately assess student performance. The following suggestions for evaluating short answer items are provided.

1   *Create an answer key and check it against the answer sheets of some of the better students before scoring the rest of the answer sheets.*
Unless a grader other than the teacher is used, the evaluation of student responses often is initiated without the creation of an answer key. Usually, this causes no problems, but students can, and often do come up with acceptable answers that were not anticipated. When there are items that have several possible correct answers, teachers should try to specify what responses are to be considered correct and which are not, before evaluating any student answers. This information should be placed on an answer key. It also is a good practice to compare the correct responses from the key, with the answers of a few of the better students, to detect

obvious inconsistencies. Students can easily interpret a question differently from the instructor. If an alternative response seems reasonable, the key should be corrected or revised to include it. For an item such as, 'Give an example of an impeachable offense,' a number of different answers could be considered correct. With this sort of item, the key constructed by the teacher may omit some correct answers. A modification of the key to include the full range of correct responses would be appropriate in this situation. Deciding how far a response can differ from what is intended and still be considered correct is the most difficult aspect of evaluating short answer items. Students are likely to enthusiastically encourage the broadening of the boundaries of what is to be considered an acceptable response. Teachers need to avoid making the range so broad that the item becomes meaningless. At the same time, teachers must strive to be fair rather than arbitrary.

2   *In addition to being told which items are correct, students should be given the correct answer for those they got wrong.*

The correct answer for each incorrect response should be written on student answer sheets or a complete set of answers should be provided when the papers are returned. When students make incorrect responses and the answer to a question is wrong, his or her misconception should be corrected during the in-class review. Incomplete knowledge is not as much of a problem as incorrect information or a distorted understanding of content. By providing students with immediate feedback, it is possible to quickly correct the misperceptions of students. Comments that explain why an answer is wrong are even better. They can increase interest and encourage students to be even more involved in the learning task.

3   *Questions should be scored as either right or wrong.*

If the short answer item poses a concrete problem to the student, it should be possible to score it as either right or wrong. Differentiating among levels of correctness using partial credits can make scoring unnecessarily complex. If partial scoring really seems necessary with a particular item it is likely that the item has strayed too far from being a short answer item and has taken the form of an essay question. Teachers are most likely to consider assigning partial credit for computational items, fill in the blank items that include more than one blank, or questions that require several answers. Although awarding partial credit for the correct methodology in a computational problem, for correctly filling some of the blanks in a completion item, or providing less than the required number of answers to a question may seem more fair to students, it contributes little or nothing to the psychometric qualities of a test. If a teacher believes that some content or skills are more important than others, the best way to reflect this is to include more questions based on the important content skill.

Essay Format Questions

The essay test item requires the student to construct a longer response than is required for a short answer item. Its length can range from a paragraph to an answer that requires multiple pages. Most essay format exams are structured so that they can be completed in a single class period, but depending on the purpose of the assessment, more than one class period might be required.

The essay test format has garnered much attention because many states have endeavored to assess writing skills using this format. In the process of setting up these exams, much has been learned about how to maximize the reliability of their scoring. Unfortunately, more precise assessment requires increased time and effort by the teacher or other graders. It also requires questions that are structured to obtain convergent responses. Unless all students are responding similarly, it is difficult to obtain satisfactory levels of reliability.

Advantages of Essay Tests

Essay tests are most effectively used to measure instructional objectives that are not easily assessed using a objective format. Examples of objectives that can be more effectively measured with an essay format are creativity, organization, and the capacity to express ideas. High level thinking skills also can be effectively assessed with well structured essay questions. This format assesses a slightly different type of high level functioning than is assessed using multiple-choice items. Multiple-choice items measure *convergent* thinking, a type of cognitive functioning associated with items that have only one correct answer. Essay questions can measure convergent thinking, but they also can measure *divergent* thinking. Divergent thinking is a form of cognitive functioning assessed by questions for which there is no single correct answer. For a given question there might be almost as many different answers as there are students. With this type of assessment, the teacher cannot be expected to prepare a scoring rubric that anticipates all possible answers.

Disadvantages of Essay Tests

The biggest disadvantage of essay tests is low reliability. This problem, along with poor content validity, is exacerbated by the small number of questions that can be included on such a test. There are two sources of measurement error that are responsible for the unreliability of essay tests: (1) lack of agreement among graders and (2), low internal consistency among items. The error caused by inconsistencies among graders can be quantified by examining the inter-correlations among the scores they assign. Grader error can be minimized by careful item construction, the delineation of scoring rubrics, and thorough training of graders. When the classroom teacher alone, scores the test, the variability associated with the graders cannot be measured. This does not mean that such error is not present. Any time student scores would be different if their responses were evaluated by a different grader, scoring error is present.

The error associated with generalizations across items is a more severe problem. On large scale assessments, this source of error is consistently identified as the most important factor causing constructed response items to have low reliability. When the overall score for a test is based on separate items, it must be assumed that each is measuring the same construct. If there is a lack of consistency across items, the reliability of the test will be impaired. With essay tests, each question tends to measure something unique. As a result, the score a student obtains on a test made up of essay questions will be a function of the particular items included on a test. This problem is less likely to occur for objective tests because there are more items and the tasks tend to be more standardized. The more highly structured and convergent the intended response, the less this factor will contribute to error. However, one of the most important advantages of essay tests is their capacity to assess divergent thinking. The procedures used to minimize the scoring error associated with variability across items tend to diminish their capacity to assess creativity and diversity in student responses.

Another important disadvantage of constructed response items is the amount of time that must be devoted to their evaluation. As the number of items and students increases, the probability that even the most conscientious teacher will carefully read each student response, declines.

The Essay Format Test and Writing Skills

One of the advantages often claimed for essay type exams is their value in fostering good writing skills by providing practice in written expression. Although students at all levels of education need practice in these skills, it is doubtful that an essay examination is the best vehicle for accomplishing this purpose. Under the pressure of the exam atmosphere and accompanying constraints of time, students are likely to do their worst writing. Having students practice poor writing habits under these circumstances is not likely to make them better writers. The types of experiences that lead to good writing skills include careful, thoughtful writing, the opportunity for proofreading, and second, third, and even fourth drafts. The ability to read what has been written and see how it can be improved is also essential to the development of good writing skills. These are not the typical experience of a student taking an essay test.

There is another way that the use of constructed response items can have an impact on student writing skills. Some states and school districts have adopted achievement testing programs that utilize constructed response items. One rationale for using essays to conduct assessments is the capacity of this practice to influence instruction. If a state or school district wants to make writing the highest instructional priority, the use of high stakes essay tests will cause teachers to focus their energies on writing skills. As of yet, evidence for the success of this strategy is scanty, but the possibility seems promising.

Types of Extended Response Questions

The three types of essay questions are as follows: (1) the extended knowledge item, (2) the application and problem solving item; and (3) the creative, divergent thinking item.

The Extended Knowledge Item

Rather than include a series of related short answer items, covering the same aspect of course content, a teacher can ask a single question that requires the student to construct an answer that includes the same content. Suppose a teacher in a seventh grade social studies class is teaching his or her students about the conditions and events that led to the start of World War I. It would be possible to frame a series of individual short answer or multiple-choice items that would assess the degree to which students are able to recall the names, dates, and events that preceded the beginning of that war. The teacher also could use a single essay item to accomplish the same task.

Example

Select the most important events and describe how they led up to the start of World War I.

A teacher might use a question like this because it requires more than the mere recall of a set of dates, names, and facts. If these were really all that the teacher wanted to assess, the short answer format might work better. The example above allows the teacher to assess the capacity of students to select what is most important and to organize, support, or defend their point of view.

Application and Problem Solving Item

If a teacher is interested in assessing the degree to which students can apply what they have learned, assess their ability to solve problems, or engage in higher level thinking, the extended response item can be used. Consider the following item.

Examples

Recall 1. What was the public response to the U.S. involvement in World War II, the Korean conflict, the Vietnam war, and the Gulf war?

Application 2. Compare the response of the public to the US involvement in World War II, the Korean conflict, the Vietnam War, and the Gulf war. What are the most important reasons for this differential response?

A student could successfully answer the first question by treating it as four different questions and describe the public reaction to each war separately. There is no need for the student to compare and contrast. To successfully answer the second question, students need to be able to correctly respond to question 1. In addition, they must understand the similarities and differences among the four conflicts and synthesize them into a coherent response.

Assessing a student's capacity to use knowledge to solve problems, to generate novel explanations, or synthesize information, are legitimate purposes for essay questions. The level of student knowledge is also assessed because the application and synthesis of information is dependent on the student's possession of factual knowledge. On an essay test, differences in knowledge of basic factual material may obscure differences in the ability of students to use and organize these facts. At the same time, students with well developed skills in problem solving, synthesis, and application may be able to produce a good response, despite a lack of fundamental knowledge.

The Creative, Divergent Thinking Item

This type of essay question emphasizes the measurement of a student's ability to express himself or herself in writing. The purpose of such an exercise is not to shape each response in the direction of a single correct answer, but to encourage the production of many equally correct answers. The use of this question type can encourage creativity and the development of problem solving skills. The most important disadvantage of this type of question is the difficulty in evaluating student responses that are qualitatively different.

Constructing Better Essay Questions

The following suggestions are presented as guides to writing more effective essay questions.

1 *Essay questions, like all other items should address the cognitive processes that are specified in the instructional objective that it is intended to assess.*

In the planning stage of test development, there is a need to determine the type of responses that would indicate the mastery of the learning objectives. It is at this point that the stimulus materials needed to elicit these responses should be specified. A teacher who wants to use an essay question to evaluate the ability of eighth grade students to think critically about historical events, may identify as evidence of critical thinking, the mastery of the following skills:

- the evaluation of the appropriateness of reliance on recognized historians;
- the identification of bias and/or emotional aspects of arguments;
- the making of distinction between verifiable and unverifiable facts;
- the recognition of the adequacy of existing information;
- the comparison of statements with known facts; and
- the determination of whether conclusions are supported by facts.

Essay questions which provide an opportunity for students to display each of these abilities should be included on a test intended to assess critical thinking skills.

2 *Use novel material to construct items.*

Questions that are creatively constructed and go beyond the obvious will encourage students to do more than provide rote reproduction of material from their text, the classroom lecture or discussion. While this practice can make the task more interesting for students, it can also make the evaluation of student responses more difficult. Consider the following essay questions.

Examples

Poor: Describe the problems faced by General Washington at Valley Forge as he attempted to build the Continental Army into an effective fighting force?

Better: Imagine that you are lieutenant stationed at Valley Forge preparing a report for General Washington on what is needed to prepare the army for its battles with the British. What recommendations would your report contain?

The first question might be correctly answered by a student who had memorized a list of the problems faced by George Washington at Valley Forge. Along with assessing a student's mastery of the same knowledge, the second question would require students to frame their response in such a way that it indicates a more thorough understanding of what was happening in Valley Forge at that time.

3   *Start essay questions with such words or phrases as 'compare,' 'contrast,' 'give the reasons for,' 'give original examples of,' 'explain how,' 'predict what would happen if,' 'criticize,' 'differentiate,' 'illustrate.'*

When combined with novel material, the use of words and/or phrases such as those above, require students to apply, rather than merely recall what they have learned. Beginning essay questions with words such as 'what,' 'who,' 'when,' and 'list,' will encourage students merely to reproduce information.

4   *Write the essay question in such a way that the task is clearly and unambiguously defined for each student.*

If an essay question is not clearly defined, students will spend too much time endeavoring to understand what they are supposed to do. The task of grading papers becomes more difficult when student responses differ depending on how they interpret each question. Consider the following essay question.

Example

Discuss the three branches of the federal government.

This question, as written, is vague and ambiguous. Students are likely to disagree about what is meant by the word 'discuss'? Does it require a listing of the branches of the federal government and their functions? A criticism and evaluation of what they do? The identification of problems in their interrelationship? Second, does the teacher expect the student to examine the question only from the perspective of modern day issues or from a historical point of view? The question as written requires that the student guess what the teacher wanted for an answer, and a student's score is likely to depend on how well he or she guesses.

114

5   *Be sure the essay question asks for the behavior that you really want the student to display.*

Teacher-made essay tests frequently include questions such as 'Give your best definition of manifest destiny'; 'What do you think is the difference between the Republican and Democratic parties?'; or 'In your opinion, what factors have contributed to the decreasing level of voting in national elections in the United States?' Usually, the teacher is not interested in the student's opinion, but instead wants to know whether the student knows the factual material underlying that position. Rewritten, better questions would read, 'Define manifest destiny'; 'Explain the differences between the Republican and Democratic parties'; and 'What factors have contributed to the decreasing number of persons voting in the United States in recent national elections?'

6   *Adapt the length and complexity of the answer to the maturity level of the students.*

Success in answering complex essay questions at a sophisticated level, depends on the writing skills and maturity of the student being assessed. It is unreasonable to expect the same organization and expression from an elementary or junior high school student that would be expected of a high school student. A teacher's awareness of the appropriate difficulty level for essay questions is acquired from experience.

7   *Do not give students a choice of questions to answer.*

Students usually prefer to select the questions they answer from a larger set of choices. Such a practice tends to compensate for the unfairness that can arise when the few items included on an essay exam are a poor sample from the domain of all possible items. However, if all the students in a class do not answer the same questions, grading will be much more difficult because student responses will not be directly comparable. The student who writes a good answer to an easy question must be compared with the student who writes a less adequate response to a harder question.

8   *Ensure that students know how much time should be spent on each question.* This can be done either by time limits or by an indication of the number of points to be awarded for each question. Such procedures prevent students from either spending too much time on an unimportant question or too little time on one that is more important. If no limits are placed on the length of student answers, the only limits may be physical. It is better to insist on quality rather than quantity in student answers. Items written to include reasonable restrictions on responses will be easier to grade and their assessment can be accomplished more objectively.

Evaluating Essay Question Responses

The appraisal of student achievement using an essay test requires more than well-formulated questions. The teacher must evaluate essay question answers carefully and consistently. Above all, the teacher who administers such a test must be willing to put forth a sufficient amount of time and effort in their evaluation. Unlike objective items, which require time and effort in the test writing phase, constructed response items require the most effort after the test has been administered. Anyone who has ever been involved in the grading of essay tests can appreciate the amount of time required and the tediousness of the task. For large classes, requiring lengthy answers, covering numerous pages, the task can be almost overwhelming. There is no way that the evaluation process for such a test can be minimized. If a teacher is unwilling to devote the hours necessary for a thorough and thoughtful evaluation, the students and the teacher would be better off with a different test format.

The competent, accurate, and fair evaluation of essay test answers begins with planning. Planning has its foundation in instructional objectives that describe what it is that students are supposed to learn. The essay question format should be selected when it provides the best method of evaluating these learning goals. The test planning stage is often skipped because it is so easy to write essay questions with a minimum of planning and effort. Generating enough items to keep students busy for the appropriate amount of time using this format is easy. However, tests constructed in this manner are unlikely to be effective in measuring what a student has learned and/or what a student can do. If the teacher has not given much thought to the sort of answers that would be considered correct, it will be difficult for him or her to effectively evaluate student performance.

There are two main approaches recommended for use in evaluating student answers to essay tests. The appropriateness of each is determined by the purpose of the tests, i.e., whether the emphasis is on assessing what students have learned or assessing what the student can do with their knowledge. Essay questions that emphasize the application of knowledge usually require students to solve problems, devise creative responses, or synthesize diverse principles and information.

If the focus is on what students know, the *analytic approach* is preferred. With this approach, the teacher specifies what is to be considered a correct answer and the number of points associated with each question. Students tend to prefer the analytical approach because it provides concrete information about how they performed on each question. It also communicates that their answer was actually read and carefully considered.

Unless the correct student response can be specified in advance, the analytical approach is not appropriate. Under such circumstances, when the focus of the extended response exercise is on broader forms of performance such as writing ability, the creation of novel solutions to problems, or the organization and synthesis of diverse information into a cogent thesis, the *global approach* is preferred. The global approach is sometimes selected because it seems to require less time than the analytical approach. This time saving may be illusory because each approach requires a similar amount of time. The time required for the analytical approach is concentrated prior to test administration while the most time consuming aspect of the global approach are the activities that occur after students have responded. If the analytic key has been prepared in advance, it should not be that difficult to match each student's response to the key and assign points.

There are two ways to implement the global approach. (1) Points can be allocated to each student's response to a question with the grader making this allocation based on his or her overall impression of the quality of the student response. (2) The response to each prompt or question can be assigned to categories according to the 'grader's' impression of their quality. Categories such as 'Excellent,' 'Good,' 'Average,' 'Poor,' or 'unsatisfactory' can be used. Sometimes the categories are made graphic and concrete by designating piles on which student responses are placed. Each pile is represented by one of the above categories. Repeated readings are used to verify and adjust the assigned score. Although there is evidence to suggest that it is possible to obtain reliable scores using the global approach, it may be difficult to defend this method of evaluation to students, who usually prefer concrete information about how points were assigned to their performance.

With the *modified global approach* the grader assigns several scores to the student response. These could include such categories as originality, quality of expression, use of correct English, and so forth.

Suggestions for More Effectively Evaluating Responses to Essay Questions

1 *For analytical scoring, the correct answer for each item must be specified in advance.*

Determining optimal answers to the questions on an essay test is time consuming and difficult because it is easier to ask than answer questions. For a question that requires students to solve a problem which has more than one correct solution, the teacher should specify each option, keeping in mind that there may be other satisfactory answers that the teacher has not included as acceptable responses.

2 *When questions refer to controversial subjects, students should not be evaluated in terms of the position(s) taken.*

Much of what is important in our society is controversial. This controversy can enhance student learning by maintaining interest and encouraging students to focus on topics about which they feel strongly. Regardless of a teacher's feeling about an issue, his or her point of view should not be imposed on students. In particular, students should not be made to feel that they should abandon their own principles to echo the viewpoint of the teacher. Instead, students should be evaluated according to what they know, and how well they can use their knowledge to support their conclusions.

3 *Reduce irrelevant factors that might influence your judgment of the quality of student answers.*

The best tests are those that provide the purest measure of the assigned instructional objectives and are not confounded by unrelated variables. One of the disadvantages of essay tests is that performance tends to be a composite of extraneous factors. Besides mastery of instructional objectives, such factors as penmanship, spelling, writing style, and general knowledge, influence student performance on such a test. Even when graders are instructed to ignore these factors, assigned scores are likely to be affected by their presence.

Spelling ability, neatness, grammar, and style of writing are important and students should be encouraged to develop these skills more fully, but they should be assessed by tests constructed for this purpose. These skills can be assessed with an essay test format, but this should be the stated purpose of the test and not a secondary agenda of the person evaluating student performance. When they are listed as instructional objectives, they should be awarded separate scores.

4   *Mask the names of students before scoring their exam.*
Poor reliability is an important problem with essay tests and subjectivity in scoring is one of its causes. This problem is exacerbated when teachers know the name of the student who wrote the paper they are grading. There is the possibility that this information will influence a teacher's perception of a student's response. An unusual answer from a poor student may be evaluated as wrong, while the same answer submitted by a student about whom the grader has a positive opinion, may be thought to be creative and original.

5   *Maintain a consistent standard for judging answers across all students.*
A careful examination of a typical set of answers to an essay exam usually reveals several student answers to the same question that appear to be of equal quality which have been scored differently. Several factors can be used to explain the discrepancy including the following: when the answer was graded — as one of the first, the middle or last; whether the teacher recognized the student who wrote the answers, or the influence of extraneous characteristics on the teacher's appraisal of the answer. This is an inherent weakness of this test format and it is quite difficult to eliminate. There are some practices that will at least minimize this propensity. First, every student's response to a question should be evaluated before the response to the next question is examined. This procedure allows the teacher to concentrate on one question at a time, making it easier to compare student responses. There is also less opportunity for a grader's evaluation of the response to one question to generalize to the others.

Another way to ensure consistency across student responses is to reread the test papers a second time or have someone else read them. Responses that get low marks when they are the first papers graded may seem better after the remainder of answers have been read. Teachers often begin their evaluation of student responses with great energy and resolve to read carefully, but as the hour becomes later, under pressure to have the tests ready to be returned the next day, they may succumb to the temptation to read less carefully. The less attention a teacher is able to devote to each student's response, the more willing he or she may be to give students the benefit of the doubt. This usually results in a lack of consistency across student responses. A final rereading of all the papers can increase the consistency of a teacher's evaluation of student responses.

6   *Put comments on the exams.*
Putting comments on papers, communicates to students that the teacher has read their responses. Students find this reassuring and appreciate the amount of effort expended on this task. It can be disconcerting for students to have a paper returned with numerical scores for each answer without any indication of how or why a particular value was assigned.

Summary

Constructed response items as their name implies, require a student to construct a response rather than select among several possibilities. There are two types of constructed response items: short answer and essay response formats. Some of the apparent advantages of the short answer are more apparent than real. They are not as objective as they appear and if not carefully planned they can end up measuring trivial content. Essay items can assess not only a student's capacity to recall knowledge in the form of facts and concepts, but they have the capacity to assess organizational, and synthesizing skills as well as problem solving ability. The biggest disadvantage to the use of essay questions is the difficulties associated with their evaluation and the restricted range of content they can cover. Responses to essay questions can be evaluated either analytically or globally. Whatever system is used for evaluation, the teacher must be willing to devote an adequate amount of time to this activity and carefully think about what is, and what is not to be considered a correct answer.

Additional Readings

CUNNINGHAM, G.K. (1986) *Educational and Psychological Measurement*, New York: Macmillan.

GRONLUND, N.E. and LINN, R.L. (1990) *Measurement and Evaluation in Teaching*, 6th ed., New York: Macmillan.

MEHRENS, W.A. and KAMINSKI, J. (1989) 'Methods for improving standardized test scores: Fruitful, fruitless, or fraudulent,' *Educational Measurement: Issues and Practices*, **8**, 1, pp. 14–22.

THORNDIKE, R.M., CUNNINGHAM, G.K., THORNDIKE, R.L. and HAGAN, E. (1991) *Measurement and Evaluation in Psychology and Education*, New York: Macmillan.

6   Alternative Assessment

In this chapter students will learn:

- about the different types of alternative assessment;
- the purposes of alternative assessment;
- why the use of performance tests has increased;
- how performance tests are used in the classroom;
- how performance tests are used for large scale testing;
- how to construct better performance tests;
- how to assess processes and products;
- how to use checklists and rating scales;
- how to establish and assess the reliability and validity of alternative assessment techniques; and
- how to construct and use portfolios.

During the 1990s, new forms of educational assessment rose to prominence and it became necessary to distinguish these new techniques from those that had dominated educational testing since its inception. The assessment methods described in the previous two chapters are called *conventional assessment* to distinguish them from the alternative assessment methodologies that will be presented in this chapter. There have been several different names given to these new approaches, including alternative assessment, performance-based assessment, performance assessment, performance testing, and authentic assessment. These terms are not synonymous and each has its own nuances. When this new form of assessment was first promoted as an alternative to conventional assessment, several authors used the term *authentic assessment*. This includes Grant Wiggins (1989) who can be considered a leader in the founding of this movement.

To illustrate the differences among conventional, performance, and authentic assessment, consider the following example. A teacher is trying to determine whether fourth grade students know how to use money and make change. A conventional approach to assessment might present the students with a worksheet which includes problems similar to the following example.

A conventional approach to assessing a student's ability to make change

---

Mark the right answer

If a candy bar costs 35¢ and you give a store clerk $1, how much change should you get back?

- two quarters
- two quarters and two dimes
- two quarters a dime and a nickel
- three quarters

To turn this task into a performance test, the teacher could use play money and have students come to his or her desk and purchase objects for which they would receive change. The students would be required to decide if they had received the correct amount of change. This task would become authentic if the students were given money, taken to a store where they actually purchased a piece of candy, counted the change they received, and determined if it was correct.

There is obviously no clear demarcation between a performance test that is authentic and one that is not. The focus of the present chapter will be on performance tests and portfolios, with the understanding that the purest alternative tests are those that are most authentic. Authenticity is not desirable in all testing settings because it can have the effect of making comparisons among student responses more difficult.

The term *authentic* is now more often used to describe a desirable characteristic of a test. The use of the term *alternative assessment* emphasizes the distinction between this form of assessment and conventional assessment. The terms *performance tests* and *performance assessment* generally refer to an authentic, alternative form of assessment in which students are assessed directly by having them perform high level, real-world tasks, often in a group setting.

When the term *performance-based assessment* is used, it usually is intended to refer to the same instructional practices that are used with *performance assessment*. At other times it is used to describe instruction that is more appropriately described as conventional. For example, in Robert Linn and Norman Gronlund's textbook, *Measurement and Assessment in Teaching* (7th Ed.) (1995), generally considered the pre-eminent measurement textbook in teacher education, the distinction between conventional and performance-based assessment has been blurred. The authors classify all assessments as either objective or performance assessments. Essay tests, along with other assessment tasks such as constructing a model, conducting an experiment in chemistry, or making a speech are classified as examples of performance-based assessment. The concepts of directness, real world applications, authenticity, and differences in underlying philosophy have been replaced by simpler requirements. In order for an assessment to be labeled a performance-based assessment, it is necessary only to have the student respond by doing something other than select the correct answer from among several choices or provide a single word answer.

The Office of Technology Assessment, likewise fails to make a clear distinction between performance-based assessment and the conventional use of constructed response or essay tests. They define performance-based assessment as '. . . testing methods that require students to create an answer or product that demonstrates knowledge or skills.' Of course all conventional constructed response tests would be included as performance-based assessment using this definition. The attributes of performance assessment that stirred so much interest among educators at the beginning of the 1990s are absent.

In some measurement textbooks, conventional test items are classified as being either *selection* or *supply* items rather than as *objective* or *constructed response* items, as is done in this textbook. Students respond to selection items by choosing their answer from among choices provided. This could include placing a *t* or *f* in front of statements on a true-false test, selecting from four or five options in response to an item on a multiple-choice test or from a list of options on a matching tests. With supply items students are required to provide a response, in the form of an answer. Completion, fill-in-the-blanks, short-answer and essay questions are all examples of supply type items. The definition from the Office of Technology Assessment provides a more appropriate description of a supply type item than it does of performance assessment.

Of course, to some extent the definition and use of words is arbitrary and if an individual or group wishes to define performance-based instruction as being synonymous with supply or constructed response tests they are free to do so. What does seem unacceptable is for these same individuals to advocate the use of performance-based assessment on the basis of the advantages of authentic, alternative, performance assessments. The use of the term 'performance-based assessment' is inherently misleading. It is being used to justify the replacement of conventional assessment with something that is supposed to be new and innovative assessment, but is really something older than conventional assessment. Berlak (1992) addresses the issue as follows:

> . . . in recent years, there have been efforts to develop so-called 'performance-based' tests. The intent is to create assessments which avoid the multiple choice format and more closely approximate real tasks, such as conducting an experiment or writing a job application letter. While some of these efforts succeeded in breaking the boundaries of the conventional testing paradigm, most do not depart significantly from the conventional standardized and criterion-referenced test technology. Rather than presenting four or five alternatives to choose from, a score is assigned to the test-takers' 'free' responses (recorded on paper or computer) on the basis of previously-determined criteria. Aggregated scores are then treated in more or less the same way as those derived from multiple choice items. For all practical purposes most such assessments are rooted in the conventional psychometric paradigm. (p. 11)

Even the most liberal definitions of a performance assessment have distinguished it from objective testing. Now, even that distinction seems to have been lost and even multiple-choice tests have been considered a form of performance assessment. For example, Burger and Burger (1994) compare the reliability of two performance assessments with the CTBS-4. The two performance assessments are a writing assessment developed by the authors and the Essential Skills Reading

Test (MEAP) a standardized reading test. Both assessments are said to meet criteria used to define a performance assessment.

The writing assessment requires students to respond to essay questions which are scored by raters. On the MEAP test, each student's ability to construct meaning from a paragraph is assessed using a multiple-choice item format. The Burgers' classification of a multiple-choice test as an example of a performance assessment constitutes a rather startling broadening of the definition. If both essay and multiple-choice tests are to be considered performance assessments, the term has lost its power to distinguish among tests and the legitimacy of a truly important new assessment methodology has been compromised. While true performance assessments may not be the best choice for high stakes, large scale assessments, it is an effective instructional tool which teachers should be encouraged to employ.

Conventional Manifestations of Performance Assessment

In some fields, such as vocational education, music, art, science, math and physical education, performance assessments are not thought of as innovations at all. They have been used for a long time. Having students exhibit behaviors that indicate mastery of instructional objectives, completion of projects, and writing term papers as a process for determining how much a student has learned, actually predates the introduction of multiple choice and other objectively formatted items. What makes the increased use of performance tests educationally significant and justifies the label of alternative assessment is the increased use of these techniques to assess students in settings where the conventional techniques described in the previous two chapters would have routinely been used in the past.

The use of portfolios to display art and photo achievements also has existed for a long time and can probably be justifiably labeled *conventional*. Now, portfolios are being used on a widespread basis to assess writing, mathematics and other subjects. These represent a different use for portfolios, which makes them legitimate examples of alternative assessment.

An Alternative to Conventional Assessment

Grant Wiggins (1989) is usually given credit for being the first to advocate the use of alternative assessment in a wider range of instructional settings and as an alternative to conventional objective tests. He used the term *authentic* rather than alternative or performance assessment. The assessment he advocated is described in an excerpt from his classic article, 'A true test: Toward more authentic and equitable assessment.' (1989, pp. 703, 704).

> I propose a radical answer, in the sense of a return to the roots; we have lost sight of the fact that a true test of intellectual ability requires *the performance of exemplary tasks*. First, authentic assessments replicate the challenges and standards of performance that typically face writers, business people, scientists, community leaders, designers or historians. These include writing essays and reports, conducting

individual and group research, designing proposals and mock-ups, assembling port-folios, and so on. (pp. 703, 704)

Ruiz-Primo, Baxter, and Shavelson, (1993) agree with Wiggin's emphasis on the need for authentic tasks stating that,

One alternative to multiple-choice testing, congruent with curricular reform and constructivist learning theories, is hands-on performance assessments. In science, for example, a performance assessment provides students with laboratory equip-ment, poses a problem, and allows them to use these resources to generate a solu-tion. This hands-on test is administered on a one-to-one basis, and performance is judged in real time as experts watch students do science. (p. 41)

Many authors view performance assessment as a means of escaping the per-ceived tyranny of multiple-choice testing. Frechtling (1991), states that, 'Propon-ents of performance assessment see these tests as offering a number of advantages over the instruments that we have relied upon for the last four decades. First, the new assessments go beyond simplistic, multiple-choice questions, requiring stud-ents to perform in situations that are both more lifelike and more complex (p. 23).'

The Increase in the Importance of Alternative Assessment

Although alternative assessment has been used for a long time, it is now being recommended for use in a much wider range of applications including state and system-wide assessment systems. There are four reasons for the remarkable support for alternative assessment: (1) concern about the negative impact of the use of standardized tests in minimum competency testing, (2) dissatisfaction with existing psychometric models, (3) the belief in a constructivist model of learning, and (4) the belief that the primary purpose of public schools is the promotion of social justice.

Concern about the Negative Effects of Using Standardized Tests for Minimum Competency Assessment

In many states, minimum competency testing was implemented in the 1980s to increase student learning by providing negative consequences to students who per-formed poorly. The usual practice was to have promotion to the next grade and/or graduation, be linked to performance on standardized achievement tests, either those normed for use across the nation or similarly formatted state tests. The use of a standardized test format for assessing the minimum competency of students seems to have had more of a negative than a positive effect on instruction. This is because the higher stakes associated with accountability tend to distort curric-ula and cause students and teachers to engage in unproductive behavior that may increase test scores, but is seldom valuable educationally.

Initially, it was the students who felt most of the pressure to perform well on these tests because they were the ones that risked being required to repeat a grade or be denied a diploma. As the stakes were raised, the chain of responsibility was altered and the failure of students became the failure of the teacher and their school. As a result, there was a tendency for teachers to alter (distort) their curriculum to increase performance on these tests.

These distortions in the curriculum, accompanied by other dubious test preparation practices, resulted in nearly all students passing the minimum competency tests. This usually happened after the test had been administered for several years and teachers and students had become familiar with the test content.

For a number of reasons, including those mentioned above, student performances on standardized achievement tests do not reflect the gloomy picture painted by educational commissions. In fact, almost every state and school district turned out to be above average on standardized achievement test (Cannell, 1988). These achievement test performances were so high that they defied any reasonable explanation other than that students were being given too much help by the teachers who were ultimately being evaluated by their students' performance. It soon became obvious that the high levels of student performance, obtained using these questionable techniques, would not come without a cost. The cost came in the form of a disproportionate amount of teacher time being devoted to coaching students to perform better on these tests and students devoting their energy to practicing test items likely to appear on the test rather than participating in more useful classroom activities. The resulting curriculum distortion led to a revulsion against the use of standardized multiple-choice format tests. The best solution to this problem would have been to lower the stakes associated with the test, but the political craving for accountability is difficult to satisfy. Instead of addressing the problems associated with high stakes testing, there has been a demand that the use of conventional tests be eliminated in favor of alternative assessment techniques. This strategy does not address the real problem. There is no reason to believe that alternative assessment techniques, used in a high stakes environment will not have the same corrupting effect on curricula as did conventional standardized test strategies.

Dissatisfaction with Existing Psychometric Theory

Conventional assessment techniques are based on a series of psychometric assumptions that provide a point of view that has been found to be useful in quantifying human attributes or constructs. These assumptions include the beliefs that:

1   the responses of students on a test are the same as physical objects which can be counted, turned into numbers, and interpreted as statistics;
2   assessment requires the use of a neutral, value-free scientific language to describe student performance; and
3   assessment is objective and takes place independently of its context.

These assumptions represent both the viewpoint of conventional measurement theory, and a scientific perspective as well. A contrary view, has emerged which has gained increased acceptance over the past several years. It is sometimes called 'qualitative assessment', 'social constructivism,' or 'post-modern thinking.' Proponents of this view reject the 'logical positivism' of conventional measurement theory. They assert that too much emphasis on objectivity will lower the quality of the interpretation of student responses. This is believed to be true because objectivity usually means context-free judgment and assessments that are context-free may ignore necessary special considerations for individual students. Furthermore, they argue that the observer can never be completely separated from what is observed and that measurement is never value-free. When conventional psychometric theory, with its emphasis on objectivity is rejected and the need for assessment continues to be recognized, adherents of this view tend to gravitate towards alternative forms of assessment.

Growing Influence of the Social Constructivist Model of Learning

During the 1990s there has been a major change in the way education is viewed in the United States. These changes involve a shift from conventional teacher-centered methods of instruction and traditional curricula to methods of instruction that are more student focused. This approach is also strongly influenced by cognitive psychology, in particular, the belief that students construct meaning rather than 'receive' knowledge from their teachers.

The most important principle associated with these new cognitive approaches is the replacement of the usual emphasis on the learning of facts, knowledge, and basic skills with a focus on the acquisition of higher level thinking skills. In other words, content is replaced with process. According to this view, if instruction and practice on high level thinking skills are put off until preliminary skills have been learned, many students will not reach the point where they get the opportunity to practice high level thinking skills. Constructivists believe that the acquisition of high level thinking skills is not dependent on the mastery of lower level skills and knowledge and therefore does not need to be delayed until they have been acquired. At the same time, they believe that asking students to solve higher level problems can motivate them to learn the underlying skills and knowledge needed to solve the problem. From this perspective, a high level discussion of a crisis in the Middle East should not be put off until students have gained a proper knowledge of the history and geography of the area. Instead, the initiation of the discussion might motivate students to learn more about history and geography. The constructivists philosophy is incompatible with high stakes accountability systems and objective testing in general. The only form of assessment constructivists can enthusiastically support is personal communications with individual students intended to directly improve instruction. They believe that the primary focus of assessment must be on the student and that accountability considerations should be secondary (Wiggins, 1996). Since it is unlikely that all assessment will ever be eliminated, they advocate the compromise position of replacing conventional, objective tests with performance assessment. Performance tests are recommended because they can be easily structured to emphasize applications and they avoid the skills-based orientation associated with conventional objective tests.

The Belief that Public Schools Should Promote Positive Social Change

One of the purposes of conventional standardized tests is to differentiate among students for the purpose of making educational decisions. Because of its objectivity and freedom from such extraneous influences as physical appearance, ethnic background, economic and social class, and family background, the use of such tests was at one time considered a force for social equality. The climate has changed and the use of standardized tests is now more likely to be labeled unfair because it inevitably identifies some students as having been unsuccessful. The problem is exacerbated when those who are identified as being least successful come from culturally different populations. Under these circumstances, standardized tests are likely to be viewed as an impediment rather than a contributor to positive social change.

Educators committed to the belief that the proper role of teachers is to encourage social justice are likely to view conventional tests as destructive. These tests are believed to play an invidious sorting-out role in the schools, where the fortunate few are singled out for rewards and success while the rest are condemned to a life of poor grades, low paying marginal jobs, and grief. The same educators that assert the school's role as a social change agent are usually equally adamant in their criticism of the positivistic theoretical underpinning of conventional measurement theory which they consider to be white, male, and Eurocentric. For these reasons the conventional standardized multiple-choice based assessment is usually rejected in favor of alternative testing techniques. The irony of this position is that there is no evidence to show that minority students perform better on performance than multiple-choice tests (Linn *et al.*, 1991) and may even do worse (Phillips, 1991, Baker and O'Neill, 1996).

The Rationale for Alternative Assessments

Using a conventional approach to instruction and assessment, teachers focus on the acquisition of *declarative knowledge* (what a student knows). Some classroom activity may also be devoted to helping students acquire *procedural knowledge* (what a student can do). A student in a high school English class would be expected to learn many facts about literature (declarative knowledge), and they would also be expected to be able to apply this knowledge on essay tests (procedural knowledge).

With conventional assessment, test scores are not ends in themselves, but are intended to be indicators of a student's status in relation to the construct being measured. Such tests can be described as indirect measures. A history test consisting of fifty multiple-choice items is supposed to tell us more than how many of those specific items a student can correctly answer. A student's knowledge of history is inferred from the number of items correctly answered. If a test is valid, legitimate inferences about knowledge of history can be made using these scores.

The rationale for the use of alternative assessment is quite different. There is no distinction made between a student's correct response on a performance assessment and the evaluation of his or her status in relation to the instructional objective it is assessing. According to Wiggins (1989), the critical attribute of performance assessment is this directness. Consider a creative writing class in which students are being taught how to write short stories. The instructional goal of the class requires that students be able to write an acceptable short story at the end of the lesson. At the conclusion of instruction, the teacher could administer a multiple-choice test to determine whether students have understood the principles of correct short story writing that were presented. This is obviously an indirect measure of student achievement and not a performance assessment because the teacher is required to infer from the number of correct responses whether or not the student has the knowledge necessary to write an acceptable short story. Alternatively, as a way of measuring whether students have reached the instructional goal, the teacher could require that the students actually write a short story. This would be a performance assessment with the important quality of directness. The teacher does not need to make any inferences about whether the student can write a short story. The short story can be directly judged as acceptable or unacceptable. There is a third possibility, the students could be asked to answer one, or a series of essay questions about how to write a short story. This would not be an objective multiple-choice assessment, but it would not be a performance assessment either. It is an indirect measure of the students' ability to write short stories because the teacher is required to infer from the quality of the responses to the essay questions, whether or not each student has mastered the basics of short story writing at a level that would make it likely that he or she would be able to produce an acceptable short story.

The use of alternative assessments is based on assumptions about how students learn, how best to teach them, and the role of assessment that are quite different from conventional assumptions in these areas. In many ways, alternative assessment can be viewed as a rejection of conventional principles of measurement, educational testing and instruction. Advocates of alternative assessment are concerned about the indirectness and artificiality of conventional methods of student assessment and the difficulties faced by teachers trying to prepare students for such tests.

Performance tests are intended to encourage 'teaching to the test' because the tasks presented to students are viewed as instructional goals rather than indicators of success in the domain of interest. Teachers are urged to teach students the specific knowledge and skills needed for success on these tasks. Frederiksen and Collins (1989) believe that test authors should structure their tests in such a way that they have *systemic validity* which they define as the match between what a test is intended to measure and the methods used to prepare students to succeed on the test. When a test has systemic validity, preparing students to succeed on it furthers the actual instructional goals, not just the indicators of the goals. Teaching students the skills needed for success on a test which lacks systemic validity may increase test performance, without affecting the underlying construct being assessed.

Even when teaching to the test is permissible, as it is with performance tests, the best strategy for preparing students to succeed is far from obvious. Practice on tasks similar to those that will be encountered on performance tests is usually recommended. However, if the student practices on items that are too similar to those that will appear on the tests, the meaning of success on the performance task will be devalued. Ideally, the skills gained from practicing one task should transfer to other similar tasks, but research on the transfer of cognitive skills among performance tasks is not encouraging (Norris, 1989).

The following example of a performance test item is provided in Grant Wiggin's (1989) now classic article on performance testing, 'A true test: Toward more authentic and equitable assessment.'

> You are the chief executive officer of an established firm. Your firm has always captured a major share of the market, because of good use of technology, understanding of the natural laws of constraint, understanding of market systems, and the maintenance of a high standard for your product. However, in recent months your product has become part of a new trend in public tastes. Several new firms have entered the market and have captured part of your sales. Your product's proportional share of total aggregate demand is continuing to fall. When demand returns to normal, you will be controlling less of the market than before.
>
> Your board of directors has given you less than a month to prepare a report that solves the problem in the short run and in the long run. In preparing the report, you should: 1) define the problem, 2) prepare data to illustrate the current situation, 3) prepare data to illustrate conditions one year in the future, 4) recommend action for today, 5) recommend action over the next year, and 6) discuss where your company will be in the market six months from today and one year from today.
>
> The tasks that must be completed in the course of this project include:
>
> - deriving formulas for supply, demand, elasticity, and equilibrium;
> - preparing schedules for supply, demand, costs, and revenues;
> - graphing all work;
> - preparing a written evaluation of the current and future situation for the market in general and for your company in particular;
> - preparing a written recommendation for your board of directors;
> - showing aggregate demand today and predicting what it will be one year hence; and
> - showing the demand for your firm's product today and predicting what it will be one year hence. (p. 707)

The best strategy for a teacher to use in preparing a student to perform well on such a performance task is not completely clear. A teacher could present instruction on some of the basic skills that would make success on the above item more likely. For instance, students could be taught graphing skills, and how to use formulas for supply, demand, elasticity, and equilibrium. Of course, this is the same strategy that would be used to prepare students for conventional tests.

When a student successfully completes a performance task item, there is no easy way of determining what cognitive skills were employed. The student may be merely repeating a task with which he or she is familiar or the performance may represent a high level cognitive response to a novel task.

Using Performance Tests in the Classroom

The use of performance testing techniques in the classroom requires relatively few adaptations to normal teacher activities. Teachers have always used these techniques and few would deny the need for even more widespread implementations of performance assessment. In the early grades, before students have been socialized to formal testing, most assessment is in the form of performance testing. In high school, many teachers routinely employ these techniques. In some subject matter areas it is difficult to imagine effective instruction that failed to include some performance assessments. For example, observing and/or conducting chemical experiments is clearly superior to filling out worksheets or reading about such experiments in a textbook. Students would learn little if algebra was taught solely through lectures to students or by having them read about how to determine the value of an unknown in an equation. The use of performance assessments is the most appropriate way to assess students when the purpose of instruction is the generation of a product or instilling the capacity to perform in some way.

Basing grades on the results of performance tests is somewhat more difficult than the usual grading practices associated with conventional pencil and paper tests. Conventional tests provide a limited amount of information. They primarily tell us how students compare with each other, which is useful for assigning grades. The information provided by performance tests is richer, telling the teacher more about what students can do than how they compare to others. This can complicate the process of making the comparisons among students necessary for the assigning of grades.

Using Performance Tests for Large Scale Testing

Interest in the widespread use of performance assessment began in the late 1980s. From the start, the literature advocating their use focused more on the inadequacies of conventional multiple-choice tests than the advantages of performance tests. The picture has not changed. There is remarkably little empirical evidence that supports the superiority of performance assessments. Shepard (1996) states that the '. . . anticipated benefits of performance assessments have been inferred by analogy from research documenting the negative effects of traditional, standardized testing' (p. 7). Of course this is a weak argument in favor of performance testing. The identification of problems with existing standardized tests in no way establishes that performance assessments provide the best way of assessing students. They must be evaluated on their own merits.

Replacing standardized achievement tests with performance assessments is difficult because they are intended for different purposes. Performance tests are intended to function as an integral part of the educational system while conventional standardized multiple-choice tests serve a monitoring function. Performance assessments need to be enmeshed in day to day instructional activities while conventional assessments are intended to record student achievement from a position of neutrality.

Quite often, the use of performance assessments in large scale accountability systems has been used to fulfill two incompatible roles. First, they are intended to provide an accountability score that can be used to evaluate students, teachers, and schools accurately and fairly. Second; they are supposed to function as a catalyst for improving instruction. Unfortunately, a test cannot serve two masters. The characteristics of a test that make it most effective as an instructional tool tend to diminish its capacity to make valid high stakes decisions, while the characteristics of a test that are most associated with reliability and validity are likely to render a test less effective as an instructional tool. If a test can't have both attributes, a decision must be made about which to favor. It is difficult to justify the identification of some teachers as successes while sanctioning others on the basis of a flawed test that cannot be justified on any other basis than its instructional value. If teachers begin to question the technical qualities of a test, it will cease to influence how they teach. Measurement driven instruction does not work when teachers fail to see the connection between measurement and instruction.

As long as the stakes are low and the results are intended to provide feedback to teachers about the effectiveness of their instruction, classroom teachers themselves can evaluate student responses on performance tests. When teachers do the scoring, costs are manageable. However, once the results are used for accountability, the school system, individual schools, and teachers have a big stake in the results. Under these circumstances, student responses must be evaluated by graders who are not stakeholders. When outside graders are required, the cost of conducting such assessments increases dramatically.

In deciding between conventional and performance tests, the high cost of performance testing, the amount of resources available for existing educational programs, and the resources that can be allocated for testing must be considered. Assuming finite resources, the authors of such plans must consider what other aspects of their educational program they are willing to sacrifice to pay for performance testing. The most important choice may not be between performance and conventional tests, but between testing and other educational programs.

Suggestions for Constructing Better Performance Tests

Most of the literature that supports the replacement of conventional with performance assessments is strong on rhetoric criticizing the shortcomings of conventional assessment, but weak in concrete descriptions of the most effective methods of implementing performance assessment. Of course, some of the rules for the writing of good essay tests, as described in the previous chapter, can be applied to alternative assessments. There are some important differences, however. Good essay tests are written in such a way that there is a single correct response. Although such a practice can greatly increase the ability of a grader to accurately evaluate a performance task, it will tend to negate the very characteristics that make performance assessments different from conventional assessments.

Educators who seek alternatives to conventional tests are unlikely to be satisfied with performance tests that adhere too faithfully to the rules for constructing conventional tests. In many cases it was dissatisfaction with the use of conventional assessment techniques that led to the search for better techniques. Instead of standardization, those seeking true alternatives to conventional assessment are likely to employ prompts that encourage a variety of student responses. They would also support evaluations of student responses that encourage unique responses and creative writing.

Authors of performance tests should examine the following suggestions for writing better performance items with the understanding that adjustments and compromises will have to be made to accommodate the specific purposes of their assessment. Remember, test construction practices that enhance reliability will usually detract from a test's fidelity to alternative assessment principles. At the same time, maximizing the alternative assessment aspects of a test will tend to detract from its technical qualities.

1   *The construction of a performance test should begin with a purpose.*
Before initiating the process of specifying the tasks to be included on a performance test, it is necessary to consider the purpose of the test. The purpose is generally expressed in the form of an instructional goal. As is true for all assessments, performance tests are administered for a reason and that reason needs to be clearly specified. Most assessments are intended for decision making, but sometimes performance tests are intended primarily for instruction. You need to ask what you expect students to be able to do at the conclusion of instruction and this should be the focus of the test. As obvious as it may sound, this is a step that is often skipped.

The specification of the purpose is of even greater importance for performance than other assessments because the tasks in the assessment must be the same as the instructional goal. By definition, no inferences should be required in the interpretation of the results of a performance assessment. If the instructional goal requires that chemistry students be able to identify an unknown substance, students should be given a test tube containing the substance and access to a chemistry lab and its equipment. Success at the task is determined by whether the correct chemicals in the test tube are identified and no inference from task to instructional goal should be required.

Providing feedback to students about their academic progress is an important function of assessment. This feedback usually comes in the form of a score on a test, a grade, or a verbal or written comment from a teacher. With conventional tests, students may have a difficult time evaluating their own performance because the only information provided to them is the number of items they have correctly answered. This is usually not very helpful to students. Well-written performance tasks accompanied by a description of the purpose and criteria used to evaluate a student's response will help students understand how well they are progressing. This is made easier when there is a clear match between tasks and instructional goals.

   2   *Selecting appropriate tasks.*

In selecting the actual tasks to be used on a performance test, care must be taken to ensure that the task to be accomplished matches the purpose of the test. This is important for all tests, but it is particularly germane for performance tasks that are intended to be direct measures of an instructional goal. Unfortunately, authors of performance assessments often face a dilemma. They may be forced to choose between engaging, clever performance tasks that unfortunately do not match designated instructional goals and less interesting tasks that do. It is important that matching the instructional goals is always the primary basis for selecting tasks for performance tests.

   3   *The task should measure the skills you want students to acquire.*

Once the purpose of a test has been specified, a test author must be careful to ensure that the particular tasks being employed, measures what is intended. This is not always an easy goal to achieve because it is difficult to know what cognitive processes are being employed by students when they respond to a task. Just because a task is intended to assess a particular skill does not mean that it accomplishes this goal. The student who has practiced a task will employ cognitive strategies different from the student for whom the task is novel. The teacher must also consider the knowledge and experience level of students. To ensure that all students are equal in previous experience, there is the temptation to construct items that are abstract and presented out of context. This practice, defeats the purpose of performance tests, which is to develop a student's capacity to solve problems in a wide range of real world contexts.

   4   *Include criteria for judging performance and make sure that students are*
       aware of how they are being evaluated.

The higher the stakes associated with decisions based on assessments, the more important carefully delineated criteria become. Teachers using performance tests instructionally can afford to be more informal. The scoring rubrics for large scale performance tests must be carefully defined to ensure an acceptable level of reliability.

   The criteria for a performance test are often defined in terms of scoring rubrics which define the correct student response for each category specified. A single performance task could be used to evaluate several different purposes, although judging tasks along multiple dimensions greatly increases the complexity of scoring. The first step in specifying scoring rubrics is the designation of categories. Grades are one example of the use of categories. To establish categories based on the use of letter grades it is necessary to differentiate among responses in such a way that an A response is qualitatively different from the response required to obtain a B and C responses are clearly different from what is expected from a B response and so forth. Alternatively, categories can be based on a more descriptive set of categories such as 'unsatisfactory,' 'satisfactory,' and 'outstanding', or 'novice,' 'apprentice,' 'proficient,' and 'distinguished.' For each task, the level of performance necessary to earn the designation for each category must be specified. The State of Kentucky uses a version of the following general scoring guide.

Kentucky Holistic Scoring Guide (Modified)

Distinguished	• The student completes all important components of the task and communicates ideas clearly.
	• The student demonstrates an in depth understanding of the relevant concepts and/or processes.
	• The student offers insightful interpretations or extensions (generalization, applications, analogies).
Proficient	• The student completes most of the important components of the task and communicates ideas clearly.
	• The student demonstrates an understanding of major concepts even though he or she overlooks or misunderstands less important ideas or details.
Apprentice	• The student completes some important components of the task and communicates those ideas clearly.
	• The student's response indicates that there are gaps in his or her conceptual understanding.
Novice	• The student shows minimal understanding.
	• The student is unable to generate a strategy or the presentation only includes recall of information.
	• Answers are totally incorrect or irrelevant.

The student should be informed about the criteria that will be used to judge them. Frederiksen and Collins (1989) call this quality *transparency*. When a task has this quality, the purpose and basis for evaluating the task are obvious to the student. Transparency also can cause problems. If the desired qualities for a student's response are presented in too much detail, the task may be too easy because the student will know exactly what it takes to be given credit for knowing the correct answer. When acceptable responses are defined broadly and a wide range of responses is expected and accepted this will be less of a problem.

5 *Performance tests need to be fair for all students taking the test.*
Performance tests like any other assessment technique must be fair for the students being evaluated. Concern about this characteristic is greatest for high stakes tests. The authors of any test should be aware of cultural differences that may influence student performance. There should be concern for cognitive styles as well as content. There is no evidence to support the assertion that performance tests are more than conventional tests for students that are culturally different. What evidence exists, tends to point in the opposite direction.

Should You Evaluate Process or Product?

In the past, it has been the final product of performance tasks that have been the focus of evaluation rather than the process. This is because products are easier to compare. A teacher is likely to be more interested in the short story a student has written than the processes used for its composition. However, this view is changing. Much of what is known about how to evaluate performance tests comes to us from research conducted on writing instruction. Research conducted on how best to cultivate good writing skills tends to support an emphasis on process rather than the product alone (Hildyard, 1992). Students should not be on their own when they write. They need to learn correct strategies. Appropriate writing strategies are believed to encourage higher order thinking, critical thinking, and reasoning.

Safety

When a performance task involves activities that could pose a potential threat to the student, there is a need to ensure that all procedures are carried out carefully. Examples of settings in which processes should be emphasized out of concern for safety are as follows: an experiment in a chemistry class, a gymnastic performance, or the use of power tools in a woodworking shop. The need to have students adhere to specified safety procedures may result in a student's evaluation being based to a large extent on his or her use of a correct procedure with correspondingly less emphasis on the quality of the actual products generated.

Tasks that Have Process as Their Main Focus

Sometimes instruction focuses more on the process than the product. Consider a group project in a social studies class. One important purpose of this instructional event might be to teach students how to work together. Even though a superior student can dominate the group and by himself or herself produce a product better than other groups, this product may not be a sufficient indicator of success. The group process might be of equal, or even greater importance.

Assessing Processes

Since processes are usually made up of a series of required behaviors, they cannot easily be evaluated globally. Instead, the focus of evaluation should be on each separate behavior. Processes are evaluated either with checklists or rating scales.

The implementation of checklists requires a listing of statements that includes all of the required characteristics of how a process is constructed. The observer places a mark next to each statement to indicate that the behavior is present. Rating scales require judges to indicate how often a student behavior has occurred or evaluate the quality of the student behavior using a rating scale. The evaluations required for rating scales are more time-consuming than those associated with checklists. Their use can limit the number of characteristics that can be evaluated.

The Use of Checklists

The construction of a checklist should include the following steps:

- the designation of the appropriate performance or product;
- a listing of the important behaviors;
- the inclusion of common errors; and
- the selection of an appropriate format.

1 *The designation of the appropriate performance or product.*
The first step in constructing a checklist is the designation of the final product. Even when it is difficult to describe the desired characteristics of a product or process precisely, they should be specified as concretely as possible. This step provides a focus for the designation of the behaviors to be evaluated.

2 *A listing of the important behaviors.*
This is the most important aspect of checklist construction. All the important and relevant behaviors necessary for the achievement of the final product or perform-ance should be included. Behaviors that are exhibited by all students or those exhibited by only a few students should not be included. Such behaviors contribute no additional useful information, and they make the checklist more difficult to use. Behavior descriptors should be written to minimize subjectivity. It should be easy for the observer to indicate whether the target behavior is present or absent.

Associated with any such list of behaviors, either implicitly or explicitly are standards. These can be as formal as the number of nails a student uses in a table being constructed in a wood shop class, or as subjective as the determination of whether a student appreciates art. The intent of standards is to increase the prob-ability that all judgments rendered have the same meaning.

3 *The inclusion of common errors.*
It is not enough to ensure that students are performing all the steps that a procedure requires. It is also important to ensure that students do not exhibit behaviors that are considered inappropriate. For instance, there are a series of behaviors that have been designated as desirable for student teachers to exhibit in maintaining class-room discipline. There are also inappropriate behaviors that a teacher should avoid. For example, the use of sarcasm would be considered an inappropriate technique for preventing unwanted student behavior. It should be included as a category on the checklist used to evaluate the student/teacher.

4 *Selecting an appropriate format.*
The organization of the list of behaviors to be observed should reflect the order in which they are most likely to occur. The behaviors to be observed should be placed on the observation forms in such a way that they are easily recognized and under-stood. Space should be provided to place a mark to indicate whether the behavior is present. Additional space also should be available for comments.

Interpretation of Checklists

Once a checklist has been administered, the results must be evaluated. When the results of a checklist are used to provide feedback to students about their performance or to help a teacher improve his or her teaching, the statements can be interpreted separately. If the results of the checklist are being used to provide summative information, the format for reporting scores becomes important. One alternative is to count the number of check marks on the checklist and obtain an overall evaluation. Of course if this approach is used, items categorized as common errors must be deducted from the total score. It also may be desirable to weight the items according to their importance.

The Construction of Rating Scales

Rating scales are used to evaluate either the overall results of a performance assessment or their separate components. Judges make an evaluation of each statement or behavior, placing their response on a scale. Checklists are usually preferred for the evaluation of ongoing activities because they are easier to implement than rating scales.

The simplest rating scale consists of a set of behaviors or characteristics accompanied by instructions specifying that each should be evaluated using a designated range of numbers to indicate the quality of each behavior. Usually the scale is presented in a graphic form with anchors at either end and numbers designating the points on the scale. Scales can take many forms. Examples are presented below.

Uses proper safety procedures in the chemistry lab

/_____/_____/_____/_____/_____/

    Never   Seldom   Occasionally   Often   Always

or,

/_____/_____/_____/_____/_____/

    1   2   3   4   5

| Is extremely careless in the chemistry lab | | | | Always uses appropriate safety procedures in the chemistry lab |

The Evaluation of Products

The products of performance assessments can be evaluated globally or their components can be evaluated separately. This latter approach is likely to be employed with high stakes tests for which reliability is of particular concern. Those advocates of performance assessment who are philosophically opposed to the use of conventional tests are more likely to adopt a global approach. They prefer this latter method because they believe instruction should be viewed holistically.

One aspect of performance assessment that make them difficult to evaluate is their emphasis on originality and creativity. It is difficult to make accurate distinctions among student responses that are intended to vary across many dimensions because any two performances can differ in a myriad of different ways. Each may be superior in some aspects while of lower quality in others. Consider a social studies project, on which a teacher is supposed to consider originality, social contribution, neatness, creativity, extensiveness and quality of narrative explanations, the use of references and so forth. How do you compare a student response that is innovative, unusual, yet poorly presented with a less creative one which is neat, carefully worded, and meticulously documented. A set of rules that standardize the evaluation of the tasks and specify what qualities are to be considered important can sometimes help. This can make it possible to limit the number of dimensions along which comparisons must be made.

The Use of Primary Traits

The National Assessment of Educational Progress developed techniques for evaluating writing skills called *Primary Traits* that can be generalized to other performance tasks (Frederiksen and Collins, 1989). The writing prompt helps the student achieve a purpose in their writing. A set of characteristics of student writing that can be expected to lead to the achievement of their goal are delineated and the student is evaluated according to the degree to which these characteristics or primary traits are present.

Use of Multiple Judges or Observers

Checklists are usually administered by the teachers who constructed them, but there are advantages to using more than one observer. The same principle is true for the responses of judges to rating scales. Comparisons can be made among the observers to obtain information about their reliability. If the responses are similar, the observations can be considered reliable. When two observers are in disagreement, it is reasonable to suspect either a lack of clarity in the scoring rules or a flaw in the observations. Statements about which there is disagreement can be examined to determine if they need to be defined more clearly. The use of more than one observer has another advantage. By pooling the responses of several observers it is possible to obtain a more accurate score than could be obtained from a single observer because errors among judges tend to cancel each other.

The Technical Qualities of Performance Assessments

When performance assessments are used for instructional purposes and decisions have low stakes, strict adherence to the conventional rules of test construction is not critically important. Likewise, there is less need to ensure acceptable reliability and validity. As long as students derive an educational benefit from the experience and instruction is enhanced, the use of performance tasks is easily justified instructionally. Of course, when performance assessments are used to make high stakes decisions, they should meet the same criteria as conventional tests.

The belief that performance assessments should be evaluated using the same criteria that are employed with conventional tests is not universally accepted. Some advocates reject conventional assessment assumptions and view performance assessment as a means for avoiding the need for adherence to what are believed to be an outmoded assessment methodology (Wolf, Bixby, and Gardner; 1991; Wiggins, 1993).

Validity

An important concern when making decisions about whether to use performance tests concerns validity. When interest in the use of performance tests was increasing in the early 1990s, there were two distinctly different points of view regarding validity. The more conservative of the two emphasized the importance of maintaining high standards of validity for performance tests. The second perspective placed less importance on the need for these assessments to meet the same technical standards as other tests. To those who consider the technical qualities of any test to be important, the lack of solid evidence for their validity is an impediment to their acceptance. They are particularly concerned about their use as a replacement for standardized achievement tests. To those who harbor suspicions about standardized tests, the lack of objectivity that characterizes performance assessments is viewed as a positive quality.

Content-related Validity

The lengthy responses required on performance tests permit the inclusion of only a small number of items. The result is a lack of content-related validity. Performance assessments can be defended against charges of poor content validity by an emphasis on the directness of their assessment of instructional objectives.

Criterion-related Validity

Criterion-related validity is not usually relevant for performance assessments. The instructional goals they address are intended to be ends in themselves. They are the criterion and this characteristic obviates the need for concern about whether performance tasks match the criterion.

Construct-related Validity

A construct is a label for a set of behaviors. The most important aspect of construct validation is the establishment of an inferential connection between items and the proposed construct. Because performance assessments are direct and do not rely on inferences, construct-related validity is not an important form of validity for this type of assessment.

Applying Conventional Techniques of Establishing Validity

According to Susan and Donald Burger (1994), 'Performance measures must be held to the same stringent standards of reliability and validity as those achieved by standardized norm-referenced assessment.' Mehrens (1992) and Frechtling (1991) take a similar stance. The problem with this view is the lack of clarity about precisely what validity means in the context of performance assessment. In such a discussion, it is important to specify the purpose of the assessment. If the performance task represents an important, high level, real world instructional goal, and it is accomplished, we know that something important has been achieved. If, on the other hand, successful mastery of a series of performance tasks is intended to be an indicator of the overall academic effectiveness of a school, it is necessary to establish a connection between success on the performance assessment and the school's instructional goals.

Modifying the Concept of Validity

Advocates of the use of performance assessment who remain concerned about their technical qualities have managed to continue their support for the use of these methods through the development of new ways of defining validity (Moss, 1992). Messick (1989) believes that the concept of validity needs to be extended beyond an emphasis on content and construct-related validity to a definition that encompasses a recognition of the consequences of assessment. If ability tests are used to track students and you believe tracking is wrong you might conclude that the use of ability tests has negative consequences and impugn its validity accordingly. Consequences also could refer to a positive effect on teaching strategies that occurs when they are altered in the direction of more emphasis on the development of problem solving skills. The use of performance tests also could lead to heightened student interest in what is taught and greater student involvement in the learning tasks. This would obviously be considered a positive consequence of assessment.

Because assessment is intended to influence instruction, tests also need to have what is called 'systemic validity' (Fredericksen and Collins, 1989). A test is systemically valid if the activities employed to help students achieve an instructional objective do not merely increase test scores, but increase performance on the construct cited in the objectives as well. An instructional objective intended to increase the vocabulary of students would not be systemically valid if students were told to study the fifty words known to be on the test. On the other hand, if the existence of the objective and the structure of the assessment process for determining a student's vocabulary, resulted in students becoming engaged in activities that increased their overall vocabulary skills, the assessment process would be said to have systemic validity.

Reliability

Determining the reliability of conventional tests is a relatively simple process and it is not difficult to obtain respectable coefficients in this area. The reliability of standardized achievement and aptitude tests are uniformly high. The reliability of a conventional test is determined through an assessment of the similarity between student performance on two parallel forms of a test. When the construction of two such tests is unfeasible, which it usually is, estimates of parallel forms reliability are obtained using Coefficient Alpha or one of its permutations such as KR-21 (for a further explanation of this topic see Chapter 2). The magnitude of parallel forms and Coefficient Alpha reliability are related to the degree to which all items on a test are measuring the targeted construct. If each item on a test is not consistently measuring the same construct, it is unlikely that an acceptable level of parallel forms reliability can be achieved.

It is more difficult to establish the reliability of a performance assessment than a conventional test. A test is reliable to the extent that it manages to avoid error variance and there are more sources of this error when performance assessments are used. Shavelson, Baxter, and Gao (1993) suggest that the reliability of performance tests can best be understood by partitioning variance. Partitioning variance is a process of quantifying the amount of error that can be attributed to different sources. The parallel forms reliability of a performance test is a function of the effect of four types of variability, each of which increases error variance and therefore lowers reliability. These include variability among raters, variability among tasks, variability across occasions, and variability across methods of assessment.

Variability among Raters

Variability among raters is quantified as *interrater reliability*. With enough care in the construction of items, scoring rubrics structured to require each student to respond in a similar way, and extensive training of raters, respectable interrater reliability can be obtained (Linn and Burton, 1994). Increased interrater reliability is purchased at the cost of alterations in the assessment process that make them more like conventional and less like an alternative assessment.

Variability among Tasks

Variability that results from the type of task used to measure a construct is called *task sampling error*. This is the type of variability that poses the greatest threat to the reliability of performance tests. Consider an assessment procedure intended to measure student ability to apply principles of science. Task sampling error would occur if student performance depended more on the type of task presented than how much students knew about science. A smaller amount of task sampling error and better reliability will occur when the most able students can do well regardless of the tasks and less able students do poorly regardless of the tasks. Performance tests typically have high levels of task sampling error.

Variability across Occasions

Variability across occasions is similar to test–retest reliability. It is possible to construct and administer performance assessments with acceptable reliability in this area.

Method Sampling Variability

Method sampling variability occurs as a result of differences in the measurement methods employed. There are many different assessment methods used with performance assessments and differences among these methods can increase the measurement error associated with performance assessments.

Conventional Methods of Computing the Reliability of Performance Assessments

Coefficient alpha reliability could be reported for a performance test made up of several discrete tasks, but the small number of items or separate tasks and the tendency for performance on one task to be unrelated to performance on other tasks, would lead to a dismayingly low reliability coefficient.

There are few studies of the parallel forms reliability of performance tasks and in those conducted so far, the reliability of performance assessments is poor. This is a major limitation, and an often heard criticism of performance tests. Without established parallel forms reliability, we cannot know whether the evaluation of a student would stay the same following a second assessment. This can be a serious problem for a classroom test, but it could be disastrous for a test that is used to make high stakes decisions about students, teachers and/or schools.

Another type of validity that is sometimes applied to performance assessments is *decision consistency reliability*. This type of reliability usually requires the administration of two forms of a performance test, but when these tests are used to evaluate schools, there are methods of computing decision consistency reliability that can be based on a single test administration. Decision consistency reliability is based on the proportion of correct decisions. If students are presented two tasks intended to determine whether or not they have mastered an instructional goal, their performance can be in agreement in two ways. Both tasks can be evaluated as successes or they can both be failures. If one is evaluated as a success and the other a failure, they would not be in agreement. The decision consistency reliability coefficient is obtained by adding the proportion of students who are successful on both administrations to the proportion of failures on both administrations. This method of computing reliability, while computationally simple and easy for the practitioner to understand, has an important limitation. The decision consistency coefficient may be biased in favor of high reliability when almost all students succeed on both tasks (or less commonly, all students fail). There are techniques for correcting for this tendency, but these adjustments introduce other more troublesome distortions.

A much better way of addressing both the reliability and validity problems associated with performance assessments is to avoid attaching high stakes to their results. Without high stakes, concern about reliability and validity recede into the background and the tasks associated with performance tests can be constructed in such a way that they maximally benefit instruction.

Portfolios

Portfolios followed the same process as performance assessment in becoming a form of alternative assessment. At one time, portfolios were used in only a few settings. Artist pioneered the use of portfolios and creative writers also have employed them, but they were seldom used to document performance in other subjects. Their use is now becoming widespread in writing and they have become an important alternative assessment tool in other areas as well.

A portfolio is a collection of information that documents a student's academic accomplishments. Arter and Spandel (1992) offer the following definition based on the extensive projects involving portfolios sponsored by the Northwest Evaluation Association. They define the student portfolio as:

> a purposeful collection of student work that tells a story of the student's efforts, progress or achievement in (a) given area(s). This collection must include student participation in the selection of portfolio content; the guidelines for selection; the criteria for judging merit; and evidence of student self-reflection.

Portfolios represent a form of alternative assessment that is even less structured than performance tests. They are primarily intended to serve instructional purposes and their assessment value is secondary to their instructional role. With conventional testing approaches, assessment is usually the first priority and instructional value is considered secondary. Performance tests fall somewhere in between, serving both roles.

Experts in the use of portfolios (Arter and Spandel, 1992) have established criteria for evaluating the usefulness of portfolios and specifying what they should contain. They generally agree that a good portfolio should include the following:

1 the designation of a purpose;
2 the provision of a plan for the selection of content;
3 a provision for student ownership;
4 an indication of student progress;

5 an opportunity for self reflection;
6 decision rules about ownership;
7 appropriate structure; and
8 other relevant information.

1 *Purpose.*

The portfolio should not be a collection of things, but should instead be a deliberate, specific collection of material that tells a story about a student's development over a long period of time. It should provide a longitudinal portrait of student progress from many different perspectives. A portfolio without a clearly defined purpose is just a disparate collection of student papers and accomplishment. Without a purpose, such an accumulation may be an interesting, but not particularly useful form of assessment.

A student's awareness of the purpose of the portfolio he or she is expected to assemble is likely to influence the depth of his or her self reflection included in the portfolio. A student will respond differently depending on whether he or she will be the only one to see the portfolio, or whether the teacher and/or others will examine it. If students are informed that their portfolio will be open to an indeterminate wide range of evaluators and interested parties, they are unlikely to be willing to share insights and self reflections that they consider to be private. Often a portfolio is intended to serve a number of different, sometimes contradictory purposes. It is difficult to structure a portfolio to maximize its usefulness as an assessment tool, which implies some degree of standardization, while at the same time maximizing its instructional value. Standardization is unlikely to effectively serve the purpose of having the portfolio accurately reflect a student's accomplishments and at the same time allow students a voice in deciding what they wish to include.

One way of solving the problem of multiple and not completely compatible purposes is illustrated by the assessment program incorporated in Kentucky's Educational Reform Act, which uses portfolios to evaluate writing skills. In Kentucky, at grades four, eight, and twelve, students maintain two writing portfolios, a Classroom Writing Portfolio, and a Writing Assessment Portfolio. The Classroom Writing Portfolio is thought of as a 'holding bin' which contains many pieces of writing in various stages of development. All drafts are stored in the Classroom Writing Portfolio including writing for subjects other than English or Language Arts. The Writing Assessment Portfolio is required to contain the following components.

- a table of contents;
- a piece of writing that the student considers to be his or her best;
- a letter to the reviewer explaining why a particular 'best piece' was selected, how it was written, and how it might be improved;
- a short story, poem or play;
- a personal narrative;
- a piece of writing in which a problem is solved or a position is defended or supported; and
- a piece or writing from a content area other than English or Language Arts.

By using two different portfolios, the Writing Portfolio and the Assessment Portfolio, it is possible to encourage creativity and risk-taking by students without sacrificing the need for some standardization of format for purposes of assessment.

2   *A Plan for the selection of content.*

The content and structure of portfolios can vary greatly. The portfolio will always include student work, but that could include a wide range of possibilities. Its content could be determined by the student, by the teacher, or it could be dictated by some outside agency. It might be the best work of a student or a sample of their work, intended to provide a descriptive picture of what he or she can do. Rough drafts should be included along with finished products. The portfolio should reflect the processes involved in creating the products found in the portfolio.

3   *Student ownership.*

Students need to feel ownership in the portfolio. This will not occur if all the decisions about its content and structure are made by others. The portfolio should be a celebration of student accomplishments with the goal of bringing students to the point where they are willing to take responsibility for their own learning. The teacher must develop a level of rapport and trust with the student sufficient to make them open to having their work inspected. They must be made to feel comfortable revealing aspects of the writing process they use that they might otherwise be hesitant to reveal.

4   *An indication of student progress.*

The reader of a portfolio should be able to recognize a pattern of growth in a portfolio. This means that earlier drafts, works in progress, and less than perfect products should be included. Such material indicates not only where the student is at the conclusion of the time period being assessed by the portfolio, but how the student was functioning at the beginning of the assessment period.

5   *Opportunity for student reflection.*

The portfolio should not be a static presentation of what a student has done. Students need to be encouraged and supported in thinking about what they have accomplished, how and why they used a particular strategy, and most importantly how they feel about this process. Students should not view their assignments as merely something to complete, which doesn't really involve them. Written self-reflection can force a student to take ownership of what they have done. It is not enough for the portfolio to provide an opportunity for the student to record their self reflection. Self reflection also needs to be encouraged and nurtured. This might require modelling by the teacher. The teacher should demonstrate his or her own self reflection in the class being taught, to increase the likelihood that students will be self-reflective.

6   *To whom does the portfolio belong?*

Decisions need to be made regarding who owns the contents of the portfolio before they are assembled. There are likely to be competing interests regarding this ownership. The student and/or the parent may assert ownership of student work, particularly creative work. At the same time there may be commitment to pass the portfolio on to the next teacher. A student's teacher may want to keep the portfolio or some part of it. If the portfolio is being used to fulfill assessment and/or accountability needs there may be a requirement that they remain available to other interested parties. It is not possible to specify here, who should have ownership of each part of a portfolio, but procedures and policies must be established regarding these issues and they should be established before these decisions need to be made.

Access to the portfolios is related to ownership. Ground rules specifying who will have access to the portfolio need to be set. Will the student be able to alter portfolio, remove and/or replace materials? Can teachers do the same? Will parents play any part in structuring the portfolio? If so, and students are able to take the portfolios home, will there be pressure on parents to 'dress up' the portfolio as tends to happen with science fair and other projects students complete at home. What happens if a student decides to delete something that the teacher believes greatly strengthens the portfolio and its absence will reflect badly on the teacher? Can a teacher veto such changes? These questions need to answered by those most closely involved with the use of the portfolios and they also should be resolved as early in the process as possible.

7   *Other relevant information.*

There are no real restrictions on what could be included in a portfolio. Official records such as transcripts, scores from standardized tests, participation in extra-curricular activities, awards, and comments from other students and teachers can all be included along with the results of the sort of performance tests described in the first part of this chapter.

8   *Structure.*

Each piece of work should be clearly labeled and dated. A table of contents should be provided to help readers understand what is included and make it easy for them to find and identify what is there.

The Portfolio as an Assessment Tool

The portfolio is a subjective method of conducting an assessment, but it can be made more objective, if that is desired, by standardizing its content. However, standardization can make the portfolio less useful for other purposes. The most important limitation of the portfolio as an assessment tool is the difficulty in ensuring that the contents of a portfolio represent the student and his or her characteristics alone. This will seldom be a problem for the teacher using the portfolio to assess classroom progress, but it can, and most likely will, be a problem when the teacher is being evaluated by the portfolio.

When the portfolio is used instructionally, the teacher will usually know the students well and be in a favorable position to judge how accurately the contents of the portfolio reflect the student's level of performance. More importantly, the teacher will have every reason to want the portfolio to be an accurate reflection of the student's achievement. Portfolios work best when students are responsible for how much they learn and the teacher is responsible for monitoring this learning. Under these circumstances portfolios can help provide students with a sense of responsibility about their accomplishments. On the other hand, when the teacher is given the responsibility for helping students assemble their portfolios and is in turn evaluated by the same portfolios, the evaluative value of the portfolios is likely to be compromised.

The more pressure that is put on teachers to have their students produce better portfolios, the more tempting it will be for them to exert too much effort improving their student's portfolios. If the teachers themselves are grading the portfolios, outside evaluators can check a sample of portfolios to make sure that teachers are not guilty of leniency or overestimating their students' performance and by inference their own. However, there is really no way to prevent a teacher, under pressure to have his or her students do well on their portfolios, from altering portfolios unilaterally. There is also no easy way to prevent teachers from putting undue pressure on students and parents to force them to generate ever more refined portfolios. The teacher might make suggestions about the content of the explanatory material that a student provides to indicate his or her capacity to engage in self reflection, they could 'help' students transfer their material onto a computer and have it printed or they could key the material themselves. As more student work requires the use of computers, it will become increasingly difficult to pinpoint authorship of student work.

Summary

The purpose of performance assessment is the determination of how well a student can use knowledge rather than how much knowledge a student possesses. The current popularity of performance assessment is a result of a reaction against the excesses of conventional pencil and paper selection type 'objective' tests. The rejection of conventional psychometric theory and the increased emphasis being placed on cognitive theories of learning have also contributed to an increased interest in performance assessment. An advantage of performance assessments is the promotion of systemic validity that makes the time spent preparing students for such tests much more productive than the activities used to prepare students for conventional tests. Performance tests are probably more appropriately used as a classroom instruction tool than as a replacement for standardized achievement. Performance testing can have either the process or a product as its focus and the strategies for evaluating each differs. The establishment of the reliability and validity of performance tests is less straightforward than for conventional tests. Unless the definitions of validity are altered it will be quite difficult to conclude that performance tests are valid. Performance tests can be constructed in such a way that they are valid, but the process of increasing their reliability tends to diminish the very qualities that make alternative assessments attractive. The best solution to problems of reliability and validity is to not attach high stakes to them. The absence of high stakes tends to make questions about reliability and validity less important.

Portfolios are a form of alternative assessment that is even less structured than performance tests. Students need to understand the purpose of the portfolio, the degree to which they are being evaluated by it, who will be examining their portfolio and the reasons for this examination.

Suggested Readings

AIRASIAN, P.W. (1991) *Classroom Assessment*, McGraw Hill: New York.

BERLAK, H. (1992) 'Toward the development of a new science of educational testing and assessment', in BERLAK, H. *et al.* (eds) *Toward a New Science of Educational Testing & Assessment*, New York: State University of New York Press.

FITZPATRICK, R. and MORRISON, E.J. (1971) 'Performance and product evaluation', in THORNDIKE, R.L. (ed.) *Educational Measurement*, Washington, DC: American Council on Education, pp. 237–70.

FRECHTLING, J.A. (1991) 'Performance assessment: Moonstruck or the real thing?', *Educational Measurement: Issues and Practices*, **10**, 4, pp. 23–25.

FREDERICKSEN, J.R. and COLLINS, A. (1989) 'A systems approach to educational testing', *Educational Researcher*, **189**, pp. 27–32.

LINN, R.L., BAKER, E.L. and DUNBAR, S.B. (1991) 'Complex, performance-based assessment: Expectations and validation criteria,' *Educational Researcher*, **20**, 8, pp. 15–21.

MOSS, P. (1992) 'Shifting conceptions of validity in educational measurement: Implications for performance assessment,' *Review of Educational Research*, **62**, 3, pp. 229–58.

WIGGINS, G. (1989) 'A true test: Toward more authentic and equitable assessment', *Phi Delta Kappan*, **70**, pp. 703–13.

WIGGINS, G. (1993) 'Assessment: Authenticity, context, and validity', *Phi Delta Kappan*, **75**, 3, pp. 200–14.

WOLF, D., BIXBY, J., GLENN, J. and GARDNER, H. (1991) 'To use their minds well: Investigating new forms of student assessment', in GRANT, G. (ed.) *Review of Research in Education*, Washington, DC: American Educational Research Association, pp. 31–74.

7   Developing Valid Grading Procedures

In this chapter the student will learn:

- about proposals for changing traditional grading systems;
- why grades are important;
- about different bases for assigning grades;
- the advantages and disadvantages of four different sources of comparisons;
- how to determine the number of each grade to be assigned; and
- the best way to combine scores.

The purpose of student evaluation is decision-making. The present chapter focuses on one particular type of decision, the assignment of grades. When a teacher assigns a grade to a student, a value is being attached to academic performance. When we label a score of 63 on a test an A, and a score of 59 a B, we have differentiated between two levels of student performance and assigned a value to them. Test scores and class ranking also tell us how a student is performing. Each of these implies a value because it is better to have a high than a low score, just as it is better to be ranked at the top of a group than at the bottom. In the case of scores and rankings, value is relative and entirely dependent on the group with whom one is being compared. You could be the best student in a class, but this would be a hollow honor if the class consisted of poor students. Similarly, you could be ranked at the bottom among professional tennis players and still be a wonderfully skilled player. While scores and ranks are relative, a grade is intended to have meaning beyond the comparison group. In practice, grades are seldom meaningful in isolation. To make a grade meaningful you need to know something about the class in which the grade was bestowed, the difficulty of the tests upon which it was based and the distribution of grades.

Eliminating or Changing Traditional Grading Systems

Assigning grades is not a pleasant activity for any teacher and most consider it to be the most distasteful aspect of the teaching profession. As repugnant as many find the grading process and as troublesome as the mechanical aspects of making these determinations can be, grades are an inevitable and permanent part of education. Attempts to alter or eliminate grades have met with limited success because parents and students are reluctant to accept alternative systems of grading.

Most schools continue to use traditional grading practices. 82 per cent of all schools use letter grades and most of those who do not use number grades (Polloway *et al.*, 1994). Most of the experimentation with the use of different methods of communicating with parents about student achievement is taking place in elementary schools. At the high school level, there is much less willingness to discontinue the use of traditional grading methods. High school administrators and the parents of students enrolled in high schools are concerned about the complications that this would introduce into the college admission process.

One proposed form of reform involves replacing letter grades with a different set of symbols. Changing the symbols does not really alter the meaning of grades. The essence of grading is the placement of students into hierarchical categories. Changing the names of the categories, for example replacing an A with an E to represent 'Excellent' or with the phrase 'Exceeds Expectations' or replacing a B with a G for 'Good' or the phrase 'Meets Expectations' does not change the underlying meaning of the name of the categories or the nature of the hierarchy.

A Perspective for Examining Grades

Grades are a deeply ingrained aspect of our culture and are seldom open to rational discourse. Thorndike *et al.* (1991) provide an excellent description of the role of grading in education as follows:

> Like any other deeply ingrained aspect of a culture, grading procedures are often taken for granted, with a minimum of rational analysis of their nature and their functions. As we examine them, our approach should be, in part, that of cultural anthropologist who looks at a set of odd but presumably meaningful behavior patterns and tries to understand the functions they serve and the manner in which they relate to the total culture of which they are a part. We should try to put aside our personal involvement, look at the phenomenon with the cold eye of the social scientist, and endeavor to identify the forces that shape and sustain present grading practices. We also need to try to understand the pressures within the educational culture that make the practices resistant to change and sometimes irrational. (p. 176)

Teachers tend to grade the way they have always graded, the way their peers grade, or the way their own teachers graded. In too many cases, this leads to a system of student evaluations that makes little sense. Rational discussions of grading methods are often avoided because existing grading practices are often difficult to defend. The process of evaluating students can have a rational basis, but unfortunately, information about the best ways of assigning grades, and the grading systems to be avoided has been poorly disseminated. College professors who lack formal training in teaching methods are usually as unaware of the accepted knowledge of how best to grade students as are certified teachers who have taken numerous teaching methodology courses.

A student's grade is not an inherent, fixed characteristic like blood type, and the goal of student evaluation should not be the establishment of this 'true' grade.

Grades are global estimates of student functioning, which like all valuing processes are subjective and dependent on the context in which they are used. A grade communicates how a student performed in one specific class, in comparison with other students. Whether that performance can be generalized into an understanding of overall student achievement is open to question.

Importance of Grades

Grades are an important and well-established part of our educational culture. Their primary purpose is to attach a value to academic achievement which can be used for decision-making within educational institutions, as well as between these institutions and the outside world. Eligibility for admission to programs or departments, for scholarship aid within a university, for membership on athletic teams, and for continuing in school is often determined by academic standing. Admission to college or graduate school is usually based on grades received at the previous academic level. Thus there are many points within the educational system where grades interact with the administrative and instructional process to affect a student's academic progress.

Effective learning also requires feedback or knowledge of results. It is difficult for students to improve their academic performance if they don't receive accurate feedback about their performance. Growing and developing requires the testing of limits and students need to know how they stand in comparison with some goal. Grades are a natural method of accomplishing both of these goals.

Parents also need to know how their children are progressing in school. This need can be fulfilled in a number of ways. Anecdotal records, teacher conferences, and/or lists of objectives mastered or not mastered are all possible means of communication, but parents understand, and respond best to the traditional methods of assigning grades. The institution of alternate systems of reporting student achievement requires a tremendous amount of parent education.

One of the more controversial functions of grades is their role in the sorting of students into different tracks within a school. From kindergarten through graduation, enormous differences arise among students. Some students are headed for prestigious universities while others barely graduate or drop out. The rest of the students find themselves lodged somewhere in the middle. The lifetime consequences of the sorting processes that take place in school, at least partially based on grades, are a significant and crucial part of our meritocracy. Whether this is a necessary part of the educational process or a harmful impediment to a student reaching his or her potential is an issue which has not as yet been resolved.

On What Should Grades Be Based

Grades should reflect the purest, best measures of achievement that can be obtained. Grades should not be based on neatness, legibility or the use of correct mechanics of written or oral expression except when these skills are included in the instructional objectives for the course. The same holds true for other factors such as attitude, motivation, effort, and personality. In most cases it would be inappropriate to include them as instructional objectives. Not only are these characteristics difficult to measure, but their inclusion as a basis for assigning grades can lead to confusion in the interpretation of the meaning of grades. Using these collateral factors as a partial basis for a grade can make it almost impossible to determine whether a student who received a B, got this grade as a result of the achievement of the course objectives or some combination of other factors, such as neatness, attitude, or personality. The use of extra credit also is discouraged. By definition extra credit refers to assignments on which only some students are being evaluated. Such a practice makes comparisons among students difficult.

Sources of Comparisons

Grading systems are intended to attach a value to different levels of academic performance. This is most easily accomplished through the use of comparisons or standards. There are five frames of reference commonly used in the assignment of grades: intuitive, ipsative, reference-to-perfection, criterion-referenced, and norm-referenced assessment. These terms do not refer to different types of tests or items. The same test and/or items could be used with any of these references. They instead refer to methods of assigning value in the form of the grade attached to a given level of performance.

Intuitive Grading

In using the intuitive method of grading, a teacher bases grades on what he or she knows about a student. It does not require a careful delineation of course requirements and grading policies. The teacher 'knows' what constitutes the appropriate level of achievement that makes a student eligible for a given grade. A subjective decision is made regarding the most appropriate grade for a student without benefit of a formal assessment or a carefully considered evaluation scheme. The intuitive approach is most often used at the primary level where the teacher has a manageable number of students and the desired level of student performance is concrete. A good, experienced, primary teacher will know how well a student should be reading or solving math problems at a given grade. With an intuitive grading system, the teacher compares each student to that standard.

The intuitive approach requires experience and insight into student behavior. Although some teachers can effectively assign grades this way, it is not recommended. It introduces the possibility of teacher favoritism or bias and it is difficult to defend this method of grading to parents disappointed with their child's grade, or to administrators responsible for ensuring the integrity of the grading system.

Ipsative Grading

In using ipsative grading, each student is evaluated on the basis of his or her own performance. The comparison can be made in two ways: (1) achievement can be compared with aptitude, or (2) achievement can be evaluated in relation to effort.

A student's grade should reflect the purest measure of achievement possible. Ipsative grading systems don't provide this important information. However, teachers find it difficult to ignore the effort of students and/or the degree to which their achievement matches their ability (Stiggins, Frisbie, and Griswold, 1989). Teachers usually require more from high ability students, assigning lower grades to those whose performance does not match their potential. At the same time, there is a tendency to give students with less aptitude, who work hard, higher grades than their achievement alone would merit.

Grades cannot easily be assigned by comparing student achievement with effort or aptitude. Achievement and aptitude are not independent student characteristics, and the separation of the two can be difficult. Quantifying effort may be even more problematic. Effort is generally estimated by comparing a student's performance at the beginning of a grading period with performance at the conclusion. The student who starts the year behind but improves, is believed to have put forth more effort and therefore deserves a higher grade than the student who is already achieving at a high level at the beginning of the year, but shows little improvement. With this system of grading, the first student might be given a higher grade, despite a final level of achievement below the second student.

For an ipsative system of grading to work, an accurate measure of initial performance is important. This is an approach to be avoided with sophisticated students who may fake a low entry skill level to achieve a large gain.

Subject Matter Areas Where Incoming Ability Level Is Important

When final performance in a class is heavily dependent on the incoming level of ability, teachers find grading difficult. This situation is most likely to occur in a course like art, music, foreign languages or physical education. Ability differences occur in all classes and teachers are often hesitant to assign a low grade to students who are incapable of performing at a high level. There is seldom as much sympathy for the student who doesn't seem to be trying. On the first day of class, there are likely to be some students who can perform at a level that far exceeds what other students with less ability can ever achieve. With minimal effort, these gifted students can remain ahead of other students who work much harder. All teachers are faced with the problem of balancing fairness with the integrity of their grading system and there is an understandable reluctance to ignore the degree of improvement or effort students with less ability exhibit over the year. The gifted music student who does nothing for a semester may not deserve an A, although at the end of the course he or she can play the violin better than anyone in the class. At the same time, it seems only fair to give credit to the student who has little music ability, who puts forth exceptional effort and improves.

Most educators are not troubled by ipsative grading in art, music or similar courses, but there may be a reluctance to grade students based on effort and potential in what are considered 'academic' subjects. This attitude persists even though an equally wide range of ability in English and algebra is likely to be encountered.

Recommendations about the Use of Ipsative Grading

The use of ipsative methods of assigning grades is strongly discouraged. Grades based on this approach are not useful for making decisions, because they do not reflect actual accomplishments. Most parents would not want their child taught by a teacher who was awarded his or her teaching certificate based on effort, or live next to a nuclear power plant, operated by an engineer who earned his or her position by showing great improvement during training. As teachers we have no right to certify students as literate and knowledgeable on the basis of their performance in relation to themselves. Furthermore, ipsative grading is based on the dubious assumption that we can know how hard someone is trying, and the nature of their true potential. Teachers should base grades on what they can most accurately measure, a student's actual achievement.

Assigning separate grades for effort is not recommended. A student who is performing poorly who receives a low grade for effort is being told that he or she can't even succeed at trying. If the poor performing student is given a high grade for effort, the message might be one of futility. They are being told that they can't succeed no matter how hard they try. Likewise, the high achieving student with a low grade for effort is being sent the wrong message.

Reference-to-Perfection-Grading

One of the most popular methods of assigning grades is called reference to perfection. 73 per cent of teachers acknowledge grading this way (Polloway *et al.*, 1994). With this approach, a range of percentages is associated with each grade. An example of this approach would be the following:

A 95–100
B 88–94
C 80–87
D 70–79
F Below 70

This is the most often used method for translating a student's score on a teacher-made test into a grade. Although the measurement and evaluation literature is highly critical of this approach, it remains a popular method of assigning grades because it has a long tradition and is easy to implement. The reference-to-perfection approach is often institutionalized by entire school systems because it creates the illusion that grades have the same meaning across courses and schools.

Since high stakes decisions often are made on the basis of grades, there is a need to believe that grades have meaning beyond the individual classroom. A system-wide grading system can help maintain this illusion.

The use of reference to perfection grading requires an understanding of what a score of 100 represents, but this is seldom possible. In general, '100' is intended to refer to complete or 100 per cent mastery of a content area. In actual practice this is not what a score of 100 really is. It is instead the more modest indication that a student has gotten all items correct, which is not particularly meaningful in the absence of information about test difficulty.

It is possible to construct tests whose items encompass complete mastery of a topic, but they are rare. Consider a test administered to third-graders, consisting of all possible single-digit multiplication problems. Such a test (albeit a prohibitively long one) would include all one hundred facts. The use of percentages to describe student performance on such a test would be legitimate because the entire domain is defined. A perfect score would mean that the student knew all such facts. A score of 80 per cent would indicate that the student knew 80 per cent of the multiplication facts. The score in this case reflects a known relationship with complete mastery. There are several other examples of curricular material that can be equally well defined, such as the symbols representing the chemical elements, the names of the bones in the body, the capitals of all the states, and names of all the presidents. When the number of items is finite and definable, all or a representative sample of the items can be included on a test, and performance can be reported as a proportions of mastery. In most subject matter areas, no such well-defined domain exists, and generalizations from item samples cannot easily be made.

Consider an eighth grade history test assessing student knowledge of the World War II, consisting of fifty multiple choice items. It is unlikely that the student who gets every item correct, knows everything there is to know about World War II. Unless the items on the test represented a true random sample of all possible items that could be asked about this war, the percentage of correct items tells us only how well that student performed on the test. Teachers don't create tests by choosing random samples of items from domains; they usually continue to write items until they have enough. The actual items included on a test might be easier or more difficult than those that would come from the domain of all items.

Another problem with the reference-to-perfection approach is that it requires the assumption that all tests using the same scale are of equal and appropriate difficulty. This is an assumption that is quite difficult to defend. If a school or school district adopts the same reference to perfection grading scale for all classes in the district, it would be necessary to assert that every test administered in the school or school district is equally difficult. If difficulty is not uniform, the grade a student is awarded in a class will be primarily determined by the factors that influence the difficulty of the tests administered. The grade assigned in one class will not mean the same thing in other classes.

Despite its limitations, the reference-to-perfection method of assigning grades frequently is used as the basis for assigning grades. Because of differences in test difficulty, a strict adherence to a reference to perfection grading approach will quite often result in a grade distribution that is different from what a teacher expects or wants. The discrepancy between the grade distribution the teacher believes is appropriate and what is obtained from the application of a reference-to-perfection scale is usually resolved by altering the ensuing grade distribution. This process is sometimes referred to as 'curving' a test (grading on the curve and curving tests are discussed in a subsequent section of this chapter). When the grades are too low the alteration can be accomplished by awarding extra credit or making the next test easier when there are too many low grades. When there are too many high grades, the teacher can grade the next test more stringently or increase its difficulty.

Such adjustments are sometimes criticized by those who believe that students should get the grade they deserve. This criticism is misguided. The reference-to-perfection approach does not tell us the grade a student deserves, which is its big promise and major failing. There is nothing innately revealing about the percentage of items a student gets right on a test.

Students are usually satisfied with explanations of grading policies based on the reference-to-perfection method because it is a familiar method of student evaluation. If students were to carefully examine this approach, it is unlikely that they would remain complacent. It is not easy for teachers to explain or defend their use of the reference-to-perfection approach because it is misleading and indirect. The adjustments used to ensure an acceptable distribution of grades are particularly difficult to defend. Students are likely to be unhappy with adjustments that award them a lower grade in order to bring the grade distribution in line with what the teacher wants or what has been imposed administratively.

The reference-to-perfection method of grading continues to be used on a widespread basis, largely out of ignorance. Students demand an explanation of grading policies and get one. It is a grading technique with a long history of use, and one with which students are familiar. Its irrationality does not seem to have deterred its use.

Criterion-referenced Grading

An alternative approach to evaluating students that became popular in the 1960s and 1970s is based on the use of criterion referenced-testing. This approach requires that the teacher list in detail, prior to instruction, all that a student is to achieve in a class. The list is compiled in the form of carefully operationalized instructional objectives (usually behaviorally stated). Grades are assigned based on the mastery of these objectives. The value of this approach to grading is that it communicates *what* a student has learned, rather than how he or she compares with other students.

Criterion-referenced assessment is an awkward method of assigning grades because it permits only two categories into which a student can be placed. A student is identified as either having achieved mastery or not having achieved mastery. This fits poorly with an A, B, C, D, or F system of grading. The dilemma can be resolved by adopting a set of arbitrary standards that designate the number of items that must be correct before it can be said that a student has mastered an objective.

The proportion of objectives necessary to earn each grade can then be specified. When this is done, the grade a student is assigned is determined directly by how many objectives are mastered and indirectly by the number of items correctly answered. A student's grade, once again, is determined by item difficulty and the cut-off scores that have been set by the teacher. The result is a system that strongly resembles reference-to-perfection grading, assuming the limitations of that discredited system of assigning grades.

Norm-referenced Grading

When absolute standards for evaluating student performance are available, they provide a solid basis for assigning grades. Typing fifty words per minute in a typing class might be considered performance meriting an A, as could successful identification of an unknown substance in a chemical class, or the successful solving of a series of quadratic equations. Unfortunately, in most educational settings, obvious, easily defined standards are not available. It is under these circumstances that the use of comparisons with other students becomes necessary. Such comparisons are labeled norm-referenced assessment.

Norm-referenced comparisons can be made with the students in a class, the total student body of the school, or more informally, the ill-defined total group of previous students that shape an instructor's impressions of what is good, average, or poor. Standardized assessments are based on carefully designed, representative national comparison groups.

The students in a class provide the usual comparison group. The obvious drawback to their use is that each class is unique and with norm-referenced comparisons, the grade a student receives may be primarily a reflection of the mix of students in a particular class. When this occurs, the grade assigned will reflect only relative standing in a classroom and reveal nothing about a student's actual level of achievement.

The norm-referenced assignment of grades is most easily justified in large heterogeneously grouped classes. When class assignment is based on ability, the implementation of a norm-referenced grading system must be tempered with judgment. Even when students are grouped according to ability, it is easier to evaluate students by comparing their performance with that of other students, than to make the absolute judgments required of the reference-to-perfection or criterion-referenced approaches.

Grading on a Curve

The phrases 'grading on a curve' or 'curving a test' are frequently used to describe the adjustment made in student scores to obtain desired grade distributions. The problem with these terms is that they have different meanings depending on the context in which they are used or who is using them. Sometimes the term 'curving' is used as a synonym for norm referenced grading, but it also can refer to the practice of assigning grades according to a rough approximation of the normal curve. With such a system, most students get a C. The same number of students get Ds as get Bs and a smaller but equal number of As and Fs are awarded. The irrationality of this approach seems obvious and it is seldom employed. More often 'curving' refers to adjustments in the cut-off points for grades which are raised or lowered to obtain a desired grade distribution. When these adjustments are used with reference to perfection grading, the effect is to turn an *absolute* grading system into a relative system. When the phrases 'grading on a curve' or 'curving a test' are used, it is a good idea to make sure that everyone involved has the same understanding of the term.

Comparing Norm-referenced Grading with Other Methods of Assigning Grades

Grades can be interpreted from two conflicting points of view. They can be viewed as independent, absolute measures of student performance or they can be interpreted relatively. The first perspective is illustrated by the reference-to-perfection, and criterion-referenced approaches to grading. With these systems, each level of student performance is assigned a grade which is intended to be independent of the grades assigned to other students. If a teacher decides that a student deserves a B, it doesn't matter how that student compares with other students. They could all have As or all have Fs, but the B performance still gets a grade of B. At the other extreme is true norm-referenced grading. With this method a student's grade is based entirely on comparisons with others. A student could do poorly in a class, but as long as his or her performance was better than others, an A would be assigned.

In practice, teachers do not adhere strictly to either of these two systems. The teacher using a reference-to-perfection approach is always going to be aware of the distribution of grades in his or her classroom and will be concerned if there are too many high or low grades. Likewise a teacher using a norm-referenced grading system will be hesitant to assign a low grade to an otherwise adequately performing student who is being compared to high achieving students.

Using Norm-referenced Grading

The implementation of norm-referenced grading begins with the specification of the criteria that will be used to determine student grades. This would include the number and nature of the tests, projects, papers, and performance tasks would be specified. The role of classroom participation would also be included as part of the criteria.

The next step is somewhat controversial. It requires that the teacher specify the number of students who are to be assigned each grade. If there are thirty students in a class, a teacher might specify that seven students would get As, ten students would get Bs, ten would get Cs and three would get Ds. The initial response to this suggestion is to argue that the number of students to receive each grade can only be determined after they have been assessed. First of all, teachers always start with some idea about the final distribution of grades they expect. Even with grading methods that are based on the use of absolute standards to evaluate student achievement, a teacher will be alarmed and start making adjustments if all students seem to be getting As or Fs. All norm-referenced grading does is make those expectations explicit.

Scores are combined (the correct methods of combining scores will be discussed in a later section of this chapter) and the students are rank-ordered based on this combined score. If it was decided that seven students were to get As, then the top seven students, based on the ranking would get the As, the next ten students would get Bs and so forth. With such a system, the grade assigned is totally dependent on how a student compares with his or her peers.

The teacher who implements such a system can expect to encounter resistance because many students believe that they should be given the grade they deserve regardless of how they compare with others. Of course the purpose of any good grading system is to determine the grade a student deserves. With some subject matter it is possible to specify exactly what it is that you want students to have learned and assign grades based on their success in achieving these goals. With large classes and subject matter that does not lend itself to the establishment of absolute standard, comparisons with others provides the best basis for assigning grades.

Up to this point, examples of grading using objective tests have been emphasized. Using constructed response and alternative assessments methods can make the assignment of grades even more difficult. Establishing standards for this type of assessment is difficult because the evaluation is subjective.

Determining the Number of Each Grade to be Assigned

When using a norm-referenced procedure for assigning grades, the number of each grade to be assigned must be specified, combined scores rank ordered and students placed on a continuum.

Grade Continuum

'F' students	'D' students	'C' students	'B' students	'A' students

Low achievement   High achievement

The highest achieving students, those who are to be given As, are at the right side of the continuum. The lower achieving students are at the left side of the continuum and they are the ones who will be getting Ds and Fs. This is obvious and easy, the hard part is deciding how many of each grade should be assigned or where on the continuum the distinction between each grade should be made. The reason this is difficult is that grades represent discrete categories while student achievement, as represented by the above continuum, is continuous. This means that the distinction between grades will be arbitrary. Placing students on a continuum can be accomplished using well established rules for the construction, administration, and scoring of assessments. Determining where to set cut-off points and by implication, how many of each grade to assign to students is difficult and subjective.

The setting of cut-off scores to determine the number of each grade to assign is based on three factors: (1) the limits imposed by the teaching setting; (2) the teacher's evaluation of the level of functioning of the class, and (3) the teacher's decision about whether he or she wishes to be an easy, hard, or middle-of-the-road grader.

The Limits Imposed by the Teaching Setting

The first factor a teacher must consider in deciding the number of each grade to be assigned in a class is the environment in which he or she functions. In every teaching setting, where grades are to be assigned, there are rules that specify what is acceptable in a grade distribution. Some schools or school districts are liberal in their designation of the number of high grades, and require few low ones. In another setting, the rules might be conservative and require teachers to assign a respectable number of low grades. Not every teacher will assign the same number of each grade in a particular school, but it would be unusual to have one teacher giving mainly As and Bs while another teacher gave mainly Cs and Ds. The rules may be explicitly stated in the form of written guidelines for grading, but more often they are based on mutual understandings. No one may ever directly tell a teacher how many of each grade to assign, but teachers will be aware of the limits and keep within them.

The Level of Functioning of the Class

If a class is achieving at a high level, awarding more *As* and *Bs* can be easily be defended. If the class is performing poorly more lower grades should be assigned. Over the years, a teacher may find himself or herself assigning different numbers of each grade, depending on the levels of student performance. In a given year, a teacher might justify a much higher distribution of grades than is generally acceptable, because of the exceptional performance of students in a given grading period. A teacher would find it difficult to justify a grade distribution that awards higher grades year after year, based on the assertion that each class is of exceptionally high ability.

The Role of Individual Differences among Teachers

There is always room for individual differences among teachers. One teacher may choose to be at the high end of the range, give many high grades and be labeled an easy grader, while another may choose to function at the low end of the range and give out more low grades. It is only when these limits are violated, that a teacher is likely to feel pressure from peers and school administrators eager to confront a teacher who has strayed outside of what is considered acceptable.

Table 7.1: Combining scores using a point system

Student	Class participation score	Final exam scores	Total points	Grade
Mary	17	74	91	B
Bob	25	72	97	A
Jane	20	73	93	B
Ralph	14	74	88	C
Joe	10	75	85	D

Combining Scores

It is often necessary to combine scores from several inputs to obtain a single value to use in determining student grades. The most common method for combining scores uses points to weight the inputs. Points are assigned to each test, paper, and project as well as for other factors such as attendance and/or class participation. The number of points assigned to an activity is intended to indicate how much that activity should be weighted in determining a student's grade. The number of points a student earns for an activity indicates his or her level of performance. If 30 points are allocated for a mid-term exam, the best student might get 28 points while an average student is given 22, and a poor student is given 10 points. No student could get more than 30.

A teacher using the point method of combining scores, creates a scale that designates the range of points needed for each grade. If points are allocated to activities in such a way that the maximum number of points is 100, the process of assigning grades becomes similar to a reference-to-perfection grading such as:

A   95–100
B   88–94
C   80–87
D   70–79
F   Below 70

It is assumed that the use of points results in the correct weighting of each factor, but this is incorrect. There is no direct relationship between the number of points assigned to an activity and how much it is weighted. Instead the amount of variability in the points assigned to an activity determines how much an activity is weighted.

Point systems don't work. Consider a tenth grade history class in which grades are to be based on a point system with a maximum of 100 points. Students are to be awarded 25 points for class participation and 75 points for their performance on a final exam with 75 items (each item counts as 1 point). Consider what would happen to five students in the class, if it were decided that there would be one A, two Bs, a C and one D and grades were to be determined using a point system. Their scores, points, and grade are listed in Table 7.1. Using the point system for combining scores, Bob who had the lowest score in the class on the final, did so

Table 7.2: *Combining scores with T-scores*

Student	Class participation	Class participation T-score weighted by .25	Final exam	Final exam T-score weighted by .75	Total	Grade based on points	Grade based on T-scores
Mary	17	12.41	74	40.13	52.54	B	B
Bob	25	15.91	72	26.97	42.88	A	D
Jane	20	13.72	73	33.55	47.27	B	C
Ralph	14	11.10	74	40.13	51.23	C	B
Joe	10	9.35	75	47.70	56.06	D	A

well in class participation he was given an A. This occurred even though class participation was supposed to only count 25 per cent. The problem of course is that there is a lot more variability in class participation than there was on the final. Compare Bob with Joe who had the highest score on the final, but didn't do so well on class participation. Even though the final was supposed to count three times as much as class participation and had that proportion more potential points, he ended up with the lowest total score.

The weighting of scores using points will only work if the tests that are to be combined are of approximately the same length and difficulty. Under these circumstances, the variability may be similar enough to justify the combining of the scores using points. When tests are of different lengths and/or difficulty, when different types of activities are evaluated such as tests, papers, and classroom participation, or when activities are not supposed to be weighted equally, summing the points assigned to activities does not weight them correctly.

A better method of combining the performance of students on different activities is to compute the mean and standard deviation of each score and change them into *T*-scores using the following formula:

$$T\text{-score} = \left(\left(\frac{\text{raw score-mean}}{\text{standard deviation}}\right)10\right) + 50$$

These T-scores can be weighted by multiplying them by the proportion they are to count in determining student grades. For the scores from the example from Table 7.1, the weighted *T*-scores for class participation and the final are provided along with sum of the weighted *T*-score for each student in Table 7.2.

The grades assigned using *T*-scores are quite different from those assigned using the point system. Bob who got an A using the point system would gets a D when his scores are combined using *T*-scores, while Joe, who had a D with the point system, gets an A using *T*-scores. What happened? Using the *T*-score method, differences in variability are controlled, but with a point system they are not. This makes class participation count far more than the final exam in the point system even though it is supposed to count one third as much as the final exam. A student

Table 7.3: Combining scores using grades

Student	Class participation	Class participation grade and numerical value	Final exam	Final exam grade and numerical value tripled*	Total	Grade
Mary	17	B-3	74	B-9	12	B
Bob	25	A-4	72	D-3	7	D
Jane	20	B-3	73	C-6	9	C
Ralph	14	C-2	74	B-9	12	B
Joe	10	D-1	75	A-12	16	A

Note: * it is tripled because the final exam is to count three times as much as class participation

who did well in class participation with its greater variability, like Bob, has an unfair advantage with a point system, while Joe is clearly a loser with that system.

The example above is clearly exaggerated. You would not expect to have students performing so differently on class participation and the final exam. However, unless the rank-order of students is the same for both inputs, the use of T-scores will yield a more accurate summary of student performance. The insidious effect of the use of point systems for combining scores is that the teachers who use it and the students graded by it, seldom know how their points are actually weighted because the variability of the measures are seldom computed. In most cases, they don't even understand the importance that variability can have in the determination of grades.

Obviously, the calculations necessary to compute T-scores by hand requires more time than is practical. A calculator helps some, but a computer can make the computations of these values fairly simple.

When first introduced to this approach, there is a tendency for teachers to protest that this procedure is too complex, too mathematical, and unnecessarily time consuming. A more important concern is the harm that can result from the failure to apply these techniques. The deleterious effect on grading depends on the degree to which tests that are to be counted as equal have the same variability. The greater the disparity in variability, the more unfair a point system will be. If a test is to count twice as much as another test, it needs to have twice the variability (not just twice the number of points). Any time the variability of tests is not proportional to how much it is to be weighted, points should not be used.

There are other ways to combine scores which are not as precise in their correction for variability but are easier to compute. One method requires turning scores into grades prior to combining them. The weight of a grade can be doubled by counting it twice. The use of plus and minus grades can make the process more precise (an A would be equal to 4, an A− to 3.75, a B+ to 3.25 and so forth). Once again consider the scores from the previous example, see Table 7.3.

As can be seen, the grades assigned are the same as those based on the use of T-scores. This would not always be the case, but the results will always be closer to the T-score results than would be obtained using the point system.

Conclusions about Grades and Grading

Grades are an important and emotionally charged aspect of educational assessment. No one likes grades much. Teachers don't like to assign them and students don't enjoy earning them. Grades do serve some important purposes. They provide feedback to students and parents, they can motivate students to work harder, and they perform a certification function. Grades can communicate to employers and the admission offices of schools how well a student can function academically.

There is strong sentiment in some quarters to eliminate or radically change the grading process. As presently structured, they tend to exaggerate academic competition and there are some studies that question their effectiveness as a method of motivating students. The problem faced by those anxious to alter the way students are graded is the lack of suitable alternatives.

Summary

The purpose of student evaluation is the making of decisions. The assignment of grades is one aspect of this process. The critical element of grading is the conferring of value on student performance. Although there has always been widespread suspicion, if not outright dislike for grades and grading practices, they seem to be a permanent feature of the educational environment. There is general agreement that grades should reflect the purist measure of student achievement possible. How hard a student is trying, ability, and other factors unrelated to achievement should not be used as the basis for assigning grades unless specified in course objectives. Five bases for making comparisons necessary for the assignment of grades are provided which are intuitive, ipsative, reference-to-perfection, criterion-referenced and norm referenced grading. The preferred method of assessment is one that is norm-referenced. Teachers are cautioned to avoid combining performance on separate activities using a simple point system. The use of T-scores is suggested as a better alternative.

Suggested Readings

CUNNINGHAM, G.K. (1986) *Educational and Psychological Measurement*, New York: Macmillan.

SLAVIN, R.E. (1991) *Educational Psychology*, Englewood Cliffs: Prentice Hall.

STIGGINS, R.J., FRISBIE, D.A. and GRISWOLD, P.A. (1989) 'Inside high school grading practices: Building a research agenda,' *Educational Measurement: Issues and Practices*, **8**, 2, pp. 5–14.

THORNDIKE, R.M., CUNNINGHAM, G.K., THORNDIKE, R.L. and HAGAN, E. (1991) *Measurement and Evaluation in Psychology and Education*, New York: Macmillan.

8   Standardized Achievement Tests

In this chapter students will learn:

- to identify the different types of standardized tests;
- which standardized achievement tests are available;
- the structure of the Comprehensive Test of Basic Skills;
- the difference between teacher-made and standardized tests;
- the differences between aptitude and achievement tests;
- how reliable and valid standardized achievement tests are;
- about the varied uses for standardized achievement tests; and
- how useful standardized achievement tests are.

Standardized achievement testing is intended to provide an objective assessment of how much students have learned in school. The results of these tests are usually interpreted using norm-referenced comparisons of a nationally representative sample of students, although some standardized achievement tests also provide absolute standards. These tests are available from several different publishers and provide information about the individual student, the entire school, school district, or state. Standardized achievement tests are usually accompanied by precise instructions for administration and scoring. They generally are intended for commercial purposes, although not all such tests were constructed for this reason.

The first recognizable achievement tests predate intelligence tests, but the widespread use and acceptance of standardized achievement tests occurred after the introduction of group intelligence tests. Arthur Otis (Robertson, 1972) is given credit for the introduction of the methodology for standardized tests, both achievement and intelligence. When the Committee on the Psychological Examination of Recruits constructed the Army Alpha and Beta tests that were used to classify recruits during World War I, they adopted many of the techniques Otis had included in his adaptation of the Stanford-Binet for administration to groups of subjects. His most important contribution was the introduction of the use of multiple-choice items and the objective scoring format. In 1918, the World Book Company published the Otis Group Intelligence Scale, closely modeled after the Army tests, which quickly ushered in an era of standardized testing. The success and acceptance of group intelligence tests led to the introduction of increasingly sophisticated achievement tests.

Achievement Test Batteries

The first objective achievement tests measured student performance in a single academic subject area. A school that wanted to assess the achievement of students in more than one academic subject, had to administer a separate test for each. This was expensive and time consuming and it required teachers to be familiar with the administrative procedures for several tests. It also made comparisons among academic subjects difficult because each test was based on a different norm group and different types of derived scores. Later, these separate, uncoordinated tests were replaced by test batteries, prepared by teams of test authors for a single publisher and administered using the same test booklet. The use of coordinated test batteries has important advantages. Planning is comprehensive and the components are designed to provide an integrated coverage of the major academic skills and curricular areas. Each subtest is coordinated with the other subtests in order to minimize duplication.

The most important characteristic of the test battery is the use of the same norm sample. Comparisons both within and between individuals are more direct and straightforward when norms for all parts of the battery are based upon the same group of students. Of course, in selecting a test battery, a school district might discover that the quality of the subtests varies. It might seem preferable to choose the reading subtest from one battery, the math from a second, and language arts from still a third. This cannot be done without paying full price for each of the batteries. The advantage of using the same norm sample and test structure compensates for the lost opportunity to choose a favorite subtest from each.

Available Standardized Achievement Tests

There are six major large-scale achievement test batteries. The two biggest sellers are the tests published by McGraw-Hill, the CAT and *TerraNova*.

The procedures necessary for the development of high quality standardized achievement tests are well known and have been developed over a long period of time. They are also costly and time consuming. Standardized test publishing is a big business and test publishers understand that the time and expense of test development are part of doing business. All of the successful tests are carefully developed and the test development and norming procedures employed are exemplary. The tests differ in their items, subtests, and techniques of test development, but the most important difference among them is the specific objectives assessed by each. For this reason, the selection of a standardized achievement test should be based on a careful analysis of the match between the objectives that a school or school district wishes to assess and the objectives included on each of the achievement tests.

Table 8.1: *Six major large scale achievement tests*

Title	Publisher	Grades covered	Structure	Content covered
California Achievement Test	CTB/McGraw-Hill	K-12	Two forms (E and F) and eleven levels.	word analysis, vocabulary, comprehension, language expression; mathematics, computation, concepts, and applications.
TerraNova formerly called the Comprehensive Test of Basic Skills (CTBS)	CTB/McGraw-Hill	K-12	CTBS Complete Battery Editions which provides both norm-referenced and objective mastery scores CTBS Basic Battery Editions is the same as the complete battery but focuses only on reading language arts and mathematics (does not include science and social studies like the Complete Battery) CTBS Survey Battery Editions includes only norm-referenced items from the Complete Battery Multiple Assessments Editions combines norm-referenced items from the Survey Battery with constructed response items. Performance Assessments Editions include extended open ended assessments.	Reading/language Arts Mathematics Science (1–12) Social studies (1–12)
Iowa Test of Basic Skills (ITBS)	Riverside Publishing	K-9	basic battery has 6 tests complete battery has 11 tests	

Table 8.1: cont'd

Title	Publisher	Grades covered	Structure	Content covered
Iowa Test of Educational Development (ITED)	Riverside Publishing	9–12	two forms: X8 and Y8 two levels: Level I for grades 9 and 10 and Level II for grades 11 and 12.	correctness and appropriateness of expression ability to do quantitative thinking analysis of social studies materials analysis of natural sciences material ability to interpret literary materials vocabulary uses of sources of information reading
Metropolitan Achievement Test (MAT)	Psychological Corporation	K-12	eight levels	vocabulary reading mathematics spelling language science social studies writing
SRA achievement series	Science Research Associates	K-12	one form eight levels	
Stanford Achievement test	Psychological Corporation	1.5–9.9	one form six levels	reading mathematics listening science social studies using information

TerraNova — The Comprehensive Test of Basic Skills

In order for the reader to gain a better understanding of standardized testing, one test, *TerraNova*, published by McGraw-Hill will be described in greater detail than the other achievement tests. *TerraNova*, formerly called the *Comprehensive Test of Basic Skills (CTBS)* is one of the best selling and technically sophisticated of the major achievement tests. *TerraNova* contains a wider range of assessment techniques than its predecessor *CTBS/4*. Part of *TerraNova* is an updating of the *CTBS/4*, but what makes *TerraNova* different from its predecessor is the introduction of open response and performance-based items. The norm-referenced and criterion-referenced parts of the test are still called the *CTBS*.

TerraNova is intended to measure concepts, processes, and skills developed through exposure to a variety of school curricula. The content of the test is inde-

Table 8.2; Grade levels and corresponding Levels of the Comprehensive Test of Basic Skills (TerraNova)

Grade level	CTBS/4 level
K.6–1.6	10
1.6–2.6	11
2.0–3.2	12
2.6–4.2	13
3.6–5.2	14
4.6–6.2	15
5.6–7.2	16
6.6–8.2	17
7.6–9.2	18
8.6–10.2	19
9.6–11.2	20
10.6–12.9	21/22

pendent of the course content found in any particular school district which makes it relevant for a wide range of school settings. If the *TerraNova* was not structured to be independent of local curricula, it could only be legitimately used with students exposed to the specific curriculum that matched its objectives.

Three versions of the *TerraNova* are currently available: the *CTBS Survey* and *Survey Plus*, the *CTBS Complete Battery* and *Complete Battery Plus*, the *CTBS Basic Battery and Basic Battery Plus*, the *Multiple Assessments*, the *TerraNova Performance Assessments*, and *TerraNova SUPERA*, the Spanish version of CTBS. The *CTBS Survey* provides norm- criterion-referenced scores for reading, language arts, mathematics and social studies. The *Survey Plus* adds word analysis, vocabulary, language mechanics, spelling, and mathematical computations. The *Complete Battery* includes the same scores provided by the *Survey*, but uses more items. The *Basic Battery* is the same as the *Complete Battery* without the science and social studies scores. The *Basic Battery Plus* adds the same additional subscales that are included on the *Plus* version of the *Survey* and *Complete Battery*.

Table 8.2 lists the grade levels and corresponding *TerraNova* levels for the CTBS tests. There is always more than one level that can be administered to a student in a particular grade level. This flexibility gives the test administrator the option of assigning the level that best matches student ability. While any one of several levels could be appropriately assigned to a student, there is always one that provides the optimum difficulty level for a student. This is important because the precision of a test is maximized when tests of appropriate difficulty are administered to students.

Norming

The *TerraNova* includes fall, winter and spring norms and was intended to reflect the school population of the entire United States. The total sample for the fall and spring norms is anticipated to be 168,000 students selected from public, Catholic, and private schools. The stratified random sampling procedure employed was based on geographic region, size, and socio-economic level.

Reporting Results

The standard scores obtained from the CTBS/4 are derived from a highly sophisticated application of item response theory (IRT). IRT focuses on underlying constructs instead of the linear transformations associated with standard scores. With standard scores, every item is assumed to make an equal contribution to a student's score. IRT is a system of interpreting scores which weights items differently. It provides a way to analyze a set of test scores so that information concerning the amount of the underlying construct possessed by an individual can be estimated very precisely. Each item is weighted according to item difficulty and the degree to which it measures the underlying construct. IRT represents the state of the art of standardized test development. Its technical complexity also is a disadvantage, because it requires interpretation with a computer. Hand scoring is not an option.

Test scoring services for the *TerraNova* are provided by the test publisher, CTB/McGraw-Hill. Alternatively, the computer programs used for computing scores and producing interpretations can be leased from that company. As is true for other major achievement tests, a wide variety of derived scores are available, including normal curve equivalents, scaled scores, grade equivalents, stanines, and percentiles. These are based on local, state, and national norms.

The Reliability of the TerraNova

The *Prepublication Technical Bulletin* (McGraw-Hill, 1996) includes preliminary reliability coefficients for each scale, level, and form. Across all of these, the reliabilities are uniformly high with most in the .90s and high .80s and only a few in the high .70s. This is to be expected because achieving high reliability coefficients for standardized achievement tests is not difficult and all large scale achievement tests are able to meet this goal.

Validity

The *Prepublication Technical Bulletin* manual for *TerraNova* provides a paragraph about each of the following types of validity: content-related, criterion-related and construct-related. Content validity is established through the establishment of a match between the instructional objectives of a school and those assessed by the TerraNova. This validation must be established by the school, state or school district adopting the achievement test. They need to examine their own objectives and determine the degree to which they match those assessed by *TerraNova*. The authors of *TerraNova* face the same problem encountered by all standardized achievement tests, they must ensure that they assess content relevant to all schools, but they must avoid content unique to only some schools. This requirement guarantees that neither the content of *TerraNova* nor any other standardized achievement test will comprehensively assess what is included in the curriculum of any school.

Criterion-related validity for *TerraNova* is established through correlations with other standardized tests such as the Test of Cognitive Skills/2 (TCS/2), the ACT,

SAT, and NAEP tests. Since all of these tests, including *TerraNova*, are dependent on reading and vocabulary ability, high correlations can be expected. A better approach would be to correlate scores with student grades in specific subjects.

The construct-related validity of *TerraNova* is to be established through the examinations of intercorrelations among the *TerraNova* tests and other assessments. Evidence for construct validity will come from the determination that correlations among similar skills are higher than those found among different skills. Although these relationships have not yet been established, such studies are currently being planned. The most important question about the construct-related validity of standardized achievement tests do not involve their capacity to assess reading/language/vocabulary or math ability. It is far more important to demonstrate that the science and social studies subscales are assessing something unique and different from reading and language ability.

Teacher-made Versus Standardized Tests

Teacher-made tests are constructed to assess student learning within the classroom. Their greatest strengths are their relevance and applicability in the settings where they are used. The most important deficiencies of teacher-made test are the technical deficiencies associated with the limited amount of time and resources available to teachers.

There is a generally accepted set of procedures that must be followed in constructing achievement tests. These procedures are well known and the extent of their implementation is only limited by their high costs. Elaborate item analyzes are employed, massive norming samples assembled, and the tests are carefully constructed to enhance content validity. The money, time, expert knowledge, and large norm samples associated with standardized tests allow them to achieve a level of technical sophistication unavailable to the classroom teacher. The large commitment of resources for the development and maintenance of standardized tests are market driven. Publishers compete for market share by maintaining a high level of technical quality. As a consequence of the commitment to technical sophistication, there are few important differences in quality among the most widely used achievement tests.

The norms provided for major standardized achievement tests are based on the administration of hundreds of thousands of tests. Publishers commit enormous resources to ensure that their norms are based on the best possible norms. Even with such massive outlays of resources, the norms established may not be optimum because the norming can only take place in school districts willing to permit such activities. In most cases these are the same school districts that have already adopted earlier versions of the achievement test being normed (Baglin, 1981).

Classroom tests are typically used once and are constructed by teachers who are unlikely to be highly skilled in test construction techniques. At the same time, they have the advantage of assessing specific course content and material relevant to the classroom. The curricular relevance of classroom tests can compensate for what may be less than ideal testing technology. Teachers also can improve their testing skills and improve the quality of their tests, thereby enjoying the best of two worlds; tests that have good technical qualities which at the same time, are closely aligned with the curriculum.

Academic Aptitude vs. Achievement

'Achievement' refers to a student's actual performance in a content area, while 'academic aptitude' refers to predictions about how a student will achieve in the future. The distinction between aptitude and achievement was once widely accepted along with the belief that it was possible to construct tests that measured these two constructs independently. Now there is little support for a belief in this distinction. There is not much difference between these two types of tests and it is not always easy to distinguish between items written for achievement and those written for academic aptitude tests. Achievement tests measure general abilities rather than actual course content because they cannot assess any instructional objectives that are not common to all of the school settings in which they might be adopted. Aptitude tests can only predict future performance by assessing current achievement using assessment methodologies similar to those used with achievement tests.

If you want to predict how well a fourth grade student will perform in math when he or she reaches high school, the best strategy is to examine fourth grade math achievement. High school performance in reading could similarly be predicted through an examination of fourth grade reading achievement. Predicting performance in high school level history would be more difficult because appropriate fourth grade history achievement tests are not available. The best way to predict performance across a wide range of subject matter, including history, would be with a test that assessed general achievement. Such a test would probably focus heavily on reading and vocabulary. This makes sense because they are necessary components for success in a history class. These skills, along with math computation, are good predictors of any academic subject.

Test publishers try to vary the format of academic aptitude tests in order to make them appear different from conventional achievement tests. These changes result in items that look slightly different, but the differences are largely cosmetic. Achievement tests generally include straightforward measures of basic skills while aptitude tests are more likely to include tasks that require a combination of knowledge and reasoning ability. For example, an achievement test might include a series of straightforward multiplication problems. An aptitude test might measure the same skills by having students examine pairs of multiplication problems and indicate whether or not each pair, is identical or different. If the student concludes that they are different, he or she must specify which of the two pairs is larger.

On an academic aptitude test, knowledge of vocabulary is often assessed by determining whether students understand the relationship among vocabulary words using an analogy format. An achievement test is more likely to have students choose the best synonym from among several options. These differences involve more form than substance. Both test types emphasize verbal and quantitative skills. The student who does well on an aptitude test using an analogy format, will usually perform equally well when asked to identify synonyms on an achievement test. Likewise, the student who does poorly on an achievement test will seldom perform better on an aptitude test. These similarities render designations of student as an overachiever, because his or her achievement scores exceed their aptitude scores, or an underachiever because the same scores are below their aptitude scores, meaningless. Such inconsistencies are best attributed to measurement error rather than meaningful learner characteristics.

Reliability and Validity

The reliability of standardized achievement tests is usually quite satisfactory. By focusing on basic verbal and computation skills, which are easily measured consistently, acceptable levels of reliability can be assured. The primary focus of the item analysis procedures used with achievement tests is the enhancement of reliability. This is accomplished by eliminating items that do not correlate well with the overall score. As a result, standardized achievement tests can be expected to have reliability coefficients in the 1980s and 1990s.

It is not easy to establish the validity of achievement tests and their technical manuals typically emphasize content-related validity. This usually involves nothing more than a determination of the degree to which items match instructional objectives. This is an important but not necessarily sufficient form of validity. It needs to be supported by evidence that the inferences made about test scores are legitimate. An achievement test can be constructed in such a way that it has content-related validity even when inferences about a student's performance are suspect.

Consider a test that contains items carefully matched to appropriate instructional objectives. What will happen if the items are primarily measures of how well students can read content related to the objectives? Such a test might appear to have good content validity because the items match the objectives. The test will most likely provide a better measure of reading ability than the acquisition of the knowledge and skills associated with the target objectives. Test publishers should include information about other types of validity such as construct- and criterion-related validity and consumers should demand that these other forms of validity be included.

Uses for Standardized Achievement Tests

Standardized achievement tests can provide information that can be used to make four types of decisions: parental decisions about whether or not their children are performing adequately; teacher decisions about how to modify their instruction; placement decisions about students; and evaluative decisions about students, teachers, schools, and school districts. Naturally, it is difficult for a single test to fulfill all of these roles and compromises in test construction must be made in order for these tests to serve the diversity of purposes listed.

Feedback to Parents about Student Performance

Achievement tests can give parents a global view of how their children are performing in school, particularly in reading and computational skills. This is particularly useful at the lower grades where most instruction focuses on these topics and where there is a wide consensus about the importance of these skills. It is much less useful at later grades because not as much class time is spent on these basic skills.

One of the most common misconceptions about standardized achievement tests is the belief that they can only measure a student's capacity to recall facts and disconnected knowledge. Actually, the contrary is more likely to be true. An examination of contemporary achievement tests reveals very little in the way of emphasis on the recall of facts or concrete information. The multiple-choice format is quite effective in assessing knowledge and facts, but test publishers are not free to construct tests that measure this sort of achievement.

One of the most important characteristics of American education is the absence of a national curriculum. Only a few states have even established a statewide curriculum. Only in the early grades where reading and basic math skills predominate, do standardized achievement tests provide a good measure of what is taught in school. After these early grades, there is really no way for a test publisher to assess what students have actually learned in school, because there is no agreement about what to include. There have been some attempts to establish national standards, but standards are not the same as the actual content listed in a curriculum. There has been no serious consideration of a national curriculum.

The lack of a national curriculum means that standardized achievement tests seldom attempt to measure anything but reading, language skills, math computation and math problem solving ability. Some tests purport to assess science and social studies, but they are really only measuring the student's ability to apply information about these topics rather than their actual knowledge. Other topics such as literature and foreign languages are completely absent.

In recent years, many educators have argued that facts and basic skills are less important than general problem solving and critical thinking skills. Making a virtue of necessity, publishers of standardized achievement tests have highlighted these attributes at the expense of more conventional knowledge. It is difficult to assess problem solving ability in the abstract. For this reason, it is necessary to provide information to the student in the form of paragraphs, charts, or graphs. The students are then asked to solve problems using this information. These procedures can provide a good estimate of how well a student can apply information, but it tells us nothing about whether students are learning what they are being taught. This is usually what parents want to know.

Using Standardized Achievement Test Results for Making Instructional Decisions

Standardized tests do not provide much useful information to teachers about how to modify their instruction because the tests are not structured to do this. First of all, tests are not aligned with what is happening in the classroom so they can not possibly tell teachers whether their instruction is effective.

Even when the tests cover the right objectives, there will not be enough items assessing the targeted objective to make a reliable decision about whether it has been mastered or not mastered. There are limits to the length of a standardized achievement tests and they can not include enough items to assess all of the objectives included.

Even when the tests assess the right objectives, and there are enough items, their difficulties will not be appropriate for making diagnostic decisions. The difficulty of items on standardized achievement tests must be carefully calibrated to maximize the accuracy of the overall assessment and thereby enhance their norm–referenced properties. On a diagnostic test, it is best to set the difficulty at a level that permits the best discriminations at the low end of the scale where you find the students for whom diagnostic assessment is most relevant.

Detailed analyzes of success and failures on specific items is sometimes available and it can be of some use to teachers, but care must exercised in using this information. Failure on an item should alert a teacher, prompting him or her to examine the proficiency of a student on the skill being measured using short teacher–made tests that focus on the specific skill covered by the failed item. Similarly, failure on an item by many students in a class should cause a teacher to reexamine how that skill was taught.

The biggest problem with using achievement test results to modify instruction is the likelihood that teachers will use this knowledge inappropriately. They may even try to improve their students' scores by teaching the specific test items that their students are getting wrong.

Standardized achievement test results are most helpful to teachers when they are made available soon after the test is administered, but there is sometimes a lengthy wait between test administration and the availability of results. High speed scoring and powerful computers can make results available quickly, but the centralization of test scoring and interpretation can cause a lag of several weeks between testing and the delivery of the test results to the teacher. Each week of delay makes the results less useful for making instructional decisions about specific children or the class as a whole. New learning has taken place, previously learned material may have been forgotten and the details of the description of student performance will be less accurate.

Although, the norms on most standardized tests are established for fall, winter, and spring, states and school districts generally prefer to administer the tests in the spring in the mistaken belief that students will have more of the year to learn and thus will obtain higher scores. When the tests are administered at the end of the school year, the results may not be available until the following fall when a different teacher is responsible for the students.

Using Standardized Test Results to Make Placement Decisions

At one time, both achievement and academic aptitude tests were used to make a wide range of placement decisions. Academic aptitude tests such as the Scholastic Assessment Test (SAT) and American College Testing (ACT) Program continue to be used routinely as a basis for admission and placement decisions at the college level. Grouping and tracking of students on the basis of academic aptitude tests, at one time, was fairly routine at all grade levels. This practice has become less common and there is considerable controversy surrounding the advantages and disadvantages of this practice.

Standardized achievement tests are not appropriate for use in making high stakes placement decisions because they are not intended for this purpose. The revision cycle for such tests is usually seven to ten years and the tests can not be considered secure. It is not difficult for anyone to obtain copies of the test and there is no way to be sure that students have not been exposed to actual test items. This can be contrasted with tests such as the SAT and ACT for which test security is a high priority. Different tests are used every year and there are many different forms in use. This security is expensive and it would not be cost effective for achievement test publishers to implement the same sort of security measures used with academic aptitude tests.

Using Standardized Tests to Make Evaluative Decisions about Students, Teachers, Schools, and School Districts

The documentation of the effectiveness of schools and teachers, the evaluation of the quality of education in a state (or the whole nation) and the making of comparisons among school districts, schools, classes and grade levels are important reasons for administering standardized achievement tests. The public, governors, state legislatures, and other politicians often view test scores as the most important criterion for assessing the effectiveness of a school district.

One of the unifying principles of educational reform is the centralization of decision-making and monitoring of student performance for purposes of accountability. High stakes testing refers to assessment systems that attach important contingencies to test performance, usually in the form of rewards or sanctions. High stakes testing was once directed at students, but it has now been broadened to include the sanctions that can befall schools and school districts when they fall below a predetermined standard or expectation.

There is a growing consensus among both proponents and critics of standardized achievement testing, that the advantages of high stakes testing programs to schools (in the form of greater accountability) are outweighed by their unpleasant consequences. Elevating the importance of scores on standardized achievement tests to the point where they become the single-minded goal of a school system can cause distortions in instruction. Instructional and testing procedures may be adopted because they promise higher scores, rather than because they address legitimate educational goals. The pressure for high test scores can restrict instructional time for anything not directly covered on the test. Teachers begin to devote large amounts of time to drill and practice on tasks similar to the items found on achievement tests. Experience in writing may be replaced by practice in identifying errors in texts and the selection of the correctly spelled word from several that are misspelled, may replace the traditional practice of spelling from dictation on the weekly spelling test. The use of alternative assessment techniques is sometimes proposed as a way to address the problems of inappropriate test preparation activities by teachers. This is likely to change the form of the inappropriate activities but is unlikely to eliminate them.

Achievement tests are neither constructed nor administered in such a way that their evaluative function is maximized, which further diminishes their use for these purposes. The following are reasons why the association of high stakes with achievement tests renders them less effective as an evaluation tool.

1 Standardized achievement tests tend to measure high level cognitive functioning rather than the specific content that students are learning in school. As a result of the emphasis on higher level functioning, student performance on standardized achievement tests tends to be more influenced by student characteristics such as the parental educational and socio-economic level, home environment and individual differences than differences in instruction.

2 The revision and renorming of standardized achievement tests are so expensive that they only take place every seven to ten years. This means that the same test is administered year after year in the same school. It is inevitable that students and teachers will become familiar with the test's contents. Teachers may be tempted to modify their curriculum to emphasize the errors students make most frequently.

3 Achievement tests are administered by those most likely to be evaluated by the test: teachers, supervisors, and administrators. These are individuals with a large stake in ensuring a high level of student performance.

4 Those who control the testing process are in a position to manipulate the results in their favor. While it is reasonable to assume a high level of ethical behavior among educators, the temptations associated with high stakes testing can become difficult to resist. This is particularly true when the possibility of detection seems remote or when it is believed that other schools are improving their scores with similar practices.

5 Those who are responsible for ensuring that appropriate test preparation and administration procedures are followed, often have the strongest stakes in ensuring high test scores.

6 Teachers seldom have students in class for more than a year. This is not enough time for a teacher to have much of an effect on the acquisition of the general abilities these tests measure. Such skills are acquired over a long period of time and also are affected by the educational and readiness activities that take place in the home.

If standardized tests are to be used to evaluate schools in such a way that it is possible to have confidence in their results, testing must be conducted by an agency other than the school district. Other test security techniques also must be employed. When students are given the Scholastic Aptitude Test (SAT), the Graduate Record Exam (GRE) or other similar tests, they must present identification. New tests are developed for each administration, different forms of the tests are used within the testing room to prevent students from copying answers from those sitting next to them, and access to items before the test is administered is severely restricted. None of these cautions are routinely employed with standardized achievement tests. There is a good reason why such precautions are not used with standardized achievement tests. It is very expensive. Achievement tests typically cost around seven dollars per student while the ACT costs twenty-five and the SAT twenty-one dollars per student. Systemwide achievement testing would be too costly if the appropriate security measures were in place.

The test security for scholastic aptitude tests focuses on preventing students from cheating on the test. When achievement tests are used for accountability purposes the emphasis has to be on the teachers and school administrators because it is they who have the most to gain from inappropriate testing activities.

Evaluating the Usefulness of Standardized Achievement Tests

The popularity and public acceptance of standardized tests are cyclical. In the 1950s, the use of both achievement and aptitude tests was an uncritically accepted as a legitimate public school function. During the late 1960s and 1970s, questions about their legitimacy began to appear in both professional journals and in the popular press. Much of the opposition was focused on mental ability tests, but demands for the elimination of those tests were generalized to all standardized tests, including achievement tests. This period of criticism was followed by an era when the importance of accountability increased. It was believed that accountability could play a key role in improving the nation's education system. This led to an increase in the use of standardized achievement tests, as well as diagnostic and locally constructed tests used to assess minimum competency.

The movement towards accountability has been tempered by a new era of criticism of standardized achievement tests. Much of this criticism has emerged in tandem with the promotion of alternative assessment techniques. The advocates of alternative assessment techniques often justify their use by identifying the flaws in conventional standardized test technology, specifically the multiple-choice item format. The conventional objective test format certainly has it limitations, and the use of standardized achievement tests, particularly in association with high stakes assessment, has led to some undesirable educational practices.

The primary objection to conventional assessment methods is philosophical. Standardized achievement testing is based on the belief that instruction can be reduced to easily measured components which must be acquired prior to the achievement of higher level functioning. Advocates of progressivism assert that the acquisition of basic skills is not a necessary prerequisite for the development of higher level functioning. They believe that students exposed to instruction in higher level problem solving will learn basic skills naturally as a part of the process. Standardized achievement tests which are believed to emphasize basic skills are not compatible with this philosophy.

Summary

The first standardized achievement tests were created after the success of early group intelligence tests. These achievement tests focused on specific academic areas, but they were soon replaced by test batteries that assessed several different academic areas. The six major large-scale achievement test batteries are as follows: the *California Achievement Test* (CAT) published by McGraw-Hill; *TerraNova* (*Comprehensive Test of Basic Skills*), also published by McGraw-Hill; the *Iowa Test of Basic Skills* (*ITBS*), published by Riverside Publishing Company; the *Metropolitan Achievement Test* (*MAT*), published by the Psychological Corporation; the *SRA* Achievement series published by Science Research Associates, Inc.; and the *Stanford Achievement Test* (*SAT*), published by the Psychological Corporation. Standardized achievement tests are created using the most sophisticated test development and norming technology available. What they lack is a focus on the content that students are taught. By necessity, standardized achievement tests can include only content that has been taught to every student. At one time it was believed that a clear distinction could be made between aptitude and achievement. It was similarly believed that it was possible to construct tests that measured these two constructs independently. The two types of tests are more similar than different and items from tests labeled as 'achievement tests' are not much different from those found on aptitude tests. The reliability of achievement tests is usually quite good, but establishing validity is a bit more difficult. Standardized achievement tests are used to provide feedback to parents about student performance and information to teachers about student performance. They can also be used as a tool for evaluating the effectiveness of schools. In recent years there has been extensive criticism of standardized achievement tests. The most important criticism concerns the perils of high stakes testing. When too much importance is placed on the outcome of these tests they tend to distort the curriculum and have an adverse impact on the way teachers structure their classes.

Suggested Readings

CANNELL, J.J. (1988) 'Nationally normed elementary achievement testing in America's public schools: How all 50 states are above the national average,' *Educational Measurement: Issues and Practices*, **7**, 2, pp. 5–9.

CUNNINGHAM, G.K. (1986) *Educational and Psychological Measurement*, New York: Macmillan.

SLAVIN, R.E. (1991) *Educational Psychology*, Englewood Cliffs: Prentice Hall.

THORNDIKE, R.M., CUNNINGHAM, G.K., THORNDIKE, R.L. and HAGAN, E. (1991) *Measurement and Evaluation in Psychology and Education*, New York: Macmillan.

9   The Ethics of Student Assessment

In this chapter the student will learn:

- where to find information about ethics;
- how and why teachers should avoid bias in their assessments;
- who is competent to administer student assessments;
- who should have access to test materials;
- appropriate test construction and administration practices;
- ownership of test results;
- ethical concerns surrounding the assigning of grades.

Ethics are discussed throughout this book in the context of the issues introduced in each chapter. The present chapter is intended to provide a more focused discussion of the topic. In the absence of clear ethical guidelines describing appropriate and inappropriate assessment practices, the content of this chapter can provide guidance to classroom teachers. It does this by distinguishing between those behaviors that ethical and unethical where there is a consensus. In other areas where no clear consensus exists, both sides of the ethical dilemma are presented.

Ethics are rules for conduct that lie somewhere between laws resulting from legislative processes and the personal nature of morals and values. Ethics represent collectively agreed upon rules for conduct, that are supported and enforced by groups of individuals or professional organizations for their members. Punishment for the violation of a law is generally stated in the law itself. The violation of an ethical standard does not imply a violation of the law, although the difference between the two is not always clear. We may obey laws because we believe in them or in the system that promulgates them, but the ultimate consequence of violating laws is some form of punishment. Ethics are also enforced, but much more loosely. The strongest form of enforcement is the group pressure that can be applied by the organization that endorses the ethical code. Organizations such as the American Psychological Association (APA) and the American Counseling Association (ACA) have ethical guidelines that cover assessment, which all members are required to follow. The consequences for violating these ethical codes include sanctions or even expulsion from the organization. The focus of these ethical guidelines is on psychological and counselling assessments and they both include statements about the misuse of tests, qualifications for administration and interpretation, professional competence, consultations, and rules for safeguarding the rights of participants in research. For a psychologist, the violation of these rules can lead to censure and/ or the loss of his or her license to practice psychology at the state level. If they are members, they could be expelled from the American Psychological Association.

Sources of Information about Ethics

There are three published ethical standards that can be applied to the assessment-related activities of teachers.

1   The Standards for Teacher Competence in Student Assessment, published in *Educational Measurement: Issues and Practices* (1990). The content of these standards was presented in Chapter 1.
2   The Code of Professional Responsibility in Educational Assessment. This document is being prepared by the National Council on Measurement in Education and is currently in draft form.
3   The 1985 *Standards for Educational and Psychological Testing* published jointly by the American Psychological Association (APA), the American Education Research Association (AERA), and the National Council on Measurement in Education (NCME). These standards are currently being revised and a new version will be available in 1997 or 1998.

While all three standards embody ethical principles, there is neither a means for enforcement nor a single professional organization from which violators can be expelled. These standards also focus on the use of standardized tests by educators and do not directly address the daily assessment activities of teachers. Additional information about ethics can be found in textbooks devoted to testing and in articles on testing and assessment published in professional journals.

Establishing What Is Ethical

It is not difficult to identify individuals willing to render judgments about which assessment practices are ethical and which are not. Unfortunately, there are no written ethical standards, endorsed by a single professional educational organization, that govern the assessment activities of educators. There is no single ethical code that applies to teachers, administrators, test publishers and the directors of testing for school districts. While members of each of these groups certainly consider themselves to be operating ethically, there is a lack of agreement about which specific behaviors should be considered ethical and which should not. No single set of published ethical standards exists that could govern the activities of all educators involved in assessment and there is therefore no way of admonishing those who violate the accepted standards.

The establishment of a widely accepted ethical code that could be used to guide a teacher's activities in the area of student assessment would be difficult to compile due to the lack of consensus regarding what is appropriate and what is an inappropriate assessment practice. For example, there is no consensus about the amount of assistance teachers should provide to a student taking an achievement test. A survey conducted by Mehrens and Kaminski (1989), found considerable disagreement among practitioners regarding this issue. The same conflicts were found by Popham (1991). The most conservative approach is to condone no test preparation activity other than better instruction. Teaching the test objectives, or practising the same or similar items that appear on the test are deemed inappropriate. Any activity that gives some students an advantage on the test not enjoyed by those who participated in the norming of the test is not permitted. At the same time, many teachers, according to the Mehrens and Kaminski (1989) believe that instruction aimed directly at test content is acceptable. Some teachers have further asserted that the high stakes use of standardized tests is unfair and have such a negative effect on instruction that any activities used to increase student performance are justified (Linn, 1983). Test publishers themselves market instructional materials specifically targeted at increasing student performance. These may include practice on items similar to those that appear on the tests themselves. Advocates of the use of performance assessment recommend a close match between instruction and assessment, believing that instruction should focus on the specific content that will be on tests. It is difficult to label an activity unethical when it is considered entirely appropriate by many professionals.

The Need for Ethical Rules for Student Assessment

It should be obvious by now that assessment can have a dramatic effect on the lives of students. If student assessment played an inconsequential role in schools, there would be less concern about the ethical implications of its practice. In the past, student assessment ethics focused on making sure that students were treated fairly, and that testing was appropriate. These remain important concerns, but educational reform has interpreted accountability more broadly and has raised additional ethical concerns. In many states, the teacher, the school, and the school district are the ones being held accountable rather than just the student. When students are the focus of accountability, it is the responsibility of the teacher administering the test to ensure that tests are administered properly and that test scores accurately reflect the true level of student achievement. When the teacher and/or the school is being evaluated, there may be a diminished commitment to ensure the proper administration of the tests used for this assessment. In particular, there may be a temptation to overlook assessment practices which result in inflated scores. Ethical transgressions are likely to occur when those with the biggest stake in student test performance are responsible for monitoring assessment practices. Without outside proctors to conduct testing, no one can monitor the behavior of teachers who have vested interests in ensuring that their students perform well. In the absence of any other control, we must depend on the personal ethics of teachers.

Legal Restrictions on Testing

There are relatively few laws regulating testing. Products sold in this country, in particular, food and drugs which have the potential for harm, are regulated at the state or federal level. Drugs cannot be sold which are either harmful or have no demonstrated medicinal value. Before a drug can be marketed, it must undergo years of rigorous testing, along with expensive and time consuming trials to ensure effectiveness and lack of side effects. Furthermore, claims about the medicinal value of vitamins or any other substance cannot be made without verification by scientific evidence. There are packaging standards for foods and other household products and restrictions on those that may be dangerous. There is no such restriction on test publishers. They can make almost any claim for a test and are not required by law to establish the veracity of their claims.

Basic Issues in the Ethics of Testing

Despite the absence of a set of enforced ethical standards for assessment related activities, there are some ethical rules that seem to enjoy widespread, if not universal support. Ethical values with the greatest support are described in the following sections.

Tests Must Be Valid

The most basic ethical standard in assessment is the requirement for test validity. As described in Chapter 2, it is not the test that is valid, but the decisions based on test scores. In other words, it is the interpretation of tests that is most important.

Test publishers are responsible for ensuring that manuals and/or promotional materials that accompany tests assert validity only when the inferences they claim can legitimately be made. At the same time, it is the responsibility of the user to ensure that their tests are valid for the purposes for which they are being used and the individuals who are being assessed.

Student Assessment Should Not Be Biased

An assessment procedure that underestimates the ability or achievement of students is labeled as *biased*. The overestimation of performance is also a form of bias but there are fewer complaints from its 'victims.' Detecting bias is difficult because it requires a knowledge of the score a student would have gotten if the assessment was completely fair and unbiased. This score is referred to as the *true score* and it is compared with the actual or *obtained score*. When a test is described as biased, it is assumed that the obtained and the true score are systematically different. The problem with using true scores to explain bias is that they are unknowable. True scores are hypothetical entities because it is the test itself (the obtained score) that provides the best estimate of a true score. We have no way of differentiating between the true and obtained score; and without precise information about the true score, it is difficult to establish the existence of such differences.

Concern about test bias usually has as its foundation poor performance by a subpopulation. However, just because an individual or an identifiable group obtains scores that are below average, lower than what was expected, or lower than what might be wished, is not evidence of test bias. The detection of test bias, like unfairness, is dependent on the perspective of those evaluating a test. It should be expected that students will label a test biased or unfair when they feel that their score underestimates their true level of achievement or aptitude.

When the performance of minorities on an achievement test is below the average of their non-minority peers, it is tempting to explain the poor performance by focusing on the test and labeling it biased. In this way, defects in the way instruction is presented to minority students can be excused. Poor achievement test performance may in actuality be an indication that there is something wrong with instruction, curriculum, or teaching methods. The glib use of 'bias' can be used to excuse the poor performance of those responsible for an educational program in which minority students are not performing well.

Types of Bias

Sometimes a distinction is made between *vernacular bias* and *statistical bias*. Vernacular bias is the term used to describe the existence of group differences. From this perspective, bias exists when groups differ. This is not a useful way to define bias because it is based on circular logic. First, differences between groups are presented as evidence of test bias and second, bias is used as an explanation of why there are differences in test score performance. It is not enough to demonstrate that differences exist, there must be evidence that the test scores are underestimating a student's true level of achievement. *Statistical bias* occurs when it can be established that an aptitude test under-predicts the performance of a student or students. For example, female students have higher grade point averages (GPAs) in both high school and college than males, but males obtain higher scores on academic aptitude tests such as the Scholastic Assessment Test (SAT). This appears to be a good example of statistical bias, although the spokespersons for the Educational Testing Service (the publisher of the SAT) deny this charge. They assert that the case for statistical bias has not been made, arguing that females have higher GPAs than their SATs predict because they take fewer math and science courses than males.

Test bias is a headache for test publishers, and contrary to popular belief, all test authors are not white males, purposefully constructing tests on which only those of their same sex and skin color can succeed. Such practices would not only be unethical, but more importantly, they would be bad for business. Publishing companies spend enormous amounts of money and put forth extraordinary effort to prevent their tests from being biased. Evidence that a test is free from bias is a marketing attribute of considerable value.

The most straightforward approach to ensuring that a test is not biased is to use an item by item approach in which the tainted items are removed. Unfortunately, this is not easily accomplished. The most obvious way to eliminate offending items is to have 'experts' examine each item individually for bias in content or construction. Unfortunately, experience has shown that constructing unbiased tests by identifying biased items is not easy. If eliminating bias was easy, there would be no biased tests because publishers would simply eliminate the offending items. They are certainly willing to expend the resources necessary to identify and remove items that appears tainted with bias. The problem with the use of experts to identify flawed items is that the results of such analyses often conflict with the empirical analyses of items. These analyses examine the difficulty of each item to determine whether or not it differs among subgroups. Experts often label items biased, that turn out to be equally difficult for all groups. At the same time, items identified by empirical analyses as being biased are often exonerated by experts who conclude that the items are completely okay. This has not dissuaded publishers from bringing together ethnically and gender balanced panels to identify items that appear unfair from the perspective of any interest group.

Only Those Who Are Competent Should Be Allowed to Administer and Interpret Tests

It is assumed that not everyone is equally qualified to administer, interpret, or possess tests. Qualification to administer one test should not imply competence in the use of others. This restriction applies to all standardized tests, but the most stringent legal restrictions are placed on psychological tests. In general, only licensed psychologists can administer or even possess these instruments, although state laws differ and there are many exceptions to these regulations. Other tests such as standardized achievement tests, should be restricted to those trained and competent in their use, but decisions about competency are left in the hands of the publisher or user. As the stakes for test performance have increased, the responsibilities for test performance have shifted from students to teachers and administrators. As a result, the credentials of those who administer tests have become even more important.

The use of standardized achievement tests by persons not qualified to use them or by those who are operating outside their area of expertise is clearly unethical, but it is not easy to determine who is qualified. Each individual must decide whether the use of a particular test is within the range of his or her expertise, and understand that not everyone who is legally qualified to use a test, is competent to do so.

Access to Test Materials Should Be Restricted to Those Who Are Competent To Use Them and Have a Legitimate Need to Possess Them

In the case of psychological tests, decisions about who should have access to test materials is straightforward. Only those who are qualified by law and training can use these tests. For other tests, issues of access can raise difficult ethical questions. Extensive training is not required for the administration of standardized ability and achievement tests, but if the public were given uncontrolled access, a diminution in validity would result. Usually classroom teachers administer standardized achievement tests, particularly in the lower grades and they obviously must have access to administer them. They also have access to copy machines. This creates an opportunity for the inappropriate dissemination of the test content. The possibility that copies of tests will end up in the hands of those who should not have access cannot be discounted. Copies of group ability tests used to determine admission to advanced and gifted classes, in the hands of the parents of children who are candidates for such programs, clearly compromise the validity of these tests.

Test publishers generally include sets of rules in their technical manuals that specify who is eligible to purchase their tests. They generally classify their tests into categories that range from those that can only be used by licensed psychologists to those that anyone is qualified to administer. In their efforts to control access to tests, test publishers sometimes are faced with a conflict of interest. They want to sell as many tests as possible and if there are restrictions placed on who can purchase tests, there will be fewer sales. In their catalogs and test manuals, test publishers generally include information such as purchaser qualification forms, information about who is and who is not qualified to order the different types of tests included in the catalog; and information about test ethics from the 1985 *Standards for Educational and Psychological Testing*, which specifies how testing should be conducted. Test publishing companies must make decisions about who will be actually allowed to purchase a particular test to an individual.

Standardized Achievement Tests Should Be Constructed and Administered in Such a Way that the Scores Accurately Reflect the Achievement of the Students Taking Them

The reporting of uniformly high standardized achievement test scores has occurred in states and school districts across the country (Cannell, 1988). Virtually every state and nearly every school district has reported mean levels of student performance that are above average. This phenomenon has been labeled 'the Lake Wobegon Effect' after Garrison Keilor's description of his hometown on the American Public Radio Program, A Prairie Home Companion, as a place, '. . . where all the women are strong, all the men are good-looking, and all the children are above average'.

From a statistical perspective it is impossible for every child or every state to be above average. Test publishers and the school districts and states that use these tests have been quick to defend themselves against suggestions of impropriety. Greater achievement by students since the tests were standardized is the usual explanation for these high scores. With a seven to eight year turn-around between revisions, there can be a sizable gap in time between the norming of a test and its use. The available evidence, however, fails to support this explanation. ACT and SAT scores have not shown a similar increase nor have the National Assessment of Educational Progress (NAEP) scores or the Armed Services Vocational Aptitude Battery (ASVAB) scores. Changes in the curriculum as a result of the testing process itself, is one possible explanation for the Lake Wobegon phenomenon. This is one consequence of measurement driven instruction. As the importance test results increases, the likelihood that the curriculum will be altered to fit what is being tested increases. Some of these alterations may be considered legitimate — to the extent that they do not involve teaching the test itself. Even in its most legitimate forms, altering curriculum to increase its match with test objectives will violate the sampling assumptions of the test and the resulting standard scores may lose their meaning.

Some teachers may teach the actual items from the test or administer the test in a non-standard way that causes scores to be inflated. They may erase or change items, point out the correct answer, or urge low achieving students not to attend school on the day of testing. Teachers also may provide inappropriate assistance when the test is administered or allow students to have more time to complete sections of the test that they otherwise would have had trouble completing in the allotted time. When high stakes are attached to achievement tests, these forms of misadministration can be expected to increase. When undue importance is placed on student performance and there is an absence of test administration supervision, the likelihood of cheating increases. All the way up the chain of command, those who are responsible for ensuring proper test administration procedures, have a second and perhaps more important interest in seeing the scores rise because they themselves are being evaluated by test scores. Administrators often face a conflict of interest and may be tempted to overlook inappropriate practices that lead to higher scores.

A teacher who is giving students too much time to complete a section of a test or helping students answer questions is guilty of cheating. Likewise, the teacher who drills students on actual items from a test is involved in a practice that would generally be perceived as inappropriate. At the other extreme, a teacher concerned about his or her student's performance on an achievement test, who works diligently to get his or her students to learn more, or who encourages students to put forth their best effort on a test, is not engaged in cheating. Such teacher behaviors would probably be viewed as exemplary. The grey area between poses ethical dilemmas. Teachers using similar items to those that appear on a test that is to be administered, or focusing instruction on those topics that are known to appear on the test, are engaging in practices that may be considered unethical. Such activities are not uncommon and are likely to be strongly defended by their practitioners. If modifications in curriculum lead to better performance on intended instructional objectives, the instructional time is well spent. If the instruction has no purpose other than raising the test scores, and does not address the learning objectives, such instruction is inappropriate and unethical.

The honest and accurate assessment of students using standardized achievement tests is dependent upon the ethics of the test publishers, school systems that adopt the test and those who administer the tests. Unfortunately, not everyone is in agreement about what the ethics should be. It is not the individual who knowingly violates ethical guidelines that is the problem. In most cases, those who appear not to be in compliance, are convinced that what they are doing is completely legitimate.

There are many who sincerely believe that all standardized testing is unethical. Those who believe this are not likely to be concerned about subtle breaches in what are considered correct procedures for test administration.

Mehrens and Kaminski (1989) describe various practices related to preparing students for standardized achievement testing. They do this by placing these practices on a continuum that ranges from those that nearly everyone would consider appropriate to those that seem clearly unacceptable. Their descriptive headings for the practices are listed below:

1 General instruction on objectives not determined by looking at the objectives measured on standardized tests.
2 Teaching test taking skills.
3 Instruction on objectives generated by a commercial organization where the objectives may have been determined by looking at objectives measured by a variety of standardized tests. (The objectives taught may, or may not, contain objectives on teaching test taking skills.)
4 Instruction based on objectives (skills, subskills) that specifically match those on the standardized test to be administered.
5 Instruction on specifically matched objectives (skills, subskills) where the practice (instruction) follows the same format as the test questions.
6 Practice (instruction) on a published parallel form of the same test.
7 Practice (instruction) on the same test (p.16).

The most difficult ethical decisions concern the acceptability of practices in the middle. According to Mehrens and Kaminski (1989), Practice 1 is always ethical, 6 and 7 are never ethical and decisions about those in between are open to debate and discussion. Based on the above list of practices, many common test preparation activities would not be considered ethical. The prevalence of such practices can be attributed to pressure on teachers and school administrators to obtain high test scores at any cost. They also may, at least partially, result from a lack of understanding about the ethical principles involved.

When high stakes assessment are administered, it is important that strict rules governing the handling of test materials and test administration procedures be in effect and that there be serious and certain consequences for violations of these rules. Susan Philips (1993) has produced a set of recommendations for ensuring test security for high stakes test administrations.

1 Ship test booklets so they arrive only a few days before testing. Require a responsible administrator sign a form acknowledging receipt and assuring that the materials will remain locked in a storage area with very limited access.
2 Allow only the minimum necessary time for testing and require all sites to test on the same day(s).
3 Require all testing materials to be returned immediately after resting.
4 Seal and number all test booklets and shrink wrap bundles of test booklets.

5   Require written assurance from test administrators at each site, that test booklets were opened only by examinees when told to do so during testing and that no booklets were photocopied.

6   Require test administrators to account for all testing materials before examinees are allowed to leave the room for lunch breaks or at the conclusion of testing.

7   Arrange for multiple-proctors in each testing room and allow only one student at a time to leave during testing.

8   Have all test administrators keep records of irregularities at the test site.

9   Investigate all reports of breaches of test security and sanction those involved in confirmed incidents.

10 Randomly audit test sites unannounced to ensure proper procedures are being followed.

11 Request that the legislature enact a statute or the state board adopt an administrative rule defining and providing sanctions for individual educators who engage in inappropriate test preparation activities and cheating.

12 Examine answer documents for tampering, excessive erasures, copying, and other signs of cheating. Screen group statistics and repeat testers for unusually large performance gains. Use suspicious findings to trigger appropriate investigations. (pp. 31, 32)

The Responses and Interpretations of a Test Belong to the Person Being Tested

The confidentiality of test results constitutes an important aspect of test ethics. Tests should be administered for the benefit of those being tested. The interpretations and responses upon which they are based belong to them. Informed consent is not required for school-related tests or job testing where permission is implicit in the job application or enrollment. Even if it is not a legal requirement, the purpose of the test and how it is to be used should be conveyed to students and their parents. In general, schools should avoid the assessment of personality, but when it is done, informed consent from parents should be obtained prior to test administration.

Assigning Grades

The grades a teacher assigns can also have an impact on the lives of students. Teachers are ethically bound to assign grades fairly, following accepted practices as outlined in Chapter 8. There is a consensus among testing specialists that grades should be based only on a student's achievement and that other factors such as effort, ability, neatness, and attitude should not influence grades. However, there is little consensus among practitioners on this issue and it cannot be easily elevated to the level of an ethical precept.

Summary

Ethics are rules for conduct that lie somewhere between the personal nature of morals and values, and laws which stem from a legislative process. Ethics represent a consensus view of how one should behave, and are enforced by organizations rather than by civil authority under the rule of laws. Although several different organizations have published ethical guidelines, there is a lack of consensus concerning exactly what is ethical and what is not with regard to student assessment. Furthermore, there are no sanctions for those who violate these ethical rules unless they also involve violations of the law or the rules of the school, school district or state. The ethics of classroom assessment are important because assessment is so important. The most important ethical issues surrounding educational assessment are as follows: bias, competence, access to test materials, appropriate test construction and administration practices, ownership of test results, and assigning grades.

Suggested Readings

AMERICAN PSYCHOLOGICAL ASSOCIATION (1974) *Standards for Educational and Psychological Testing*, Washington, D.C: Author.

AMERICAN FEDERATION OF TEACHERS, NATIONAL COUNCIL ON MEASUREMENT IN EDUCATION AND NATIONAL EDUCATION ASSOCIATION (1990) 'Standards for teacher competence in educational assessment of students,' *Educational Measurement: Issues and Practices*, **9**, 4, pp. 30–2.

CUNNINGHAM, G.K. (1986) *Educational and Psychological Measurement*, New York: Macmillan.

THORNDIKE, R.M., CUNNINGHAM, G.K., THORNDIKE, R.L. and HAGAN, E. (1991) *Measurement and Evaluation in Psychology and Education*, New York: Macmillan.

Appendix A: Assumptions and scaling

We use models to explain causal relationships among variables. A model is constructed from a series of statements that we believe to be true. We have no way of establishing the truth of these statements. They may be untestable, the cost of finding out about them may be prohibitively high, or they may represent an assertion that is either obvious or trivial. The unverified aspects of a model are handled by means of assumptions. An assumption is an assertion that we neither prove nor disprove, but that must be true in order for any conclusions about our model to be valid. Once an assumption is proven true, it is no longer an assumption, it is an established fact. In the event that our assumptions are not true, the conclusion drawn from any analysis based on them is invalid.

When you examine the results of a reading achievement test for an individual student you make a number of assumptions. You assume that the test was administered in a standardized fashion, that the student was given neither too much or too little time, and that there were no disruptions that interfered with his or her performance. Furthermore, you assume there was no mechanical breakdown in the scoring process, that the score reported is the correct one for the student and is not a transposition of another student's score. There is no easy way of testing all of these assumptions, but if one or several of them are not true, the results of the test may be invalid. If a child who has always been an excellent student — who has obtained good grades and high scores on similar tests — gets a low score on a reading achievement test, it may be appropriate to question some of the assumptions surrounding the test results.

Scales

The appropriateness of the mathematical treatment of numbers is a function of characteristics that we call scaling properties. The scaling properties of test scores and other data used in the social sciences are of interest because they determine the type of statistical analysis that can be employed. Concern about scaling has declined over the years, but during the 1950s and 1960s it was one of the hottest topics in the field of statistics. During that period, it was believed that much of the statistical analysis being performed in the social sciences was inappropriate because the data being analyzed was not of the proper scale for the statistical analyses being used. Eventually this view was altered, partially as a result of the consequences that were likely to result from a rigid adherence to scaling dogma. The statistical analyses appropriate for lower level scales are more difficult to implement, harder to understand and less sensitive than those developed for use with interval scale data. Diminishing concern about the problems of scaling also were the result of simulation studies which quantified the loss in precision that could be expected when statistical analyses were performed on data that was not of the correct scale. These analyses, made possible by the availability of more powerful computers, demonstrated the robustness of these statistics when scaling assumptions were violated.

Types of Scales

The scale of a set of data is not inherent, it is a function of what we designate it to be. In a more formal sense, it is determined by the assumptions we make — and of course the same assumptions are not reasonably associated with all scores. By definition assumptions are never tested. When assumptions are inappropriate, the resulting analysis of data may be flawed and the inaccuracy introduced will be unknown.

Data can be classified into one of four scales: nominal, ordinal, interval, or ratio.

Nominal Scales

The most basic type of measurement involves placing objects or person into categories. For example, we can divide a group of people into males and females and label them *M* or *F*, *A* or *B*, or any other code that we might find appropriate or convenient. Often numbers are used, such as a 1 for males and a 2 for females. Other examples of nominal data are religious affiliation, ethnic background, and marital status. The main assumption on which the nominal scale is based is the requirement of *equivalence*. This means that subjects in the same category cannot be different with respect to the classification attribute, and subjects in different categories cannot be the same with respect to that attribute. If we assign numeral 1 to freshmen, numeral 2 to sophomores, numeral 3 to juniors, and numeral 4 to seniors, everyone assigned numeral 2 must be a sophomore and no one assigned numerals 1, 3, or 4 can be a sophomore.

When we use numerals as labels, they indicate differences, not ranking or hierarchy. For instance, in a school district there might be four high schools. Each student is in one high school, and a student can not simultaneously be in two different schools. We could label them 1, 2, 3, and 4, but this would not mean that school 4 was better than the other three or had more of any attribute than the others.

Suppose a group of judges observes the behavior of children on a playground. The judges provide a set of scores assessing each child's behavior on a number of different dimensions. The judges are particularly interested in studying the misbehavior of children in this setting and decide to classify misbehavior into one of three categories: (1) overly aggressive behavior, (2) dangerous behavior, such as jumping off the top of a jungle gym; and (3) whining and crying behavior. In order to simplify the recording of the children's behavior it is convenient to use a code.

A 1 could be assigned to the first category, a 2 to the second, and a 3 to the third. It should be obvious that these assigned numerals should not be treated as numbers and included in mathematical computations as though they were. They are clearly nominal scale data.

Ordinal Scales

When it is possible to assume that categories can be ranked, they take on the properties of the next higher level, which is the ordinal scale. For instance, the judges, observing behavior on the playground, might focus on aggressive behaviors and categorize children into three groups according to the frequency of their aggressive behavior. We have now established a relationship between three categories, and the magnitude of the numbers takes on meaning because they indicate order. We could give the children who are most often aggressive a score of 3, those who are least often aggressive a score of 1, and those in between a score 2. We could just as easily use the number 5, 7 and 132, but their use would likely cause confusion.

Numerals are an efficient way of indicating rank order, but they do not bear any direct relationship to the actual amount of the attribute. If we administer a math test to 35 students in a class, the number of items correct could be used to rank order the students with the best student assigned a rank of 35 and the worst a rank of 1. The student ranked 35 may have gotten 3 more items correct than the student ranked 34, but the difference between the 34th and 33rd student could only be one item or it might be 10. Knowledge of rank order tells us nothing about how much difference there is.

When we have an ordinal scale, if two subjects are placed in separate categories, one or the other must have a higher ranking. They cannot be equal. If $A \neq B$, then either $A > B$, or $A < B$. This characteristic is called *connectedness*. If $A > B$, then B cannot be greater than A. This quality is *asymmetry*. Furthermore, if A has more of a quality than B and B has more of a quality than C, then A must have more of the quality than C. This is called *transitivity*.

Not all ordinal scale data are the same, and it makes sense to think of two kinds. First of all, there are ordinal data that consist of mere ranking categories. They are just a step up from nominal scale data and should not be treated in any other way than as though they were pure ordinal scale data. This sort of ordinal scale data will be referred to as Type 1 ordinal scale data. Occupations ranked according to their status is an example of a Type 1 ordinal scale. Contrast this with the results of a teacher-made test. Strictly speaking, they are not interval data because the intervals between scores are not precisely uniform. However, treating them as nothing more than Type 1 ordinal scale data, would also be a mistake. They are almost, but not quite, interval scale data and are therefore called Type 2 ordinal scale data. The intervals between occupations, ranked according to their status, does not have such regularity, but classroom tests do. Test scores that are deemed to be Type 2 ordinal scale data can be and are treated as though they were of an interval scale.

Interval Scales

With interval scale data, the numbers attached to objects or persons refer to the amount of the attribute, rather than mere relative position in a series. We not only can say that *A* has more of a trait than *B*, but also how much more of the trait *A* has. A ruler is an interval scale (as you shall see, it is also a ratio scale) and it is legitimate to conclude that 3 inches plus 4 inches is the same as 5 inches plus 2 inches. This characteristic is called 'additivity'; without it we can not justifiable add, subtract, multiply, and/or divide. For individuals ranked in terms of tennis ability, it would be wrong to say that the difference between the first and the second and the ninth and tenth rated players is the same. Furthermore it would not be fair to make up a doubles team consisting of the first- and fourth-rated player and think that they would be equal to one consisting of the second- and third-rated players, even though their rating in both cases sums to five. The number 1 player might be far superior to the other three or the 4th rated player could be far worse. Only if their ability was measured on an interval scale would a tennis match based on these pairings be fair. The importance of the assumption of an interval scale resides in the mathematical properties it confers. Mathematical computations on actual scale can only be conducted on either interval, ratio, or Type 2 ordinal scale data and not with nominal or Type 1 ordinal data. Test scores and the results of most psychological instruments are assumed to have meaningful intervals, which permits mathematical computations.

With interval scales we do not know about the relative magnitude of scores because we have not established an absolute zero. It is incorrect to say that one student is twice as intelligent as another. This is because psychological measurements typically use the mean as a point of reference, and a person's score is interpreted in terms of variability around the mean. We do not really know what it means to say that a person has an IQ of zero or what a zero would mean on a self-concept scale.

Ratio Scales

Ratio scales differ from interval scales by having a zero point that is not arbitrary. With a ratio scale, zero represents the complete absence of the relevant trait. When a scale has this characteristic, statements about the relative amount of the trait possessed by an individual are permitted. It is correct to say that one child is twice as tall as another child because height is measured on a ratio scale; but it is not acceptable to assert that one child has twice the reading ability of another child. This is because reading ability is measured only on an interval scale. Test scores are never ratio scale data and one must search diligently for examples of the use of ratio scales in the social sciences. Height, weight, and time are examples of ratio scales, as is Kelvin Temperature (Fahrenheit and Celsius are only of an interval scale).

Table E.1: Description of scales

Scales	Assumptions		Descriptions	Examples
Nominal	Equivalence		Individuals are placed into categories	Occupation Sex Race
Ordinal	Equivalence Connectedness Asymmetry Transitivity	Type 1	Individuals are placed into categories and are ranked	Ranking of tennis players Class rank
		Type 2	Individuals are placed on a continuum characterized by a scale on which the units may not be completely uniform	Classroom test scores Grade point average
Interval	Equivalence Connectedness Asymmetry Transitivity Additivity		Individuals are placed on a continuum characterized by a scale on which the units have uniform intervals.	IQ scores Standardized test scores Fahrenheit and Celsius
Ratio	Equivalence Connectedness Asymmetry Transitivity Additivity An absolute zero		The same characteristics inhere as for interval data, except ratio scale data have an absolute zero	Height Weight Kelvin temperature

Assigning the Appropriate Scale to Data

The four scales are cumulative. Ordinal scale data are at the same time nominal, and data that are interval are both nominal and ordinal. Ratio scale data, therefore, have all of the properties of nominal, ordinal, and interval scales, along with those characteristics that make ratio scales unique. Each step up the scaling ladder assumes the characteristics of the subordinate levels. The different scales are described in Table E.1.

Assumptions

The relevance of assumptions must be kept in mind when the scaling properties of sets of data are considered. We make assumptions about the scaling characteristics of data that we have no easy way of verifying. In the event that our assumptions are wrong, the validity of our results is likely to be adversely affected.

Continuous and Discrete Data

Another way of illustrating a distinction among these scales is in term of *continuous* and *discrete* data. With discrete data there are no decimal values. A subject is assigned a 1, a 2, or a 3, with no values in between. Nominal data and most ordinal data are discrete. Interval and ratio data are generally considered continuous and can have values that are intermediate between integers, in the form of decimals. You must be aware, however, that it is possible to have data reported in decimal values, which does not meet the criteria necessary for an interval scale.

Appendix B: Computation of the standard deviation

Instead of a single formula, as is the case with the mean, there is a family of algebraically equivalent formulas for computing the standard deviation. Included are a definitional and several computational formulas. The definitional formula is used to help students understand how the standard deviation reflects the amount of dispersion in a set of scores. Computational formulas, as their name implies, provide the easiest method of computing the standard deviation with a calculator. Developments in computer software and the availability of increasingly powerful hand calculators have diminished the importance of the computational formulas.

The definitional formula is as follows:

$$\sigma = \sqrt{\frac{\Sigma x^2}{N}}$$

σ = the standard deviation
Σx^2 = the sum of the deviations squared
N = the number of cases

An example of the computation of the standard deviation using the definitional formula appears in Figure E.1.

To compute the standard deviation using the computational formula as illustrated in Figure E.2, you need only know the sum of the scores ΣX, the sum of the square of each score (ΣX^2) and N. It is important that you understand that these are large Xs representing scores not small xs representing deviations such as were used with the definitional formula. The standard deviation obtained using the computational formula will always be the same as the standard deviation obtained from the definitional formula because the two are algebraically equivalent. Although it may seem more complex, the computational formula includes simpler mathematical operations than those used with the definitional formula, particularly when the standard deviation is being computed for a large number of scores. If a calculator with two memory stores is used, the apparent complexity of the computational formula is diminished.

It is possible to examine the definitional formula and get a feel for what mathematical processes are taking place, but the computational formula is of little use in conveying the underlying mathematical meaning of the formula. The computational formula is seldom used anymore because of the availability of powerful calculators and more convenient statistical computer software.

Figure E.1: Computation of the standard deviation using the definitional formula

Score (X)		Mean $\bar{X}$	Deviations $x = X - \bar{X}$	Squared Deviations x^2
7	–	4	3	9
4	–	4	0	0
2	–	4	−2	4
1	–	4	−3	9
7	–	4	3	9
4	–	4	0	0
4	–	4	0	0
3	–	4	−1	1

$\Sigma X = 32 \qquad \Sigma x = 0 \qquad \Sigma x^2 = 32$

$$\sigma = \sqrt{\frac{32}{8}} = \sqrt{4} = 2$$

1 The first step in computing the standard deviation is to compute the mean. Remember the mean is the sum of all of the scores (ΣX) which in this case is 32, divided by the number of scores (N). The mean of these scores is therefore 32 divided by 8. The mean is therefore 4.
2 Next the mean (4) is subtracted from every score. The resulting value is called the deviation which is represented by a small x.
3 The deviations are squared and summed. This value is represented by the following symbol: Σx^2. In this case Σx^2 equals 32. It is a coincidence that both ΣX and Σx^2 are the same value.
4 The standard deviation is computed by finding the square root of the Σx^2 divided by N. Since 32 divided by 8 is 4 and the square root of 4 is 2, the standard deviation is 2.

Figure E.2: Computation of the standard deviation using the 'computational' formula

Score (X)	Score squared X^2
7	49
4	16
2	4
1	1
7	49
4	16
4	16
3	9

$\Sigma X = 32 \qquad \Sigma X^2 = 160$

$$\sigma = \sqrt{\frac{\Sigma x^2 - \frac{(\Sigma x)^2}{N}}{N}} = \sqrt{\frac{160 - \frac{1024}{8}}{8}} = \sqrt{\frac{160 - 128}{8}} = \sqrt{\frac{32}{8}} = \sqrt{4} = 2$$

Estimating Populations from Samples

It is not unusual to see either the computational or definitional formulas written with $n - 1$ as the denominator instead of just N, which we have used up to this point. This is because the meaning and interpretation of the standard deviation changes depending on how it is being employed. Up until now, we have viewed the standard deviation and variance as measures of variability that stood alone as descriptors of the set of data with which we were interested. However, in the field of statistics, we are often concerned with the relationship between samples and populations and in using statistics to estimate the parameters of the population.

The mean of a sample is an unbiased estimator of the mean of the population. In other words, the estimate of the mean of a population, based on the mean of a sample drawn randomly from the population is just as likely to overestimate as underestimate this value. This is why the mean provides a good estimate of the central tendency of the population. The standard deviation and variance, when computed using the formulas presented up to this point, are biased estimators. They consistently underestimate the population parameter. This underestimation is greatest for small samples and less noticeable for larger samples. For this reason when one wishes to make inferences about the variability of the population, it is necessary to change the formula for computing the variance and standard deviation in such a way that they no longer underestimate these values. This is done by changing the denominator from N to $n - 1$. The symbols for the standard deviation and variance changes from σ and σ^2 to s and s^2 when $n - 1$ is used as the denominator. These changes in symbols are not made merely to confuse students, but to inform the consumer of such statistics about whether sample or population statistics are being employed.

Appendix C: Description of the normal curve

The term 'normal curve' refers to a mathematically defined curve such as is shown in Figure E.3. Along with its mathematical properties, the normal curve has a distinctive shape (a bell shaped curve). If you measure a randomly occurring phenomenon repeatedly and create a graph in which frequencies are represented vertically, the resulting curve can be expected to take on the characteristic bell shape of the normal curve, tall in the center and shorter at both extremes (it will resemble the curve seen in Figure E.3). Similarly, if you examine the results of students' performance on a test, you will find that most students are about average and there are relatively few scores at either extreme. Of course, there are naturally occurring phenomena that do not yield a normal distribution. Classroom tests that are either too easy or too hard will have scores piled up at the extremes and will not be normally distributed.

Take a coin and flip it ten times. Count the number of times it comes up heads, and then repeat the process many times. If you construct a histogram of the number of heads you get in each ten flips, you will have a bell shaped normal distribution similar to the one in Figure E.4. The number of heads you get most often will be 5. The frequency of 4 or 6 will also be high. Less often, it will be heads either 3 times or 7 times. Very seldom will heads come up ten times or zero times, but this will occur occasionally if there are enough trials. Although a small number of trials may not provide a very good approximation, of a normal curve, the more trials you use, the closer you will approach the classic bell shape. If the first several trials deviate from the expected shape, do not expect the next trials to compensate. Each new trial is independent of what happened before. The reason large samples, or a large number of trials, leads to closer approximations to the normal curve is that the values that do not fit the model — which can be expected to happen occasionally — will have a minor effect in the presence of many other trials. It is of course possible, in a finite number of trials, for any shape to emerge. It is possible, although certainly unlikely, to have every flip of a coin come up heads in trial after trial.

The same shaped distribution we get by flipping coins can also be obtained by tossing dice, spinning a roulette wheel, dealing cards or utilizing the results of other games of chance or other processes in which chance plays the dominant role. It should not come as a surprise that naturally occurring events, such as the height of a large number of army enlistees, trace a normal curve similar to that obtained by tossing dice or flipping coins. In very large samples, the genetic and environmental factors that determine height involve chance combinations that can reasonably be

Figure E.3: A normal distribution

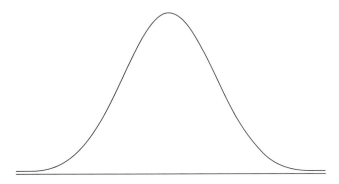

Figure E.4: A distribution of 100 trials of 10 coin flips

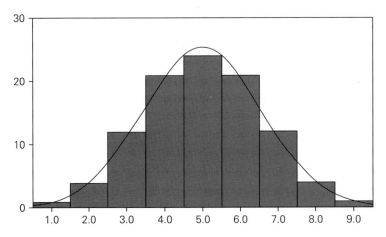

considered random. Some factors may raise a person's height above the mean and others may push it below, but with a large sample, these various factors will cancel each other causing most heights to be close to the mean.

The investigations of the normal curve was prompted by attempts to understand probability and was partially a response to the needs of gamblers. They believed they could use a knowledge of the probabilities of certain events happening to improve their chances at gaming tables. One of the earliest mathematical treatments of probability is found in *Ars Conjectandi* written by James Bernoulli in the seventeenth century. Bernoulli developed a method for determining the probability of an event occurring a specified number of times over a given number of trials when the probability of the event occurring in one trial was known.

When Bernoulli was developing these formulas, computers and calculators were of course not available and the required computations are quite daunting to even the most skilled mathematicians. Not only are they complex, the actual computations take a prohibitively long time. In the search to discover a solution to this

Figure E.5: *Normal curve with points of deflection*

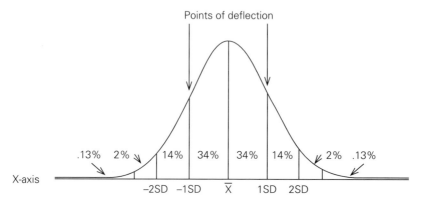

Points of deflection

.13%   2%   14%   34%   34%   14%   2%   .13%

X-axis

−2SD −1SD $\overline{X}$ 1SD   2SD

problem, an interesting phenomenon was discovered. It was found that a graph of probabilities computed using the Bernoulli formulas traces a bell shaped curve. This led mathematicians to the conclusion that a mathematical function that defined the curve could be used to solve probability problems more easily than the Bernoulli function.

To satisfy this need, De Moivre devised a mathematical formula that approximated the naturally occurring normal curve and greatly simplified the problems of computing probabilities. The formula is too complex to reproduce here, but sophisticated calculators as well as computers with the appropriate software can compute the probability of a wide variety of chance occurrences.

Characteristics of the Normal Curve

The normal curve has three important characteristics. The point of deflection, or the place where the curve switches from concave to convex, occurs one standard deviation on either side of the mean. This is illustrated in Figure E.5. The second is that the normal curve never touches the X-axis. No matter how far along the axis one goes away from the mean, the possibility of a score still exists. The third is that with the normal curve there is a fixed proportion of cases between any two points along the X-axis. This third characteristic can be seen in Figure E.5 where the proportion of cases for different standard deviations away from the mean are indicated. These are not the only differences that are known. Many statistics books contain tables which include the difference between the mean and the decimal value of the standard deviation to two places.

This last characteristic of the normal curve is of particular importance for two reasons. (1) It is this characteristic of the normal curve that permits the probability statements used in inferential statistics. It provides the rationale for a researcher, to conclude that the difference between the mean score of two samples would occur by chance, less than 5 per cent of the time. (2) It also permits the computation of the normalized standard scores described in Appendix F.

Figure E.6: Examples of deviations from normality

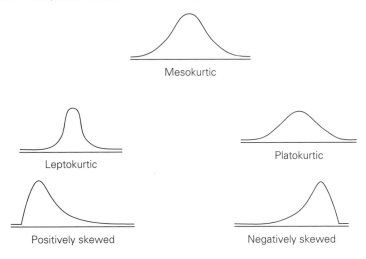

Mesokurtic

Leptokurtic

Platokurtic

Positively skewed

Negatively skewed

Variations in the Normal Distribution

There is not one normal distribution but a family of distributions. Some of these may not look like the classic normal distribution, but may still possess the mathematical properties of the normal curve. The classic bell-shaped curve is a standard normal curve with a mean of zero and a standard deviation of one. Two important variations from the classic bell shape are defined as *kurtosis* and *skewness*.

Kurtosis refers to the degree to which a curve tends toward being more pointed (leptokurtic) or flatter (platykurtic) than the classic bell shape, which is described as mesokurtic. The larger the standard deviation, as compared to the mean, the more platykurtic the distribution, and the smaller the standard deviation the more leptokurtic. The kurtosis of a distribution can vary, and the distribution may still meet the requirements for normality.

Regardless of the relative size of the mean and standard deviation, the normal distribution is always symmetrical around the mean. Lack of symmetry is referred to as skewness. If you construct a histogram of the results of a test and the test is too easy, the scores will pile up at the high end. In this case we say that the curve is skewed negatively (the direction of the skewness is determined by the location of the tail of the curve). If the test is too hard, the scores pile up at the bottom end of the distribution and we label the curve as positively skewed. Kurtosis and skewness are illustrated in Figure E.6.

There are many other ways that a distribution can differ from the classic bell shape of the normal distribution. It could be rectangular — that is, every score could occur with equal frequency. Instead of one peak at the center of the distribution, it could have two and be bimodal or have many peaks and be multimodal.

Appendix D: Computation of correlation coefficients

As was the case for the standard deviation, there are both definitional and computational formulas for computing correlation coefficients. The computational formula is quite intimidating to the non-mathematically inclined, although it is really more lengthy than complex. Only examples of computations using the definitional formula are provided. The two formulas for computing correlations are as follows:

The definitional formula

$$r = \frac{\sum z_x z_y}{N}$$

The computational formula

$$r = \frac{N\sum XY - \sum X \sum Y}{\sqrt{N\sum X^2 - (\sum X)^2}\ \sqrt{N\sum X^2 - (\sum Y)^2}}$$

To compute a correlation using the definitional formula, you must first convert each raw score into a z-score. The formula for computing z-scores is as follows:

$$z\text{-score} = \frac{X - \overline{X}}{\sigma}$$

where:
X = a raw score
$\overline{X}$ = the mean
σ = the standard deviation

The paired z-scores are cross multiplied, summed, and divided by the number of pairs of scores to obtain the correlation coefficient.

An Example of a Positive Correlation

In Table E.2 the correlation coefficient between reading and math scores for eight students is computed using the definitional formula. Consider student A who has a raw score of 70. Since the math test has a mean ($\overline{X}$) of 40 and a standard deviation (σ) of 20 that student's z-score is 1.50 (70 minus 40 divided by 20 is 1.50). The remainder of the raw scores are converted to z-scores in a similar manner.

Table E.2:   An example of a positive correlation

Student	Math		Reading		Cross-products
	Raw score	z-score	Raw score	z-score	
A	70	1.50	80	1.00	1.50
B	40	0	30	−.67	0
C	20	−1.00	30	−.67	.67
D	10	−1.50	10	−1.33	1.99
E	70	1.5	100	1.67	2.50
F	40	0	80	1.00	0
G	40	0	30	−.67	0
H	30	−.50	40	−.33	.16

$$\overline{X} = 40 \qquad\qquad \overline{X} = 50 \qquad\qquad \sum z_x z_y = 6.81$$
$$\sigma = 20 \qquad\qquad \sigma = 30$$

$$r = \frac{\sum z_x z_y}{N} = \frac{6.81}{8} = .85$$

The correlation coefficient is obtained by multiplying the z-scores for math by the z-scores for reading, summing these cross-products and dividing by the number of pairs. The cross-products sum to 6.81 and when this is divided by the number of pairs, a correlation coefficient of .85 is obtained. Notice how positive z-scores are multiplied by positive z-scores and negative z-values by negative z-values. In both cases the result is a positive cross-product. Under these circumstances the sum of the cross-products is relatively large, and when divided by the number of pairs it yields a fairly high correlation coefficient.

An Example of a Near-zero Correlation

In Table E.3 the computation of the correlation between a math test score and a test of physical education proficiency (PEPT) is computed. As can be seen, a near zero correlation coefficient is obtained. The two variables are obviously unrelated. In some cases (for example, Student E) a high score in math is associated with a high PEPT score; in others a low score in math is associated with a low score on the PEPT (for example, student C). In both situations the resulting cross-product is positive because positive values multiplied by positive values and negative values multiplied by negative values both yield positive products. In other cases high scores in math are paired with low scores on the PEPT (for example Student A), or a low score in math is paired with high scores on the PEPTS (for example, Student D). In both of these situations the resulting cross-products are negative because when a positive and a negative value are multiplied, the product is negative. When all of the cross-products are added, the sum is a small value because the negative values cancel the positive values. In the case of the data in Table E.3, the sum of the cross products is .34. When this is divided by the number of students (N=8) the resulting correlation coefficient is only .042.

Table E.3: *An example of a near zero correlation*

Student	Math		PEPT		Cross-products
	Raw score	**z-score**	**Raw score**	**z-score**	
A	70	1.50	30	−.67	−1.00
B	40	0	40	−.33	0
C	20	−1.00	10	−1.33	1.33
D	10	−1.50	100	1.67	−2.50
E	70	1.5	80	1.00	1.50
F	40	0	80	1.00	0
G	40	0	30	−.67	0
H	30	−.50	30	−.67	.33

$$\overline{X} = 40 \qquad \overline{X} = 50 \qquad \sum z_x z_y = .34$$
$$\sigma = 20 \qquad \sigma = 30$$

$$r = \frac{\sum z_x z_y}{N} = \frac{.34}{8} = .042$$

Table E.4: *An example of a negative correlation*

Student	Reading		Hours of TV		Cross-products
	Raw score	**z-score**	**Raw score**	**z-score**	
A	80	1.00	3	−.5	−.50
B	30	−.67	4	0	0
C	30	.67	4	0	0
D	10	−1.33	7	1.2	−1.99
E	100	1.67	1	−1.5	−2.50
F	80	1.00	2	−1.0	−1.00
G	30	−.67	7	1.5	−1.00
H	40	−.33	4	0	0

$$\overline{X} = 40 \qquad \overline{X} = 4 \qquad \sum z_x z_y = -6.99$$
$$\sigma = 20 \qquad \sigma = 2$$

$$r = \frac{\sum z_x z_y}{N} = \frac{-6.99}{8} = -.874$$

An Example of a Negative Correlation

When two sets of data are negatively correlated, positive z-value are paired with negative values and vice versa. As a result, the sum of the cross-products is negative and relative large when compared to the denominator. When the sum of the cross-products is negative, the correlation coefficient will also be negative. This is illustrated in Table E.4, where reading test scores are correlated with the average number of hours of television watched per day. Notice how the best readers are the ones who watch the least television and vice versa.

Why the Correlation Can Never Exceed ± 1

In order to understand why the correlation can never exceed 1, positively or negatively, consider how a variable could be related to another variable in such a way as to yield the highest possible correlation. This would occur in the correlation of the performance of students on two tests on which every student performed the same on both tests. When this occurs, the z-scores for each pair of scores will be the same. When this happens, the mathematical procedures for computing the correlation between the two scores becomes the same as those used to compute the standard deviation of the z-scores of the scores. To compute the standard deviation of a set of z-scores, you square the z-scores, sum them, divide by the number of scores and determine the square root. There is no need to compute the deviations, because for z-scores the deviations are the same as the z-scores. (Subtracting a mean of zero from z-scores does not change their value.) When you compute the correlation between two sets of identical scores, the z-scores for each pair are the same. In effect you are squaring the z-scores and dividing by the number of scores. Since the sum of the squared z-scores always equals the number of scores, both the computation of the standard deviation of z-scores and the correlation of the same scores yields a value of 1. With the standard deviation you must compute the square root, but this does not change anything because the square root of 1 is 1.

Computational Formula

Other than for instructional purposes, correlations are seldom computed without the aid of a computer. There is seldom any practical use for the computational formula. Even a calculator sophisticated enough to compute correlations directly is not of much help because the amount of data and number of buttons to push results in a high likelihood of error. When an error is made, the entire process of entering data must be started again. Even when no error occurs there is a tendency to think that there was, and it is difficult to suppress the urge to repeat the computations as a check. If the results of the two computations are not in agreement, a third computation must be performed in hopes that it will match one of the previous two. This problem is exacerbated by the fact that we seldom compute a single correlation, but are unusually interested in a series of correlations or intercorrelations, which makes the computation of correlations without the aid of a computer impractical.

Appendix E: Computation of percentiles

The percentile ranks of students in a class are computed by dividing each student's rank in the class by the total number of students and multiplying by 100 to eliminate the decimal. For example, a 60 item test is administered to 35 students in a class. To compute percentile ranks, the students must be placed in rank order with the best student ranked 35 and the poorest performing student ranked as 1. Suppose Bob is ranked 25th in his class. His percentile rank is computed by dividing 25 by 35 which is .7143. When this number is multiplied by 100 and rounded off he is assigned a percentile rank of 71. As you can see the computation of percentiles is easy if you know a student's rank. Establishing rank becomes difficult when each student does not have a unique score. This will occur when several students get the same number of items correct.

There is a slightly different, more mathematically complex system for computing the percentile rank when more than one student gets the same score. It is called the *cumulative midpoint* method of computing percentile ranks and it requires the assumption that each score is represented by an interval and the appropriate rank of a score is the midpoint within the interval. The cumulative midpoint is determined by adding a value equal to one half of the number of scores in an interval to the number of scores below the interval. This is done whether the interval contains one or several scores. In Table E.5 you will note that no one received a score of 40 or 41 and therefore they have percentiles of zero. One person received a score of 1. The cumulative midpoint of 1 is .5 and .5 divided by 12 is .04166. When this value is multiplied by 100 and rounded, the percentile is 4.

Consider the percentile rank of a score of 47. There are six students who obtained scores below 47 and three who obtained scores of 47. The cumulative midpoint of 47 is obtained by adding one half the scores in the interval ($\frac{1}{2} \times 3 = 1.5$) to the number of scores below 47. Adding 1.5 to 6 results in a cumulative midpoint of 7.5 for a raw score of 47. The percentile rank is 62.5 [$((7.5 \div 12) \times 100) = 62.5$].

Table E.5: Computation of percentiles

Score	Frequency	Cumulative Midpoint	Percentile
50	0	12.0	100
49	1	11.5	96
48	2	10.0	83
47	3	7.5	62
46	2	5.0	42
45	2	3.0	25
44	1	1.5	12
43	0	1.0	8
42	1	.5	4
41	0	00	0
40	0	00	0

Appendix F: Computing normalized *T*-scores

Non-normalized *T*-scores, like *z*-scores, are linear transformations that maintain the shape of the original distribution. If a set of raw scores is negatively skewed, it can be anticipated that the distribution of *T*-scores will also be negatively skewed. Likewise, if the raw scores have a bell shape, so will the transformed distribution. Under some circumstances it is desirable to take a distribution of raw scores that is close to being normally distributed and adjust the scores so that they are normally distributed. This should only be done when the normality of the distribution is supported by an underlying theoretical rationale.

In the normalization process, the *z*-scores used to compute normalized *T*-scores are not obtained with the usual *z*-score formula. It is instead derived from statistical tables found in the appendices of many statistics books that provide the proportion of the normal curve between the mean and points along the x-axis. This distance along the x-axis is defined in terms of the proportion of standard deviations or *z*-scores. To transform a set of raw scores into normalized *T*-scores, each raw score must be changed into a percentile rank which obliterates the original shape of the distribution by forcing it into the characteristic shape of all percentiles, which is rectangular.

Percentiles must be changed into proportions of the normal curve which can be transformed into *z*-scores using statistical tables. To do this for percentiles greater than 50, subtract 50 from the percentile and place a decimal to its left. If the percentile is less than 50, it is subtracted from 50, a decimal is placed to its left and a negative sign attached. Consider a percentile of 67. If you subtract 50 and add a decimal to its left the proportion of the normal curve will be .17. In the appropriate statistical table, this proportion of the normal curve is equivalent to a *z*-score of .44. To compute the *z*-score of a percentile of 33, subtract 33 from 50 which is of course 17. A decimal is affixed to its left making it .17. From the statistical table a *z*-score of .44 which would be read as −.44. Few statistical tables are detailed enough to include every possible decimal value for proportions of the normal curve. In interpreting the table, the nearest proportion of the curve should be chosen or interpolation can be used to obtain the exact value.

Figure E.6 is a graph of the percentiles from Table E.5. As can be seen this is not a normal distribution. It is skewed negative. Figure E.7 is a graph of the same set of scores that have been normalized. Although the distribution is not now perfectly normal, the normalized *T*-scores provide a closer approximation of such a distribution.

Figure E.7: Non-normalized T-scores

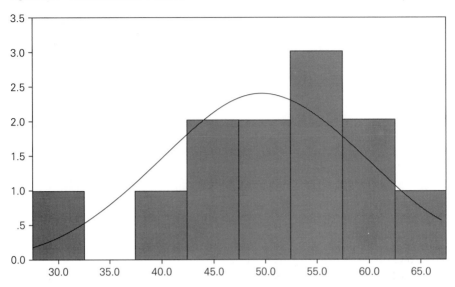

Figure E.8: Normalized T-scores

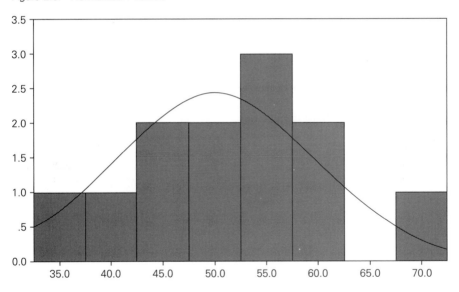

Appendix G: Computation of coefficient alpha and KR-21

The most powerful method of computing reliability is through the use of Coefficient Alpha. It can be used to determine the reliability of tests that are made up of objective items scored as right or wrong, or essay items assigned a wider range of scores. It can also be used to evaluate the reliability of personality tests made up of a series of statements to which the respondent indicates their position on a scale. Typically a scale with 'strongly agree' as one anchor and 'strongly disagree' as the other is used with 5 to 7 points in between. The formula for the computation of Coefficient Alpha follows:

$$\text{Coefficient Alpha} = \frac{k}{k-1}\left(1 - \frac{\sum \sigma_i^2}{\sigma_t^2}\right)$$

where

k = the number of items
σ_i^2 = the variance of each item
$\sum \sigma_i^2$ = the sum of the variance of each item
σ_t^2 = the variance of each item

To perform this computation it is necessary to know the mean, number of items, and the variance. These are easily obtained, but you also need to know the variance of each item. Hand calculation of these values is not practical. A spreadsheet can be used to perform these computations, but the response of each student to every item is required. A 50 item test administered to 35 students requires the entry of data into 1,750 cells. Realistically, the computation of Coefficient Alpha really requires machine scoring of answer sheets and computer analysis.

For tests made up of items that are scored as right or wrong there is an easier method based on a formula called KR-21 which provides an estimate of Coefficient Alpha. This formula requires the assumption that all items have the same difficulty. When this assumption is violated, KR-21 will underestimate reliability. The KR-21 formula is as follows:

$$\text{KR-21 reliability} = \frac{k}{k-1}\left(1 - \frac{\overline{X}(k - \overline{X})}{k\sigma^2}\right)$$

where
k = the number of items
$\overline{X}$ = the mean of the test
σ^2 = the variance of the scores

This is a convenient computation which should routinely be used with all classroom tests. It requires only information about the number of items, the mean, and the variance for each item; all of which can be easily obtained with a calculator. It does not require the statistics for individual items which greatly simplifies computations.

If a test has forty questions, a mean of 30 and a variance of 16, the reliability would be .54

$$\text{KR-21 reliability} = \frac{40}{40-1}\left[1 - \frac{30(40-30)}{40(16)}\right] = .54$$

References

AIRASIAN, P.W. (1991) *Classroom Assessment*, McGraw Hill: New York.

AMERICAN PSYCHOLOGICAL ASSOCIATION (1974) *Standards for Educational and Psychological Testing*, Washington, DC: American Psychological Association.

AMERICAN FEDERATION OF TEACHERS, NATIONAL COUNCIL ON MEASUREMENT IN EDUCATION, & NATIONAL EDUCATION ASSOCIATION (1990) 'Standards for teacher competence in educational assessment of students', *Educational Measurement: Issues and Practices*, **9**, 4, pp. 30–32.

AMERICAN PSYCHOLOGICAL ASSOCIATION, AMERICAN EDUCATIONAL RESEARCH ASSOCIATION, & NATIONAL COUNCIL ON MEASUREMENT IN EDUCATION (1985) *Standards for Educational and Psychological Testing*, Washington, DC: American Psychological Association.

ANGOFF, W.H. (1971) 'Scales, norms, and equal scores', in THORNDIKE, R.L. (ed.) *Educational Measurement*, Washington DC: American Council on Education, pp. 508–600.

ARTER, J.A. and SPANDEL, V. (1992) 'Using portfolios of student work in instruction and assessment', *Educational Measurement: Issues and Practices*, **11**, 1, pp. 36–43.

ASHBURY, R.R. (1938) 'An experiment in the essay-type question', *The Journal of Experimental Education*, **7**, pp. 1–3.

BAGLIN, R.F. (1981) 'Does "nationally" normed really mean nationally?', *Journal of Educational Measurement*, **18**, 2, pp. 97–107.

BAKER, E.L. and O'NEIL, H.F. Jr. (1996) 'Performance assessment and equity', in KANCE, M.B. and MITCHELL, R. (eds) *Implementing Performance Assessment: Promises, Problems, and Challenges*, Malwah, NJ: Lawrence Erlbaun Associates, pp. 183–99.

BAIRD, L. and FEISTER, W.J. (1972) 'Grading standards: The relation of changes in average student ability to the average grades awarded', *American Educational Research Journal*, **9**, pp. 431–42.

BERK, R.A. (ed.) (1984) *A Guide to Criterion-referenced Test Construction*, Baltimore: John Hopkins University Press.

BERLAK, H. (1992) 'Toward the development of a new science of educational testing and assessment', in BERLAK, H. *et al.* (eds) *Toward a New Science of Educational Testing and Assessment*, New York: State University of New York Press.

BLOCK, J.H. (1971) *Mastery Learning*, New York: Holt.

BLOOM, B.S. (1968) 'Learning for mastery', UCLA-CSEIP, *Evaluation Comment*, **1** (Whole No. 2).

BLOOM, B.S. (ed.) (1956) *Taxonomy of Educational Objectives, Handbook I: Cognitive Domain*, New York: Longman, Green and Company.

BURGER, S.E. and BURGER, D.L. (1994) 'Determining the validity of performance based assessment', *Educational Measurement: Issues and Practice*, **13**, 1, pp. 9–15.

CANNELL, J.J. (1988) 'Nationally normed elementary achievement testing in America's public schools: How all 50 states are above the national average', *Educational Measurement: Issues and Practices*, **7**, 2, pp. 5–9.

CARROLL, J.B. (1963) 'A model of school learning', *Teachers College Record*, **64**, pp. 723–33.

Comprehensive test of basic skills pre-publication technical bulletin (1988) Monterey, CA: McGraw-Hill.

CUNNINGHAM, G.K. (1986) *Educational and Psychological Measurement*, New York: Macmillan.

DOWNING, S.M. (1992) 'True-false, alternative-choice, and multiple-choice items', *Educational Measurement: Issues and Practices*, **11**, 3, pp. 27–30.

EBEL, R.L. (1972) *Essentials of Educational Measurement*, Englewood Cliffs: Prentice-Hall.

EBEL, R.L. (1979) *Essentials of Educational Measurement*, (3rd Ed.), Englewood Cliffs: Prentice-Hall.

EBEL, R.L. and FRISBIE, ?? (1991) *Essentials of Educational Measurement*, (5th Ed.), Englwood Cliffs: Prentice Hall.

EDWARDS, A.L. (1957) *Techniques of Attitude Scale Construction*, New York: Appleton.

FELDHUSEN, J.F. (1961) 'An evaluation of college students' reactions to open book examinations', *Educational and Psychological Measurement*, **21**, pp. 637–46.

FELDT, L.S. and BRENNAN, R.L. 'Reliability', in R.L. LINN (ed.) *Educational Measurement* (3rd Ed.), New York: Macmillan, pp. 105–46.

FITZPATRICK, R. and MORRISON, E.J. (1971) 'Rerformance and product evaluation', in THORNDIKE, R.L. (ed.) *Educational Measurement*, Washington DC: American Council on Education, pp. 237–70.

FRECHTLING, J.A. (1991) 'Rerformance assessment: Moonstruck or the real thing?', *Educational Measurement: Issues and Practices*, **10**, 4, pp. 23–25.

FREDERICKSEN, J.R. and COLLINS, A. (1989) 'A systems approach to educational testing', *Educational Researcher*, **189**, pp. 27–32.

GLASER, R. and KLAUS, D.J. (1962) 'Proficiency measurement: Assessing human performance', in GAGNÉ, R.M. (ed.) *Psychological Principles in Systems Development*, New York: Holt, Reinhardt and Winston.

GLASER, R. (1963) 'Instructional technology and the measurement of learning outcomes: Some questions', *American Psychologist*, **18**, pp. 519–21.

GRONLUND, N.E. and LINN, R.L. (1990) *Measurement and Evaluation in Teaching*, (6th Ed.), New York: Macmillan.

GUION, R.M. (1977) 'Content validity — the source of my discontent', *Applied Psychological Measurement*, **1**, pp. 1–10.

GULLICKSON, A.R. and ELLWEIN, M.C. (1985) 'Post hoc analysis of teacher-made tests: The goodness of fit between prescription and practice', *Educational Measurement: Issues and Practices*, **4**, 1, pp. 15–18.

HAMBLETON, R.K. (1994) 'The rise and fall of criterion-referenced measurement?', *Educational Measurement: Issues and Practices*, **13**, 4, pp. 21–30.

HILDYARD, A. (1992) Written composition. In Handbook on Research on Teaching. In ALKIN, M.C. (ed.) *Encyclopedia of Educational Research*, New York: Macmillan, pp. 1528–38.

HOPKINS, K.D., STANLEY, J.C. and HOPKINS, B.R. (1990) *Educational and Psychological Measurement and Evaluation*, (7th Ed.), Englewood Cliffs, NJ: Prentice-Hall.

HUGHES, H.H. and TRIMBLE, W.E. (1965) 'The use of complex alternatives in multiple-choice items', *Educational and Psychological Measurement*, **25**, pp. 117–26.

KRATHWOHL, D.R., BLOOM, B.S. and MASIA, B.B. (1964) *Taxonomy of Educational Objectives, The Classification of Educational Goals, Handbook II. Affective Domain*, New York: David Kay.

LINN, R.L., BAKER, E.L. and DUNBAR, S.B. (1991) 'Complex, performance-based assessment: Expectations and validation criteria', *Educational Researcher*, **20**, 8, pp. 15–21.

LINN, R.L. and BURTON, E.B. (1994) 'Performance-Based Assessment: Implications of Task Specificity', *Educational Measurement: Issues and Practices*, **13**, 1, pp. 5–15.

LUKHELE, R., THISSEN, D. and WAINER, H. (1994) 'On the relative value of multiple-choice, constructed response, and examinee-selected items on two achievement tests', *Journal of Educational Measurement*, **31**, 3, pp. 234–50.

MAGER, R.F. (1975) *Preparing Instructional Objectives*, (2nd ed.), Belmont, CA: Fearon.

MARSHALL, J.C. (1967) 'Composition errors and essay examination grades reexamined', *American Educational Research Journal*, **4**, pp. 375–86.

MEHRENS, W.A. and KAMINSKI, J. (1989) 'Methods for improving standardized test scores: Fruitful, fruitless, or fraudulent', *Educational Measurement: Issues and Practices*, **8**, 1, pp. 14–22.

MEHRENS, W.A. (1992) 'Using performance assessment for accountability purposes', *Educational Measurement: Issues and Practices*, **11**, 1, pp. 3–9.

MESSICK, S. (1989) 'Validity', in LINN, R.L. (ed.) *Educational Measurement*, (3rd Ed.), New York: Macmillan, pp. 13–104.

MOSS, P. (1992) 'Shifting conceptions of validity in educational measurement: Implications for performance assessment', *Review of Educational Research*, **62**, 3, pp. 229–58.

NATIONAL COMMISSION ON EXCELLENCE IN EDUCATION (1983) *A Nation At Risk: The Imperative for Educational Reform*, Washington, DC: US Department of Education. Nation at Risk (1983).

NEDELSKI, L. (1954) 'Absolute grading standards for objective tests', *Educational and Psychological Measurement*, **14**, pp. 3–19.

NICKERSON, R.S. (1989) 'New directions in educational assessment', *Educational Researcher*, **18**, 9, pp. 3–7.

NITKO, A.J. (1983) *Educational Tests and Measurement*, New York: Harcourt, Brace, Jovanovich.

NORRIS, S.P. (1989) 'Can we test validly for critical thinking?', *Educational Researcher*, **18**, 9, pp. 21–26.

PHILIPS, G.W. (1991) 'Performance assessment: A national perspective — cautions and concerns', In Performance Assessment & KERA Conference Proceedings.

POLLOWAY, E.A., EPSTEIN, M.H., BURSUCK, W.D., RODERIQUE, T.W., MCCONNEGHY, J.L. and JAYANTHI, M. (1994) 'Classroom grading: A national survey of policies', *Remedial and Special Education*, **15**, p. 162.

POPHAM, W.J. (1980) 'Domain specifications strategies', in BECK, R.J. (ed.) *Criterion Referenced Measurement*, Baltimore: Johns Hopkins.

POPHAM, W.J. and HUSEK, T.R. (1969) 'Duplication of criterion-referenced measurement', *Journal of Educational Measurement*, **6**, pp. 1–9.

POPHAM, W.J. (1990) *Modern Educational Measurement*, New York: Prentice Hall.

POPHAM, W.J. (1991) 'Appropriateness of teachers' test-preparation practices', *Educational Measurement: Issues and Practices*, **10**, 4, pp. 12–15.

ROBERTSON, G.J. (1972). The development of the first group mental ability test. In BRACHT, G.H. and HOPKINS, K.D. (eds) *Perspectives in Educational and Psychological Measurement*, Englewood Cliffs, NJ: Prentice-Hall.

RUIZ-PRIMO, M.A., BAXTER, G.P. and SHAVELSON, R.J. (1993) 'On the stability of performance assessments', *Journal of Eduational Measurement Assessment*, **30**, 1, pp. 41–53.

SHAVELSON, R.J., GAO, X. and BAXTER, G.P. (1993) 'Sampling variability of performance assessments', *Journal of Educational Measurement*, **30**, pp. 215–32.

SCHAFER, W.D. and LISSITS, R.W. (1987) 'Measurement training for school personnel: Recommendations and reality', *Journal of Teacher Education*, **38**, 3, pp. 57–63.

SHAVELSON, R.J., BAXTER, G.P., GAO, X. (1993) Sampling variability of performance assessments, Journal of Educational Measurement, **30**, 3, pp. 215–32.

SHEPHERD, L.A. (1993) 'Psychometricians' beliefs about learning', *Educational Researcher*, **20**, 7, pp. 2–16.

SHEPHERD, L.A. (1996) 'Effects of introducing classroom performance assessments on student learning', *Educational Measurement: Issues and Practice*, **15**, 3, p. 7.

SKINNER, B.F. (1954) 'The science of learning and the art of teaching', *Harvard Educational Review*, **24**, pp. 86–97.

SLAVIN, R.E. (1991) *Educational Psychology*, Englewood Cliffs: Prentice Hall.

STIGGINS, R.J. (1991) 'Relevant classroom assessment training for teachers', *Educational Measurement: Issues and Practice*, **10**, 1, pp. 7–12.

STIGGINS, R., CONKLIN, N.F. and BRIDGEFORD, N.J. (1986) 'Classroom assessment: A key to effective education', *Educational Measurement: Issues and Practice*, **5**, 2, pp. 5–17.

STIGGINS, R.J., FRISBIE, D.A. and GRISWOLD, P.A. (1989) 'Inside high school grading practices: Building a research agenda', *Educational Measurement: Issues and Practices*, **8**, 2, pp. 5–14.

SULLIVAN, R.G. and CHALNICK, M.K. (1991) 'Measurement-related course work requirements for teacher certification and recertification', *Educational Measurement: Issues and Practice*, **10**, 1, pp. 17–19, 23.

THORNDIKE, R.M., CUNNINGHAM, G.K., THORNDIKE, R.L. and HAGAN, E. (1991) *Measurement and Evaluation in Psychology and Education*, New York: Macmillan.

TITTLE, K.T. (1989) 'Validity: Whose construction is it in the teaching and learning context?', *Educational Measurement: Issues and Practice*, **8**, 1, pp. 5–13.

WIGGINS, G. (1989) 'A true test: Toward more authentic and equitable assessment', *Phi Delta Kappan*, **70**, pp. 703–13.

WIGGINS, G. (1993) 'Assessment: Authenticity, context, and validity', *Phi Delta Kappan*, **75**, 3, pp. 200–14.

WIGGINS, G. (1996) 'Assessment at a crossroads', *Harvard Educational Review*, **66**, 3, p. 638.

WOLF, D., BIXBY, J., GLENN, J. and GARDNER, H. (1991) 'To use their minds well: Investigating new forms of student assessment', in GRANT, G. (ed.) *Review of Research in Eduation*, Washington DC: American Educational Research Association, pp. 31–74.

Index